OLYMPIC EVENTING MASTERCLASS

OLYMPIC
EVENTING
MASTERCLASS

Behind the Scenes with the World's Top Competitors

Debby Sly

DAVID & CHARLES

AUTHOR'S ACKNOWLEDGEMENTS
My greatest thanks go to all those featured in this book for their generosity in giving their time
and co-operation so willingly; to Billy and Suzy; and, as always and forever, to Martin.

PHOTOGRAPH ACKNOWLEDGEMENTS
Horse and Hound Library: pp6 (Leslie Lane), 8, 9, 10 (Svenskt Pressfoto), 13, 16 (Associated Press
Photo), 76 (Keystone Press Agency), 89 (Findlay Davidson), 153 (Leslie Lane), 166
Kit Houghton: pp19, 20, 35, 36, 37, 38, 42, 46, 47, 58, 61, 63, 64, 69, 82 (top), 91, 94, 95 (top),
126, 136, 147, 151, 158, 167, 175, 178, 179, 186, 190, 191
Helen Revington: pp30, 31 (top), 33, 34, 87, 99
Bob Langrish: pp26, 27
Nick Morris: pp48, 49, 50, 51, 53, 54, 55
Stephen Sparkes: pp66, 71, 72, 73, 79, 82 (inset), 83, 95 (below), 100, 102, 104, 105, 106, 113,
114, 115, 122, 123, 128, 129, 130, 131, 132, 133, 134, 135, 137, 138, 139, 140, 141, 142, 143,
144, 145, 146, 182, 184, 185
Iain Burns: pp108, 109, 110, 112
Sue Williams-Gardner: pp117, 118, 119, 120, 121, 122 (top), 124
Martin Ewing: p187

PAGE 2–3
Having survived this jump with neither reins nor stirrups to record
one of the fastest clear rounds, disappointment followed in the
showjumping phase. Andrew Nicholson and Spinning Rhombus on
their way to team silver at the Barcelona Olympics

A DAVID & CHARLES BOOK

First published in the UK in 1996
Copyright © Debby Sly 1996

Debby Sly has asserted her right to be identified as author of this work in accordance with
the Copyright, Designs and Patents Act, 1988.

A catalogue record for this book is available from the British Library.

ISBN 0 7153 0375 9

Typeset by ABM Typographics
and printed in Italy by New Interlitho SpA
for David & Charles
Brunel House Newton Abbot Devon

Contents

1
The Olympic Ethic

The exciting spectacle of an Olympic Games is guaranteed to provoke strong emotions in even the most casual of observers. The athlete standing head bowed to receive a medal, then proudly at attention as his or her national anthem is played should touch an emotional chord in the most stoic, as for one brief moment in history he or she is acknowledged as the best in the world. But with its sporting ideals trying to rise above the controversy of its growing commercialism, the Olympic Games attracts both the purist and the sensationalist. The value of an Olympic gold medal is recognised the world over, and simply to participate in an Olympic Games categorises the sportsman or woman as being one of the finest and most élite of competitors. At its best it epitomises true sportsmanship, personal endeavour and team spirit, a shrine to the conviction that what matters is not the winning, but the taking part – what is important is not to conquer but to fight well. At its worst it involves the greed and selfishness of drug-taking and corruption.

At one time, be it very many years ago, the Olympic Games were all about true amateurism; nowadays however, as some of the participating sports such as basketball and tennis become ever more commercial, the boundaries are much harder to define.

• *The sport of eventing has attracted competitors from all walks of life.*
Princess Anne and Goodwill at the 1976 Montreal Olympics

The Early History of the Games

The concept and structure of the Olympic Games evolved from the religious festivals celebrated by the Ancient Greeks. Amongst these were four great sporting festivals: the Olympic Games in honour of Zeus and held in Olympia, the Pythian Games at Delphi, the Nemean Games at Nemea, and the Isthman Games in Corinth. There are records of Olympic champions dating from 776BC, and the Games were of such importance to the early Greeks that time was measured by the interval between them, four years being an olympiad. The Games were always held between 6 August and 19 September; participants had to be free-born Greeks, and the competitions were truly amateur in that the only prize for any one contest was a wreath or garland. But as the Games grew in status, great prizes and fame were to be had and the athletes became specialists in their chosen field, training full time and even in those early days fuelling a deepening divide between amateur and professional. In the second century BC Greece lost its independence to Rome, and support for the Games died away. The Romans considered that it was beneath man's dignity to appear naked (as it was the custom for most athletes to do) and to perform in public, and the Games were abolished in AD393 by the Roman Emperor Theodosius.

Subsequent emperors proved more supportive, however, and could see the value of the traditional Greek festivals. Similar Games were re-started, and before long Rome was allowing 150 holidays for the purpose of participating in or spectating at such events. But there was a vast difference between the Greek attitude and that of the Romans as to the *raison d'être* of these Games: the Greeks called them 'Contests' and organised them purely as sporting festivals with the competitor in mind; whereas the Romans saw them as Games in the true sense of the word and organised them with the spectator in mind – they saw them as a form of entertainment. The Greek attitude was more in the amateur spirit, the Roman's more professional.

Over the centuries mankind's competitive spirit has been sated either by war or by sporting contests of one sort or another, and it was not until the late nineteenth century that the Olympic Games were re-established; in 1892 a certain Baron Pierre de Courbertin suggested that the spirit of the great Games should be revived and proposed that a new olympiad should begin. In 1894 he formed the International Olympic Committee (the IOC) and in April 1896 the Olympic Games were reborn, appropriately enough in Athens. The first running was somewhat chaotic, entries were unlimited and it would be fair to say that those participating did not necessarily reflect the greatest talent available at the time; but it was a start.

The first three-day event to be held in Britain was at Aldershot for the 1948 Olympics. The winner, Captain Chevallier of France (right) is congratulated by runner-up Lt Col Henry (USA)

At the Stockholm Olympics of 1912 twenty-eight nations participated, sending a total of 2,500 competitors. It was at this Games that the three equestrian disciplines of eventing, dressage and showjumping were introduced for the first time. At Los Angeles in 1932 the idea of the Olympic village was conceived and put into practice, accommodating all the athletes and their officials; since then the number of nations and sports involved has continued to grow.

The Games have not been without controversy: just before the start of the Mexico Olympics there was a demonstration by students protesting against the dictatorial government; this was broken up by machine-gun fire. Then during the 1972 Munich Games nine Israeli athletes were kidnapped by Palestinian terrorists; two other Israeli athletes were murdered in this attempt, and all nine hostages, five of the terrorists and a West German policeman died when the police rescue attempt failed. Again, at the 1976 Montreal Olympics there were protests and boycotts staged by countries who objected to the presence of the New Zealand team because of New Zealand's affiliation through rugby to South Africa, a country which at the time still operated a policy of apartheid. More political storms were experienced at the Moscow Olympics of 1980 when sixty nations boycotted the Games in protest at the USSR invasion of Afghanistan. These Games were further tainted by allegations of bias in the judging by Eastern European officials, and also by the revelation that some athletes were using anabolic steroids as performance enhancers.

Into the Twentieth Century

The 1952 Helsinki Olympics featured a high-tech scoreboard; flashing lights recorded each competitor's progress around the course

AMATEUR VERSUS PROFESSIONAL • As the Olympic Games continue to grow ever larger and ever more commercial, and the distinction between amateur and professional sportsmen becomes increasingly blurred, the Games can never hope to be completely free of controversy. The purists believe in the original spirit of the Olympics, that the Games are for amateurs and not for professionals, and a significant rule change made by the IOC in 1976 did little to satisfy them: this ruling altered the guidelines regarding the eligibility and definition of the Olympic athlete, stating that competitors were not to receive any financial or material benefit in connection with their participation in their sport *except* those allowed by IOC bylaws. These concessions still hold good, and permit athletes to receive personal equipment, clothing, and also hotel and travel expenses; further, competitors may be compensated for loss of possible earnings due to their absence from work as a result of time spent training for and participating in their sport. This last wide concession in effect

Course design often left a lot to be desired from the horses' point of view. The timber was often very small, and the fence profiles uninviting. The siting of this particular fence at Stockholm 1956 gave the horse little chance of a comfortable jump; fortunately the fallen horse was safely extricated

allowed professionals in through the back door, because competitors could now devote as much time to their sport as they wished, provided they could find someone to compensate them for loss of potential earnings. This is no more than a thinly disguised way of paying someone to participate in a chosen sport. Moreover an athlete whose sport succeeds in attracting extensive television and media coverage will inevitably find it easier to gain sponsorship than those who participate in lesser known sports or, as in the case of three-day eventing, sports which are expensive to televise; less television coverage means less public interest and awareness, which is obviously of less benefit to a potential sponsor. As it stands, therefore, the system allows the successful track athlete to earn a very good living simply by following his sport; he can train and compete full time and still make a good deal of money.

The Three-Day Event: Its Place in the Olympic Ideal

The three-day event rider has to prove his amateur status to his national federation in order to ride at an Olympic Games. He can perhaps make a living by receiving payment to keep and school horses on a livery basis for outside owners, but this means that much of his time will be spent training and competing young, inexperienced horses rather than concentrating on training himself and his top horse for championship competitions. Within the sport of three-day eventing there are those who compete purely as a hobby and those who compete full time, but there is still a far greater discrepancy between the financial rewards reaped by a top track athlete and those received by an Olympic three-day event rider.

The sport of three-day eventing undoubtedly embodies the whole spirit of the Olympics, combining as it does speed, courage, fitness, endurance, skill and, on the part of the rider, selflessness; it is truly a reflection of the Olympic motto *Citius – Altius – Fortius* (Faster – Higher – Stronger). At the Barcelona Olympics, sports writers who normally have little interest in anything equine were moved to write about the courage and sportsmanship of the three-day event rider. And yet the sport has often been the butt of rumours perpetrated by the IOC that it will be dropped from the Olympic movement. Some regard it as élitist, others begrudge the cost of building the three-day event cross-country course.

The IOC has become a very powerful body, and decisions regarding the hosting of the Games and which sports to allow into the Olympics are far too often dictated by politics and commercialism. But for as long as the Olympic movement clings to any semblance of its original spirit, it should be proud to include the three-day event.

The Evolution of the Three-Day Event

The sport of three-day eventing is not particularly well understood by the general public; where many might have heard of Badminton Horse Trials, the vast majority still assume that if you ride a horse over jumps you must be a showjumper. Of the spectators at Badminton itself, only a relatively small percentage would even be aware of the full speed and endurance test; most only observe Phase D, the cross-country. In this respect the Olympic three-day event does the sport a world of good because it brings eventing to the attention of a far greater number of people.

Since eventing's first appearance at the Olympic Games in 1912, the type of competitor and the number of countries taking part has altered dramatically; to appreciate the change it helps to understand a little regarding the origins of the sport. It is easy to forget that the three-day event was conceived on the Continent. Today, Britain is most definitely seen as the centre of the eventing world; it hosts the largest number and widest range of events, and is the home of the most famous and prestigious three-day event of them all, Badminton Horse Trials. Whenever a British team fails to cover itself in glory at an international competition the criticism is blunt and free-flowing; in particular the attack on the British riders who failed to secure a medal at the Barcelona Olympics was ferocious and would have had anyone believe that Britain was surely the mother and maker of the sport!

EUROPEAN ORIGINS • But it was in Europe that the three-day event was born, largely as a consequence of the musings of cavalry officers who wanted to devise a competition which would test their horses. The cavalry charger had to be obedient and well schooled to accomplish his parade duties, but he had also to be fit and courageous enough to cross any country to search out and then engage the enemy. And once that task was completed there was rarely time to rest – it was on to the next battleground and hopefully another victory. Thus the format of the first three-day events was the same as it is today: a simple dressage test to test the horse's obedience, followed by a course to test his stamina, speed and jumping ability across country, and finally a round of showjumping just to prove that he was fit to continue work after the rigours of 'battle'. The competition was known as 'The Military', and it provided cavalry officers with a challenge and some respite from the 'boredom' of peacetime duties.

An imposing fence, but one with a much kinder profile than that shown in the photograph on pages 10–11. Stockholm 1956

THE BRITISH APPROACH • In Britain, cavalrymen found challenge and respite by taking their horses hunting, and this well illustrated the fundamental difference in the attitude to riding between Europeans and the British. On the Continent it was usual for horse and rider to be trained in a manège (a riding arena) where the training was very disciplined and regimented, concentrating on improving the obedience and suppleness of the horse. This became a sport in itself, today's dressage. If the horse and rider did any jumping at all it tended to be as an extension of their 'school' work. On the Continent the best horses and riders aimed to perform 'Haute École' – High School – movements, made familiar to us today by the Spanish Riding School and also the cavalry school of Saumur.

In Britain there was foxhunting, and every horseman wanted to hunt: hunting entailed galloping fast across country and jumping, with various degrees of success and expertise, whatever crossed your path. Any 'schooling' of the horse was aimed at getting it to the stage where it could jump, and therefore hunt, as quickly as possible. The British boasted that for every continental riding master, there was a British Master of Foxhounds!

As far back as the eighteenth century there is evidence of how much at odds the British and the 'Continentals' were with each other. France in particular produced a string of brilliant horsemen whose classical training ideas are still relevant today; one of the most influential must be Sieur de la Guerinière, born in 1688, who taught at the Spanish Riding School for fifteen years and who was chief instructor to Louis XIV. He taught what is now seen as the basis for the correct training of the horse, embracing fluidity, free forward movement and controlled impulsion, and he sincerely believed that every horse needed these basics if it was to enjoy its job, be it dressage, hunting or military work. But the British remained unconvinced, one nobleman commenting during a High School demonstration that if his horse behaved like that he would shoot it! The British even considered the deep-seated dressage saddle, favoured on the Continent, to be unsporting as it was harder to fall out of! And even of the things that the British *were* good at – riding fast across country over fixed obstacles – there was still much ignorance. For example, nowadays we ride across country with our weight out of the saddle to relieve the pressure on the horse's back thus allowing it to bowl along, unrestricted, underneath us. The foxhunting noblemen of the eighteenth century rode in a similar way but for another reason entirely: 'to avoid friction of the bottom'!

This difference in attitude is reflected in the way that equestrian sport evolved in different countries. Dressage, showjumping and eventing developed on the Continent, whereas point-to-pointing, steeplechasing and hunting thrived in Britain and Ireland. Thus Britain's first taste of three-day eventing would have been via the experience of British officers venturing abroad to compete against other nations. When the first Olympic three-day event was held in 1912, however, the British team had still had very little practice at this sort of competition, and this was reflected in the fact that they failed to complete. Sweden dominated the early Olympics, taking the individual and team gold in 1912 and in 1920. From then until 1936 the honours were shared between Sweden, Germany, France, USA, Italy, Belgium, Denmark, Norway, Poland and the Netherlands. Britain, the great cross-country experts, did not feature at all until they won the team bronze in 1936, and during all this time the sport was very much the domain of the military. In Britain, Bertie Hill and Reg Hindley became the first civilians to represent their country in the sport, in 1952. And it was not until 1964 at the Tokyo Games that women were allowed to compete in the three-day event; the first being an American, Lana Dupont. Britain's first Olympic lady rider was Jane Bullen, a twenty-year-old nurse at the time, who rode Our Nobby in the gold medal-winning team in Mexico in 1968 (see Chapter 8).

It is also interesting to note that the sport of eventing is one of the very few sports in which men and women compete on equal terms. If anything, female riders are discriminated against by the minimum weight rule which stipulates that in Advanced classes and at three-day events, all horses must carry at least 11st 11lb (70kg) (this includes saddle and fully kitted-out rider). As liveweight is much easier to carry than dead-weight, and since very few men, if any, have to carry lead, the horse ridden by the lightweight generally female rider is at a greater disadvantage. But in spite of ongoing discussions and grievances on the subject (which could become a chapter in itself!) the FEI will not be moved to abolish the rule.

Another peculiarity of the three-day event and one which has caused debate and dissent in recent years within the IOC, is the fact that both team and individual medals are awarded to riders in the same competition; this was the case for Matt Ryan in Barcelona, where one riding performance won him an individual gold medal and a team medal. There was talk of abolishing the team competition, but this proposition was met with dismay by most participating countries because it is the team competition that encourages some of the nations less experienced in equestrian pursuits, those who would have little hope of ever winning an individual medal. Thus the discussions on the subject were dropped almost as quickly as they were started, and for the time being the team competition still stands. However, almost as if to give themselves the last laugh, the IOC did decide, in 1992, that medals would only be awarded to the three team members whose scores actually counted.

In 1996 at the Atlanta Olympics there will be a separate team and individual competition for the first time – that is, a rider can compete either in a team, or as an individual but not both unless it is on two different horses – which is certainly going to give the selectors some teasing choices. It will be interesting to see if Britain, in particular, which has always been a believer in the importance of putting the team before the individual, will put her best riders in the team or allow them the opportunity of a more personal victory.

THE THREE-DAY EVENT IN BRITAIN • The very first three-day event held in Britain was at Aldershot, for the 1948 Olympics. By this time Britain's usual pool of potential competitors had been somewhat diminished: the army had become far more mechanised, the number of mounted units had been greatly reduced and their rôle and character was changing. A team of three entered the competition but was eliminated when one horse became lame. The USA won the team gold and a Frenchman, Bernard Chevalier, took the individual medal. But although this was a disappointing result for Britain, in the long term it was the prelude to a success story both for the sport of three-day eventing and for the nation itself, because out of the Aldershot three-day event was born the inspiration for Badminton Horse Trials.

The spirit of the three-day event had captured the hearts and minds of many horsemen in Britain, the most influential being the 10th Duke of Beaufort MFH. He could see that Britain simply lacked competition experience and training facilities, and offered to run a three-day event on his Gloucestershire estate with the ultimate intention of better preparing a team for the 1952 Olympics in Helsinki. (The story of what happened there is related by Bertie Hill, in Chapter 9.) The first Badminton Horse Trials were held in 1949 and marked the beginning of a string of successes for British event riders. In 1952 the first one-day event was held, and the number of these competitions increased rapidly; their purpose was to provide experience, stepping stones in the preparation of horse and rider towards the ultimate goal of a three-day event. Thus by the second half of the century the sport of eventing had well and truly arrived in Britain. For those horsemen who took part in the early Olympic Games, the cross-country course that faced them for this, the pinnacle of their careers, would most definitely have been the biggest thing they had ever encountered, a state of affairs which would have been true certainly until the 1960s. Now, the majority would concede that the Badminton cross-country course is the most awesome. When the late Frank Weldon took over as director of Badminton he was determined that never again should British riders compete abroad and be frightened by the size of the fences or the questions asked. His determination to ensure that the British were as well prepared as possible has given the sport of eventing an annual competition which most riders look upon as an unofficial World Championships for individuals.

Britain's first gold medal-winning team at the 1956 Stockholm Olympics; from left: Lawrence Rook (Wild Venture), Bertie Hill (Countryman) and Colonel Frank Weldon (Kilbarry)

In terms of physical size, all fences at four-star CCIs and CCIOs – Badminton, Burghley, Punchestown, the World and European Championships, and the Olympics – can go up to the same maximum dimensions, but it is the skill of the course builder, not the size of the fences, which dictates the difficulty of the course. Before the 'star' system of grading three-day events was introduced, the Olympic fences were allowed to be physically larger than at other competitions. However, because the team championship competitions want to encourage as many teams as possible to compete and complete, the Olympic course nowadays is designed accordingly; thus there will still be some very difficult questions, but the alternatives are designed so that as many countries as possible are able to complete. So whatever the rule books may say about the height and width of fences, Badminton still reigns supreme in the event rider's mind.

Success in this particular sport demands good all-round horsemanship. Countries such as Australia and New Zealand, even later converts to eventing, have proved to be extremely successful because they produce naturally good all-round horsemen. Australia, New Zealand, South Africa, Argentina and Mexico, for example, have vast unpopulated areas of land where the horse is still very much a part of working life. Horses in these wilder rural areas have a job to do – there is neither time, place, nor opportunity for the luxury of months of quiet schooling – and work-riders in these countries are accustomed to jumping on a relatively inexperienced horse and getting some work out of it quickly. Thus those who decide to take up eventing as a sport and have time to devote to training a competition horse, also have the benefit of being all-round, efficient horsemen already. It was not until the 1950s that, for example, Australia and New Zealand formed their own national equestrian federations, a move which allowed them to compete internationally. Within ten years Australia had reached the top, winning the team and individual gold medals at the 1960 Rome Olympics. For many years Bill Roycroft formed the backbone of the sport and the team in Australia, and joined the heroes of sports' folklores at the Rome Olympics: he had suffered a very heavy fall from his horse, Our Solo, at the notorious Drainpipe Fence, a line of concrete drainage pipes which had to be jumped lengthways, giving them a five-foot (1.5m) spread and a totally unforgiving construction. He completed the course but was in hospital that night with a broken shoulder. However, on hearing that another team member had been eliminated but that Australia was still in the lead if his score could count, he discharged himself and returned to jump a clear round and help Australia to the gold. In 1968 and 1976 Bill was joined in the team by his son Wayne, and on both occasions Australia won the team bronze. Team and individual gold eluded the country again until Matt Ryan's decisive victory at the 1992 Barcelona Olympics.

New Zealand's introduction to the sport came even later, but they have since made a tremendous impact on the eventing scene; 1984 and 1988 saw Mark Todd win two consecutive individual gold medals, and team bronze in 1988. He should also have earned a team silver in 1992, but with the retirement on Phase C of Mark's ride, Welton Graylag, his became the discard score and under the new rules, medals were only given to the three riders whose scores counted. There would be few to disagree that Mark is one of the world's greatest horsemen, and New Zealand has also produced two world champions, Blyth Tait (Stockholm, 1990) and Vaughn Jeffries (The Hague, 1994). On the latter occasion, ironically, the hotly favoured New Zealand team fell apart when both Mark Todd and Andrew Nicholson fell at the same fence, and Blyth Tait retired after a fall.

Success at the highest level in eventing is all about everything coming right for the big occasion, and so it is not surprising that being the hot favourite is no guarantee of success. It is not that straightforward, and certain titles and competitions continue to elude even the best horsemen:

The Implications of the Eventing Test

OVERLEAF
The Olympic three-day event often comes under attack because the high cost of the necessary facilities is lavished on a relatively small number of competitors. The training area at the 1988 Seoul Olympics

Mark Todd, for example, has never won a World Championship title; and it took America's Bruce Davidson, who has competed with tremendous success at international level, twenty-one years to win Badminton Horse Trials – having ridden there for the first time in 1974, victory eluded him until 1995, and even then he was lucky in that the original overnight leader, Britain's William Fox-Pitt, had the misfortune of having his horse fail the final veterinary inspection. Ireland, a country to which many nations turn when buying an event horse, has never yet won an Olympic medal. But it is this broad spectrum of success that encourages so many nations to take part. For example, at the Barcelona Olympics in 1992, fifteen different nations successfully completed the team competition.

Equestrian sport nowadays is no longer the domain of the military or the rich, and many other people from completely non-horsey backgrounds are taking up eventing and other equestrian sporting disciplines. These aspiring riders tend to be taught in the same way as many of our continental cousins, learning first within the confines of the manège before going out to compete. With attitudes in Britain becoming frighteningly surburban, traditional training grounds such as the hunting field are often dismissed and despised with the result that many riders of today, and of the future, know much in theory but have not had the practical experience of riding a horse over unknown country and across varying ground conditions (this is a point discussed by Richard Meade in Chapter 6).

The sport has also been through a period of subtle re-emphasis. For a while course builders were moving away from the big bold galloping course which called for speed, courage and sheer guts, with perhaps less in the way of athleticism and technique, and increasingly were building more technical combinations which required accuracy and therefore a more highly schooled, nimble and athletic horse. Some critics believe that as a result riders lost a degree of the dash and determination which had long been the hallmark of the event rider. However, the balance between the two is probably more even now, besides which riders are more inclined to understand and appreciate that if they acquire some of the subtleties of technique required at the more technical fences, then their overall performance is bound to be enhanced: a more athletic, well schooled horse is going to perform better throughout all the phases than one that relies merely on scope and stamina to gallop across country over large but straightforward obstacles.

It is because eventing is such an undeniably complete test of all-round horsemanship that it is such a challenge in the first place. Moreover there are so many things that have to come right at the same time in order to *win*: horse and rider must be fit to compete, they must be 'on form' in all three phases, and at a three-day event there is the added hurdle of the horse having to pass two veterinary inspections. With so many variables to contend with, it is not surprising that the sport continually throws up different stars from different countries. And looking back at its history, no one country has the divine right to expect to be the leader of the pack!

Herbert Blocker and Feine Dame, individual silver medallists at the 1992 Barcelona Olympics

OLYMPIC THREE-DAY EVENT RESULTS

Year	Team	Individual	Year	Team	Individual
1912 STOCKHOLM	Sweden Germany USA	Alex Norlander, Sweden Harry von Rochow, Germany Jean Cariou, France	1960 ROME	Australia Switzerland France	Laurie Morgan, Australia Neale Lavis, Australia Anton Buhler, Switzerland
1920 ANTWERP	Sweden Italy Belgium	Helmer Morner, Sweden Age Lundstrom, Sweden Etore Caffaratti, Italy	1964 TOKYO	Italy USA West Germany	Mauro Checcoli, Italy Carlos Moratorio, Argentina Fritz Ligges, West Germany
1924 PARIS	Netherlands Sweden Italy	A. van der Voort van Zijp, Netherlands Frode Kirkebjerg, Denmark Sloan Doak, USA	1968 MEXICO	Great Britain USA Australia	Jean Lacques Guyon, France Derek Allhusen, Great Britain Michael Page, USA
1928 AMSTERDAM	Netherlands Norway Poland	Charles Pahud de Mortanges, Netherlands Gerard de Kruyff, Netherlands Bruno Neumann, Germany	1972 MUNICH	Great Britain USA West Germany	Richard Meade, Great Britain Alessandro Argenton, Italy Jan Jonsson, Sweden
1932 LOS ANGELES	USA Netherlands –	Charles Pahud de Mortanges, Netherlands Earl F. Thomson, USA Clarence von Rosen, Sweden	1976 MONTREAL	USA West Germany Australia	Edmund Coffin, USA Michael Plumb, USA Karl Schultz, West Germany
1936 BERLIN	West Germany Poland Great Britain	Ludwig Stubbendorf, Germany Earl F. Thomson, USA Hans Mathieson, Denmark	1980 FONTAINEBLEAU (alternative Olympics)	France West Germany Australia	Nils Haagensen, Denmark James Wofford, USA Torrence Watkins, USA
1948 LONDON	USA Sweden Mexico	Bernard Chevalier, France Frank S. Henry, USA Robert Selfelt, Sweden	1980 MOSCOW	USSR Italy Mexico	Federico Roman, Italy Aleksandr Blinov, USSR Yuri Sainikov, USSR
1952 HELSINKI	Sweden West Germany USA	Hans von Blixen Fenecke Jnr, Sweden Guy Lefrant, France Wilhem Busing, West Germany	1984 LOS ANGELES	USA Great Britain West Germany	Mark Todd, New Zealand Karen Stives, USA Virginia Holgate, Great Britain
1956 STOCKHOLM	Great Britain West Germany Canada	Petrus Kastenmann, Sweden August Lutke Westhues, West Germany Frank Weldon, Great Britain	1988 SEOUL	West Germany Great Britain New Zealand	Mark Todd, New Zealand Ian Stark, Great Britain Virginia Leng, Great Britain
			1992 BARCELONA	Australia New Zealand Germany	Matt Ryan, Australia Herbert Blocker, Germany Blyth Tait, New Zealand

2
Breeding the Potential Olympic Horse

There are those who dream of riding an Olympic three-day event horse, and those who dream of breeding one, and it is difficult to say which would be the hardest to achieve. However, statistics do show that an event rider has a much greater chance of riding at more than one Olympics, than a breeder has of producing more than one Olympic event horse. There are plenty of breeders who believe they might have produced a horse with Olympic potential, but whether or not this is fully realised depends on the calibre of his eventual rider, and also on a degree of luck. Sam Barr has devoted more than thirty years of his life to breeding the Welton event horses: he has achieved a measure of success in that he bred the winner of Badminton in 1993 (Welton Houdini, ridden by Ginny Elliot, then Leng), and the 1995 European Champion Welton Romance (Lucy Thompson), and his stallion Welton Crackerjack also sired Welton Greylag, the winner of Burghley 1991; an Olympic champion, however, eludes him still. Welton Greylag was ridden by Mark Todd at the Barcelona Olympics 1992, but pulled up lame after the steeplechase and could not continue, which just proves that a winning Olympic partnership requires not only a good horse and a good rider, but also good luck.

Another popular eventing sire, Ben Faerie, owned by Diana Scott, produced two of Ginny Elliot's horses: Night Cap and Priceless. But of the two only Priceless went to the Olympics, winning team silver and individual bronze in Los Angeles. Here we had two horses by the same sire, produced and ridden by the same rider, but the timing and form essential for Olympic selection came together for only one of them.

• *Leslie Law and Welton Apollo; over a five-year partnership this combination was unplaced only five times*

23

■ In racing, where details of every horse must be registered with Wetherby's its pedigree and performance are recorded; whereas in eventing, the breeders of many of the world's top class horses are unfortunately unsung heroes, unknown and untraceable. An event horse is usually about eight years old before it starts to compete at Advanced level and to show whether potentially it is top class, but by this time it may have passed through several homes and its breeder been forgotten. Even if the breeder is found, it is not unusual for him or her to have no idea at all as to the pedigree of the dam that produced the successful eventer. As regards breeding policy, Britain has always been one of the worst culprits for being haphazard, to say the least, as far as competition horses are concerned: she produces some of the best in the world, but generally they are hardly traceable in terms of their pedigree. Most other European countries have a system of assessing any stallion that stands at stud, and records are kept of the competition success of its progeny; often the breeding industry itself receives heavy government funding, too. None of this happens in Britain, however: no one even knows how many stallions there are in the country, let alone the performance potential of their offspring.

In 1994 the British Horse Database was founded with the aim of recording pedigrees and performance data. It did not have an easy start – there was discontent amongst people who had already paid to register their horses or ponies with a particular breed society, and those with a competition gelding of unknown pedigree were even less willing to spend money recording what, as far as they were concerned, was useless information. But the supporters of the Database insisted that in order even to begin to catch up with the sophisticated European systems, Britain had to make a start somewhere. The Database received a much-needed boost in 1995 when the Horse Trials Group, amongst others, made it compulsory for affiliated event horses to be on its register. It will be some years yet before the British Horse Database has any real influence in terms of the information it provides for both potential buyers and breeders; besides which, many in the industry argue that we will always lag behind other European countries unless some control is instituted regarding the quality of stallions that may stand at stud.

In the United Kingdom it has often been the case that little or no thought is given to the breeding potential of a particular mare. A predominant attitude has been this: 'If she can no longer be ridden but we can get her in foal, why don't we breed from her?', with the result that many unsuitable and unsound mares have been used to produce the next generation. A little more thought than that is usually given to the choice of stallion, but often

significantly relevant information such as the performance of his progeny has not been available, so if the mare owner likes the look of him and the price is right, then he will be used, the assumption being that he could, in some miraculous way, overcome any failings that the mare might have. The offspring would, of course, be born perfect! But gradually attitudes have started to change – and it is important for the future of all equestrian sports that they do change, especially as many breeders consider that the mare's genetic influence on her offspring may be up to 75 per cent; and whether or not the mare is a good jumper is particularly important, as this seems to come through strongly to the offspring.

In Europe, the performance testing of stallions is an accepted part of the breeding industry; young Warmblood and Arab stallions (Thoroughbreds are tested separately) have to be approved for breeding as two-year-olds; in the August of their third year they are taken to a testing centre (very often state sponsored) where they stay until mid-November. At the centre they are broken in and trained to the standard required by the performance test by the testing station staff. At the end of the 100-day period they undergo the performance test, when they are assessed for the following: ridden work and ridability; free jumping; ridden showjumping and cross-country jumping; paces and gallop; character and temperament. Their marks are totalled and they are graded accordingly, as grade one, two or three. Stallions awarded less than the minimum acceptable mark are no longer considered approved for breeding.

A performance test which followed the European system precisely would probably never be accepted in Great Britain by the breeding industry. There is no state funding and so the cost would fall on to the stallion owner, but a more fundamental reason is that the British are used to 'doing their own thing' – even if they were persuaded to pay to send their potential stallion to a testing centre, it is impossible to imagine that agreement would ever be reached as to which trainer and training methods to adopt.

The resentment already caused by the introduction of the British Horse Database is largely because the British have a deeply felt and wonderfully simple belief that they have bred many of the best performance horses in the world, and that Britain has the best Thoroughbred stock in the world, too; and they are convinced that these are good enough recommendations for any would-be breeder or purchaser, without the need for more red tape.

However, this naïve sentiment is no longer good enough. The continental-bred horses, with their documented pedigrees and performance data, generally earn higher prices at the more prestigious sales than do

The stallion Welton Louis competing at his first Novice horse trial.
He should have won the event but Sam missed a fence when he walked the course, and was subsequently eliminated!
Louis went on to compete at Advanced level in both horse trials and pure dressage

British-bred horses, and this is particularly true in the case of dressage and showjumping animals. The event horse with British blood is still much sought after, but this may not last: as other breeds prove that they too can sire a top class eventer – as, for example, some Trekehner and Warmblood stallions are doing – the price and demand for the British horse will drop. Foreign buyers attending British sales are attracted by the class of horse they see, but they want to see papers as proof of breeding and performance potential before they will consider buying.

An encouraging development in Britain which is now slowly gathering momentum is the National Stallion Association's (NASTA) performance test; it emulates the European system in that a performance test is carried out, but it has been modified to satisfy British reticence in that stallions are not expected to be broken and trained at a national centre. Instead, young stallions can be declared by the owner as being prepared and ready for performance testing in any season up until their fifth year. In whichever season they are declared they have to obtain qualifying certificates in the three disciplines of dressage, showjumping and cross-country. This equates roughly to the horse being capable of competing at, say, Novice one-day event level. The horse must also pass a veterinary examination at the end of the test.

At present this facility is taken up by relatively few stallion owners; in 1993 twenty stallions were tested, and thirteen in 1994, mainly Arab, Trekehner and Irish Draught stallions. But as the British become more accustomed to the availability of breeding and performance data via the British Horse Database, the attraction of also having your stallion performance tested should increase, and this can only be to the benefit of performance horse breeding.

The horse-breeding industry will always have two main facets: professional establishments whose aim is to earn a living by selling the youngstock they produce, and those who wish to breed a foal for their own enjoyment, often for reasons of sentimentality, by making use of that faithful old mare which has broken down or retired. Those in the latter category often have no greater ambition than to produce just another reliable hack for their own use, and so it is perhaps easier to forgive any lack of research or thought as to how suitable the mare is, or which stallion to choose. But the professional breeding establishments should have done their homework regarding the optimum match, the mating which will produce the world-beater they all dream of. In spite of the lack of breeding and performance information presently available, most serious breeders and competitors have a good idea of the type of horse that is suitable for the work required: temperament, conformation and movement are all very tangible qualities, and generally it is easy to see whether a mare, stallion, or youngster possesses them and to what

degree; after that the success or otherwise of the horse is dependent upon the training he is given.

In an ideal world, the breeder who believes he has produced a potentially top class competition horse would contact a suitable rider who would buy it to produce and compete – and the world should be at their feet. But as Sam Barr points out, 'When we assess a really good home-bred horse we might think it would suit Mark Todd very well, or Ginny Elliot for example, but when you ring them up to suggest it, they can rarely afford to pay you the horse's true value.' Thus it very often happens that the best horses are sold to the riders with the deepest pockets, rather than those with the greatest ability. In many other parts of Europe – for example France and Holland – the government provides enough money to keep top class horses in the country for their best riders. In Britain, the very best horses are often sold abroad to the highest bidder in order to

defray the ever-rising costs of competition, and British riders are left with an ever-diminishing pool of top class horses to choose from.

In a way, however, this all contributes to the appeal and challenge of the sport of horse trials for its enthusiastic participants: it is an amateur sport, and whilst many riders do make their living from it, either through sponsorship or because owners pay them to ride their horses, the vast majority of horse trials' enthusiasts are the one- or two-horse owner-riders for whom the sport is a hobby rather than a career. Nevertheless, when it comes to choosing an Olympic team it is generally only the 'career riders' who merit selection. Their talent has meant that they attract either sponsorship, or the owners of good horses, and once they have a string of

quality horses on which to compete, they continue to improve and earn good results because the number of horses they ride means they gain far more experience than most other competitors. Andrew Nicholson may have ten competition rides over one weekend; most of us would be lucky to have two! Leslie Law may have the chance to ride a string of world class horses in his career; other riders just have to hope that somewhere, sometime, they will 'click' with one really good horse and so together will be able to achieve dizzy heights – even if it is only once in a lifetime!

Breeders may bemoan the many variables that affect whether or not they succeed in producing an Olympic star, but they should be thankful that they do have a very varied and committed market to sell to.

Sam Barr's young 'Weltons' are reared in large groups, ensuring that their upbringing is as natural as possible

The Welton Event Horses

SAM & LINDA BARR

■ Sam Barr is a well known character in the eventing world: he and the Welton prefix are synonymous. Sam and his wife, Linda, can often be seen watching the performance of Welton progeny at anything from a Pre-Novice one-day event to the Olympic Games. Many would describe Sam as very single-minded, maybe even dogged, in his belief that the Welton horses have shown the way forwards in the competition breeding world. But to do what he has done certainly did need supreme confidence in his, at the time, innovative theory: that it was quite feasible to breed event horses using stallions whose performance and temperament were thoroughly tested in competition. Today it is commonplace to see stallions competing in all equestrian disciplines, but this shouldn't detract from the fact that when Sam first did this in the 1960s, many considered it a foolhardy thing to try to do. Now the Barrs have six stallions, all of which have, or will, prove themselves worthy of being event horses in their own right as well as sires, so perhaps Sam can be forgiven his forthright views!

Sam describes himself as a 'bit of a funny mixture', the child of a Polish father and a Yorkshire mother. He was born in the farmhouse next to what is now Limbury farm and stud, and rode from the age of four, having been taught bareback. He was a keen foxhunter and showjumper, and rode Welton Louis' dam to Grade A level. He achieved his greatest ambition in 1984 when, at the age of sixty-four, he completed Burghley three-day event on his home-bred Welton Friday. Friday was a 17hh half-bred gelding by Welton Gameful out of an Irish Draught mare. Amazingly for someone who has always paid so much attention to detail in the eventing world, Sam took the wrong course in the showjumping and was technically eliminated. However, his age seems to have been taken as a pardonable factor, and he duly received his commemorative plaque for completing the event. A close second to this remarkable achievement was breeding Welton Houdini, the 1993 Badminton winner.

Sam met Linda, the woman who was to become his third wife, when he first went to Radnege House, Buckinghamshire, for some dressage lessons. Linda was training there as a working pupil under the strict eye of the proprietor Pat Smallwood, and headgirl Gill Watson (now trainer of the British Young Rider squad).

Linda's interest in horses started when she was allowed to go on a riding holiday. After that she spent weekends and holidays helping out at local stables, before taking a job looking after hunters and then going to Pat Smallwood's. 'Pat was a stickler for doing things just right,' recalls Linda, 'and although it was actually Gill Watson who gave Sam his first dressage lessons, it was Pat who, some years later, found herself judging Sam in a competition; she commented that she would never have believed he would have come to enjoy his dressage as much as he obviously was that day!'

Linda was nineteen when she accepted the position of headgirl at the Limbury Stud. Sam recalls that she rode very nicely on the flat but was not at all keen to jump, and had never competed. Sam decided to rectify all that and sent her out hunting on Welton Gameful. The horse was a keen hunter, and every time the Ledbury Field Master glanced behind him he found Linda and Gameful breathing down his neck. After that Linda started to compete the stallions at horse trials for Sam. She rode Crackerjack through Novice level, but after the pair had completed a two-day event she found him too strong to hold. She had quickly come to enjoy the cross-country phase very much and went further with Welton Apollo, completing Osberton three-day event with him and then riding him at Advanced level.

Now her priorities are organising the stud work and the breaking and schooling of the youngsters. 'I used to hate the stud work because the mares could be so stroppy,' says Linda, 'but now I find it very rewarding. New technology such as scanning has made it so much easier to keep track of exactly what is going on, and it has helped us be far more successful at getting mares in foal.'

Sam and Linda have been breeding and producing potential event horses since 1961, and in spite of their depth of experience they are the first to admit that getting it right doesn't become any easier. To succeed at the top, the 'text-book' event horse should have excellent conformation combined with courage, willingness and an easy temperament, but very few horses have all these attributes, and plenty of Olympic champions have not measured up to the ideal – usually it is their courage, willingness and trainability that enables them to overcome anything else they might be lacking physically or

Sam and Welton Friday at Thirlestane Castle as part of their preparation for the Burghley three-day event

mentally. Nevertheless a breeder must have an ideal in mind; for Sam, this is a horse with the carefulness of a Grade A showjumper and the boldness of the stallion Welton Crackerjack.

Crackerjack was born in 1974. He was by Sam's foundation stallion, the Thoroughbred Welton Gameful, out of an Irish Draught × Thoroughbred mare. He competed at Advanced level, finishing thirteenth at Burghley, and has sired the winners of six international three-day events, amongst these Welton Houdini who won Badminton with Ginny Elliot (then Leng) in 1993, and Welton Greylag, the 1991 winner of Burghley; Greylag was also Mark Todd's ride at the Barcelona Olympics. Crackerjack was very bold and extravagant across country, and he was also a very careful showjumper – but probably his greatest asset was his marvellous temperament. 'He had a tremendous willingness to please,' said Sam 'and if we had had then the experience that we have gained in the years since, he would almost certainly have been an Olympic horse.'

Crackerjack's dam bred several show horses; she hunted for nine seasons before she came to Sam at the age of fifteen, and then proceeded to have four foals for the Welton Stud, all colts and all of which competed at Advanced level. It takes a really good mare as well as a good stallion to produce world-beating offspring: Crackerjack's dam proved she was a bit special by taking herself off, at the age of nineteen, to follow the Ledbury hounds whenever they were hunting locally. She would jump everything the field did, and then find her way home in time for tea!

One of the reasons that Crackerjack has been such a popular and prolific sire of good event horses is because he is three-quarter bred: it is easier to find proven Thoroughbred mares than it is good three-quarter- or half-bred mares, although this situation is changing as more people see the wisdom of competing on mares. And many riders show a preference for something which is, say, seven-eighths Thoroughbred, rather than full Thoroughbred, a way of thinking which has helped Crackerjack become the first choice stallion for many well bred mares.

The other tried and tested formula that Sam adopts is to use his full Thoroughbred stallion, Welton Apollo, on a three-quarter-bred mare, ideally one which is a Grade A showjumper. Welton Apollo is also by the stud's foundation stallion Welton Gameful, out of what was a very well bred Thoroughbred mare, Water Rights. Apollo competed at Advanced level until he was fifteen, when he was retired sound, having just finished fourth in the British Open Championships at Gatcombe.

One factor which is shared by all the Welton stallions is their remarkable temperament. According to Sam: 'Temperament is an inherited trait, and it continues to be one of the defining features of all our stallions, even after three generations. It is the major quality contributing to the fact that the Welton horses can be ridden successfully by such a wide variety of riders.'

Any breeder will be quick to tell you that having bred a really nice horse you are still only half-way there: after that, it depends on the rider. Some horses seem able to succeed in spite of their riders; they will put up with mistakes and just keep going. Others will only take so much, however, and then become unco-operative and difficult: if a horse has a somewhat unreliable temperament – maybe lacking in courage or generosity, perhaps highly strung – he will not put up with his rider making too many mistakes. As Sam Barr has found, if you can place your horses with the best riders, then you have given them the best chance. The Welton Stud's most successful horses so far have been Welton Houdini, ridden by Ginny Elliot (formerly Leng), and Welton Greylag, ridden by Mark Todd. Although Sam believes that Houdini could have been successful with a number of different riders, he concedes that Welton Greylag's general *joie de vivre* would have set a limit on the riders capable of competing him to his full potential.

When trying to breed or buy the ultimate event horse, Sam considers that it is no longer enough to select an animal simply because it is bold across country; today's competition horse needs to be a careful jumper, and it must also perform well on the flat. It is harder to improve a horse that has a naturally poor canter or

RIGHT: Linda, Sam and Welton Crackerjack. BELOW RIGHT: Sam's foundation stallion Welton Gameful has passed his easy-going temperament through three generations of stallions and on to countless offspring.
It is this temperament that has allowed the stallions to compete so successfully, and which has helped produce very rideable competition horses for riders of all abilities
BELOW: Linda and Welton Crackerjack, sire of Welton Greylag who won Burghley with Mark Todd, and Welton Houdini, winner of Badminton with Ginny Elliot

walk, than it is to teach boldness across country: thoughtful and logical training will produce a bold cross-country horse, but there may be very little anyone can do to improve the horse that is a genuinely poor mover.

Sam believes that potential starts to show at the yearling stage, and it is important that the breeder is able to assess a horse's talents early on since buyers tend to be looking for younger horses these days because they are cheaper; so the breeder must be able to put a sensible price on his youngstock. Sam watches his young horses working loose in the school and over small fences; he assesses their movement and attitude, and the shape they make over a fence. He is not worried about a bit of spookiness in a youngster as this tends to make a very careful jumper. In an ideal world he would not sell any of them until they had been broken in and had competed lightly, because if the basics have been well established it is harder for a rider to spoil a horse. But as a result of rising costs and falling prices it is becoming more difficult to make this system viable, and many breeders are forced to sell youngstock sooner than they would like.

Once a young horse has been backed, his good and bad points generally come to the fore. Sam is looking for a horse that genuinely wants to go forwards: 'They must want to go forwards, also they must naturally carry their hocks more underneath them than the average Thoroughbred and they should not be built "downhill" – their conformation should not be such that they are naturally on their forehand.' This is the ideal attitude and conformation the rider should be looking for; nevertheless having said that, there are – and always will be – successful horses which may have many physical faults but whose integrity of character outweighs these: they rise to the top because of their outstanding courage, or their overriding desire to please.

THE FOUNDATION STALLION, WELTON GAMEFUL

Welton Gameful was the first stallion Sam bought, in 1961, and brought back to his farm which was to become the Limbury Stud. He went on to breed the three stallions Welton Louis, Welton Crackerjack and Welton Apollo, all of which were competed to the highest levels as well as being expected to stand at stud. At the time this was an extremely unusual thing to do: stallions were generally looked upon as highly strung creatures that needed to be kept separate from other stock, and very few continued to be ridden once they were standing at stud; but Sam was determined to prove the performance ability and temperament of his stallions.

Welton Gameful was by the classically bred,

Thoroughbred stallion Prince's Game. Prince's Game was bred by the Aga Khan but never raced due to injury as a youngster; however, he carried some of the best flat-racing bloodlines. 'All my life I had admired a particular mare by this stallion,' said Sam. 'She was called "Princess Grace" and won in the show ring throughout her life. She was a fabulous mare, probably one of the all-time great lightweight show horses. She was beautifully deep with a tremendous gallop; it was always a

THE LIMBURY STUD, HOME OF THE WELTON HORSES

Far from the formality and grandeur of Newmarket's Thoroughbred studs, the Limbury Stud was formerly a dairy farm, worked by Sam's grandfather and father. A covered yard has been converted to internal stabling, a purpose-built stable block was erected to house some of the stallions, and an indoor school was built in a former farm building half a mile from the main farm. The land consists of undulating grass paddocks and wooded hillsides, and the horses are reared very much in a herd environment. Whilst the younger stallions are kept in a separate stable block, Welton Crackerjack resides at one end of the double row of internal stables, keeping a fatherly eye on proceedings.

In 1995 there were six stallions standing at the Limbury Stud: the three older stallions Louis, Crackerjack and Apollo, all by Welton Gameful; plus Welton Ambassador (by Welton Louis) who was competed to Advanced level by Leslie Law; Welton Emissary by Welton Crackerjack, and a full brother to

great thrill watching her do her lap of honour. So when I saw a colt foal by Prince's Game offered for sale, I didn't waste any time going to see it. He wasn't very big, and the mare didn't seem to be doing him very well, but I liked him enough to have him. His dam, funnily enough, had been given to the man because her previous owners couldn't get her in foal; he was a coal miner who also had a smallholding, and he bred four foals from her!'

So the newly weaned Welton Gameful was brought south to Gloucestershire, with the idea of standing him at stud to breed top class hunters from some Irish Draught mares that Sam already owned. Welton was the name of Gameful's dam, and has been used as a prefix – the hallmark of the Limbury Stud – ever since. One of Sam's daughters, Dawn, competed on Gameful throughout her Pony Club days, and he went on to become an Advanced event horse. Sam himself soon realised the value of his foals as potential event horses, and his career set the stud on the course it still follows today: breeding event horses from proven eventing stallions.

Advanced eventer Welton Envoy; and a newcomer to the scene, the New Zealand Thoroughbred Kiwi Selection. Sam and Linda decided to import a New Zealand stallion as they believe such a horse would make a very good cross for many of the Welton mares owned by themselves and clients. Kiwi Selection will follow in the path of the other Welton stallions in that he will be expected to prove himself as a competition horse. Since 1985 the stud had taken approximately 100 to 120 mares each season, but this number will increase with six stallions now at stud. The Barrs also have fifteen broodmares of their own.

Linda is the heart and soul of the day-to-day running of the stud. She is up and about just after six o'clock, when she checks round all the horses and gives the morning feeds; the staff – two or three, depending on the time of year – come in just after seven. Duties vary throughout the year, beginning with the covering and foaling season generally from March until September, followed by the breaking in and bringing on of the youngstock in the winter.

The general philosophy at Limbury is to bring up the young horses in as natural and cost-effective a way as possible. The foals are all weaned in the middle of November: they are yarded in groups, and the mares are moved to a field out of ear-shot. The routine feeding plan is based on pit silage, which surprises many horsemen, and a home mix of cereals which is adjusted to complement the quality of the silage. All hay and silage at the stud is analysed. Sam believes that horses thrive best when fed just short of appetite, and so if any feed is left in the mangers the ration is reduced the following day.

The weaned foals are fed four times a day: three times this is a small feed of the home mix which is based on barley, oats, 10 per cent dried sugar beet, soya bean meal, molassed palm kernel, salt, ground limestone and biotin; the fourth feed is high dry-matter silage. Hay is fed to appetite. All the youngstock are group housed and fed in yards throughout the winter months.

The rising two-year-olds receive one feed of silage, one feed of hay and 2lb (1kg) of home mix. The three- and four-year-olds are fed a mixture of hay and silage, with added salt and ground limestone. Sam positively dislikes seeing over-weight youngsters as he is convinced this is detrimental to their long-term ability to compete and remain sound. 'The harder you can bring them up consistent with steady growth, the better,' states Sam.

The colts are gelded as yearlings, before being turned out in the spring. From this point onwards the youngstock may be sold at any stage, although the Barrs are happier if they have had the chance at least to back them first. If Linda had her way, nothing would leave the stud until it was at least five years old, as she has seen too many good horses fail to achieve their full potential through lack of correct basic training. Between twelve and fifteen young horses are broken in every year, and this work is done during the winter months. Linda does the actual backing of the young horses herself; Sam is the only person whom she will allow to lead the horse when it is first mounted, and he

LEFT: Sam with some of the first mares to have been put to Welton Gameful. The stud's original aim was to produce top class hunters
BELOW: Linda with the New Zealand stallion Kiwi Selection

A mare by Welton Louis with her foal, sired by a New Zealand stallion

jokes that she must be totally oblivious to his advancing years because any of the young horses could knock him flat without even realising they had done it! But perhaps Linda's confidence is not misplaced, because backing a young horse is one of those situations calling for trust and understanding between all those involved, rather than sheer strength.

All the Welton youngstock used to be produced and competed before being sold at the age of five, but it is harder to make the economics of such a policy work any longer, and the Barrs sell more and more young horses now – although the unbroken ones are often returned to them to back, which makes you wonder why people buy such young horses if they are not in a position to break them in themselves. Sam says, cynically, that it is because they think this way of going about it is cheaper – and wonders whether perhaps he should put up his breaking and schooling fees!

The stallions are usually the only horses at the stud to be competed seriously; this used to be done by Linda, but in more recent years it was the responsibility of local rider Leslie Law. He rode Apollo successfully at

Badminton three times, and brought the younger stallion Welton Ambassador up through the grades to Advanced level. However, Sam now feels that Leslie has 'outgrown' what the Welton horses can offer; he is at a stage when his life is ready to take an independent turn. Besides: 'I want to start again by helping to produce a young rider on our own horses,' explains Sam. 'The feedback, the enthusiasm and the excitement are all much greater when you are working with a new talent. Also, it is then easier to forgive the odd mistakes that a young rider is bound to make while he or she is learning.'

Sam feels very strongly that too many riders try to advance themselves too quickly. 'They need to become proficient before they become professional. If only they would learn their craft thoroughly first, then sponsorship and success would come automatically. But too many riders rush out and try to make a living from the sport before they are good enough. They struggle on, riding large numbers of horses as that is the only way to get enough money in, and often find themselves riding mediocre horses. In this way they can never develop what ability they might have,' concludes Sam.

The Brendon Hill Stud

DIANA SCOTT

■ When Diana Scott talks about the success of Brendon Hill Stud she is always quick to apologise for the pun, but can't resist telling you that 'faerie' stories really do come true! The stud's best known stallion, Ben Faerie, has sired a great number of competition horses, the most successful to date being Night Cap and Priceless, both ridden by Ginny Elliot (née Holgate) to become European champions in the 1980s. Priceless was also Ginny's ride at the Los Angeles Olympics (1984) where they won team silver and individual bronze medals. Priceless went on to win Badminton the following year, and Diana's proudest moment was being presented with the prize for the best British-bred horse for that performance. Ben Faerie also produced the dam of Schiroubles, one of the horses which represented South Africa at the Barcelona Olympics in 1992.

Diana and Ben Faerie at home

Diana's husband Maurice always used to stand a stallion on his Somerset farm, to use on mares belonging to the local farmers, mainly to produce hunters capable of surviving the tough conditions of Exmoor. In 1970, however, the farm was without a stallion. Diana was expecting their second child, and she decided it would be fun to choose a stallion herself, and take charge of it while she was unable to ride. She describes how she went about it, still smiling fondly at the memory and coincidence of it all:

'I went to Ascot Sales, and the very first head to look over the door at me was Ben. I had a vision in my mind of what I wanted: it had to be a bay horse, very handsome and with lots of quality. I wasn't interested in bloodlines – I just had a type in mind. I had £250 to my name, and luckily Ben came early in the sale and for 240 guineas he was mine! I then had to do a deal with a friend to get him home, as I had no money left for transportation. Ben was 2½ years old and had raced; he had been second in his first race, and won on his next outing – so it was strange that he was up for sale. He may have been a bad debt, or perhaps he had become too "colty" because when he covered his first mare he certainly seemed to know what he was meant to be doing!

'We stood him at stud when he was three, and his "vintage" year – when he produced Nightcap and Priceless – was when he was five. Although I had hacked him out and hunted him lightly, he never really had to prove himself. Once he had produced Night Cap and Priceless he was never short of mares, and we began to realise his value – which then made me worry about him getting loose or hurting himself if we competed him or continued to hunt him. So although he never had to prove himself as a jumper, it didn't seem too important because he was built right – he has a wonderful shoulder and back end, and a lovely hind leg.

'Our aim then was to breed tough, sound staghunters [at the time of writing Diana is Joint Master of the Devon and Somerset Staghounds] and Ben has proved time and time again that these, too, are qualities that he passes to his offspring. And he has the most marvellous temperament – he has been a lovely horse to own and to work with. He takes everything in his stride; one winter he had to share a shed with a Hereford bull!

'When I think of what I look for in a good staghunter – stamina, courage, soundness, toughness and a comfortable ride, a horse powerful enough to carry you across rough terrain, but sensible enough to think about what it is doing – these are the very things that you also need in an event horse. The mares we use have always been tough, sound hunters, and Ben seems to stamp them with the right amount of quality to produce both hunters and eventers. Priceless was only three-quarter bred, and plenty of people said he would not have the speed or the stamina for eventing, but he did. The part-bred horse just needs to be fitter than the blood horse does in order to compete successfully.

'Looking to the future, our intention is to continue with the same principle of producing horses that will fulfil a role both in the hunting field and in competition.

Ben's reign is nearly over, and he will only cover a few more select mares; however, we will continue to stand his son, Hot Rumour and grandson It's Without Doubt. We also have an exciting young stallion called Future Role.'

Hot Rumour has proved his temperament time and again when carrying Diana in her capacity as Joint Master of the Devon and Somerset Staghounds. He is a son of Ben Faerie, out of an Armagnac Monarch performance mare. It's Without Doubt is by Welton Louis and is out of Doubtless, a full sister to Priceless. So both of these stallions are seven-eighths Thoroughbred.

Ben Faerie is a full Thoroughbred, and having enjoyed such success with him, Diana chose the two-year-old Thoroughbred stallion, Future Role, in much the same way as she chose Ben.

'I bought him at Doncaster sales as a yearling. He is a lovely mover, but what really influenced me was the same gut feeling that I had when I found Ben. His first foal will be out of Doubtless. As far as the stallions are concerned we have not deviated far from the original: we are now standing two of Ben's offspring, and the young stallion was chosen in the same way as Ben was. But as far as mares go, we like to experiment, and we have been fortunate in that our stallions do seem to cross well with a wide variety of mares. I am not averse to using a mare with pony blood as this puts self-preservation into the offspring, and we have also successfully used Shire mares, which give their offspring tremendous substance and movement. My son Michael has a super all-rounder by Ben out of a Shire mare which has won sixteen horse trials points, and is consistently placed in dressage and showjumping competitions.'

In spite of the boost which she thinks the British Horse Database scheme will bring to British breeding, Diana is adamant that more needs to be done to improve the quality of stallions which are allowed to stand at stud. At present anybody can stand a stallion of any description: as a consequence, some of these are very inferior animals, and a great many poor quality offspring are produced. Too many people think it is an easy way to make a living – but this is certainly not the case if it is to be done properly. And because of the British reticence to spend too much money on young-stock, it is not an easy way to make money, either. Very few British buyers appreciate what it costs to breed and produce a young horse. As Diana pointed out, whilst the Brendon Hill stud fees have gone up to reflect inflation – from £20 when Ben was a three-year-old, to £1,000 in recent years – the price of young horses has not gone up enough to cover the increasing cost of producing them.

Diana is excited about the future for the Brendon Hill Stud, and it is refreshing and encouraging to see, in her establishment, such a strong link between hunting and the production of competition horses. As long as there is hunting in Great Britain we will produce the best foundation mares in the world because there is no better place to test their stamina, courage and temperament. It has always been said that one reason for the British being so good at cross-country riding was because of the strong connection between riding to hounds and competitive cross-country riding. Horse and rider learn to remain balanced and in a rhythm across all kinds of terrain and over unknown obstacles. Sadly it seems that too few of our younger riders learn their trade in the hunting field, and this situation needs to change. The modern world of eventing does not seem to appreciate how much it has been helped by Britain's tradition of hunting, and if hunting is ever banned in this country the eventing world will suffer more than it realises.

PRICELESS BLOODLINES

Ginny Elliot's 1985 Badminton winner and European champion was Priceless, a son of Ben Faerie out of a mare called Reckless. Reckless was owned by Diana's father-in-law and had already bred several foals before she came to Brendon Hill. In all she produced fourteen foals, and every one of them proved to be a very good horse. Reckless herself was a wonderful hunter; she had a very bold eye, and plenty of bone and substance, but she also had a great deal of quality about her. She bred her last foal at the age of twenty-four – he became an Advanced event horse – and was eventually put down when she was twenty-seven.

Priceless was bred to be Maurice Scott's hunter, but

Diana pinched the ride on him first and 'hunted the legs off him as a four-year-old, he worked very hard'. The Holgates by this time had already acquired Night Cap, who was by Ben Faerie, and rang Diana to see if she had anything else for sale by Ben. Although Diana thought Priceless was very special from having ridden him, compared with some of the other youngstock on the farm he didn't look that great. She recalls:

'He was quite plain-looking, and he didn't have a great eye, which is something so many people judge a horse on. To look at, you wouldn't have said that he'd ever be a world-beater – but when you rode him you felt that he just might! However, he was the first horse the Holgates asked about! Ginny rode him round the farm and popped him over a little log – now known as Priceless' log – and asked to buy him. I said he couldn't go until the end of the hunting season, so it was agreed that he should be vetted in May.

'When hunting finished he was turned out in the field until the vetting was arranged, and in that time he developed a thoroughpin [a swelling in the hock]. I wasn't worried about it, but the vet was when he heard that it had only just come up! Much discussion followed between the Holgates as to whether they should now risk buying him. Finally they decided to go ahead as long as he jumped the ditch in our front field without hesitating. Needless to say he did, and the rest was all part of Ben's fairy story!'

Reckless' first foal was the filly Doubtless, a full sister to Priceless, who was kept by the Scotts as a broodmare. Like her mother, she too has produced a string of good horses, including the stallion It's Without Doubt; his full brother Some Doubt, who is standing at stud in Germany (bought by a breeder over there who was fed up with Warmbloods!); and No Doubt, who was sold to America to go eventing. She is now twenty-three and about to foal down to the new stallion Future Role. The Scotts have retained a filly of hers to use as a replacement broodmare when she finally retires. With such a record, who can blame any breeder for continuing the quest to produce an even better horse next year?

LEFT: *Diana and her husband Maurice out hunting on Exmoor*
BELOW: *Ginny Elliot (formerly Leng) with Priceless on the cross-country phase at the Olympics in Los Angeles, 1984*

3
Producing the Young Event Horse

Those wishing to produce and ride a top-class event horse have a long long road to follow! First they must breed or buy a horse with the potential, in terms of temperament, ability and soundness, to be trained to the highest level, and then they must systematically undertake that training and education. There are no shortcuts, or at least none that pay off in the long term, but the process of training a horse well is endlessly rewarding, and worth every ounce of effort put into it.

Karen Dixon and Get Smart on their cross-country round at the Barcelona Olympics

Karen Dixon

A PROFILE

■ When Karen Dixon was selected for the 1988 Seoul Olympics, she was undoubtedly considered to be the 'baby' of the team. Just twenty-three years old, her international experience was minimal compared to that of her well established team colleagues, Captain Mark Phillips, Ginny Elliot (then Leng) and Ian Stark; but her grit and determination made up for anything she might have lacked in terms of experience. These qualities are enjoyed by Karen in abundance, possibly the ultimate consequence of being the youngest member and the only daughter in a fiercely competitive and very sporting family – Karen has four older brothers, the youngest being nine years her senior.

Karen's parents once ran an international equitation centre from their farm and, as Karen puts it, 'With four older brothers there were always plenty of left-over ponies for me to ride! The equitation centre generally had over forty horses, and up to twenty students from all over the world would come to learn and train, and so I was brought up amongst all this equestrian activity. My mother was also chief instructor for the Zetland Pony Club, which I joined as soon as was practically possible.

'In spite of all the facilities and staff on the premises, my parents were very strict about the fact that if I wanted to ride then I had to be completely responsible for my pony, and this was very good discipline.

'I always loved cross-country riding, and once I was in the Pony Club I opted for eventing rather than any of the other disciplines. When I first tried for the Junior team I rode a horse that we had bred out of my first really good pony; she wasn't considered good enough to make the team, but I rode her at the unofficial team competition and she won that! My next horse was loaned to me by my brother, who had joined the army. Barclay was 16.3hh, but he was very short-coupled. I was just fifteen, and rode him in the Junior trial at Windsor – we finished seventh and were long-listed for the Junior Championship. Tragically Barclay injured himself in the stable about three weeks before the championship and had to be put down.

'Mum then gave me two options: first, we had been offered Susie Brooks' horse Superstar on loan; he had finished third in the Junior Championships and would

have been a first class ticket into the team for me. Or we could buy an ex-racehorse called Running Bear, which had been sent to Mum to school. She really liked him, and she particularly liked the idea of us producing the horse ourselves. We had brought on and produced all our ponies from scratch and Mum thought it would be good to follow the same approach with my first horse. So we bought him, and he really started me on the road to my eventing career.

'Running Bear was then eight years old, and eighteen months later, in 1982, we won the Junior European Championship. I rode him at my first Badminton, and he took me through into the Young Rider teams. We went to Badminton when I was eighteen. The late Colonel Frank Weldon tried his hardest to prevent me riding there – he thought I was too young and inexperienced, but that made me more determined than ever to do it! Besides, I felt secure in the knowledge that Running Bear was a fantastic machine across country. We finished twelfth, and that same year, 1983, we took second place at the Young Rider Championships as well as team gold.'

The Young Rider and Junior systems have produced many apparently promising event riders, but very often these young people do not go on to repeat their successes once they move into the senior ranks. Somewhere along the line they seem to lose their way, and often the problem lies in the fact that all their early success has been gained on one particular horse: they find a horse they get on with in their teens, they compete successfully at Pony Club level and then take the same horse through to Junior and Young Rider trials. By this time, however, the horse is getting on a bit, and just when they need to make the transition to senior competition, it is ready to retire. They then find it very hard to build up the same confident partnership with another horse. Karen did not fall victim to this sort of situation, however: her next horse, Get Smart, was bought as a four-year-old in 1984, and she rode him the following year in the associate members' section of the Pony Club Championships where they finished second. As a seven-year-old he finished twelfth at Burghley, and as an eight-year-old he was fourth at Badminton. It was on this 'Pony Club' horse that Karen then went on to represent the UK at the Seoul and Barcelona Olympics, as well as at World and European championships.

'I knew Get Smart was special as soon as I sat on him. Mum had seen him in a field of young horses and liked him immediately, and so did I.' The characterful 16hh gelding by Garnered has matured over the years to become one of the most consistent event horses in the world; when he first graduated to the four-star scene, dressage was probably his weakest point, but with help from Jane Bartle-Wilson this steadily improved. Across country he has always been honest and reliable – and Karen, too, has honed her own performance, relying less on pure dash and determination as she did earlier, and more on style and technical accuracy, an approach that she usually maintains today; it is now a pleasure and an education to watch this combination tackle a cross-country course.

THE YARD AT WYCLIFFE GRANGE
Karen's yard is based at her mother's home, Wycliffe Grange, Barnard Castle in Co Durham; there are very often up to fourteen horses in work. Karen's own string includes four Advanced horses, two Intermediates, one Novice and two Pre-Novices, and a four-year-old. The other inhabitants of the yard comprise schooling liveries, or horses belonging to the girls that work in the yard.

The staff consists of three or four college students on their 'sandwich' year, plus the travelling headgirl, Liz. There is also an Italian girl who helps out with riding the younger horses. Work starts at 7am, and as a rule Karen is riding her first horse by 8.15am. 'I usually ride five or six horses each day' explains Karen, 'and prefer just to keep riding until I have finished. In that way, once I stop for lunch, whether it's at one o'clock or three o'clock, I know the rest of the day is free for paperwork and so on. My mother helps with some of the riding out when she is around, and although I do all the schooling of the older horses, a couple of the girls school and jump the younger ones.'

EARLY TRAINING
'Most of our own horses are bought as unbroken youngsters, and they would generally be backed as three-year-olds then turned away. As four-year-olds, if they are up to it and brave enough, they are aimed at the Burghley Young Event Horse class held at Bramham in the spring. I like to have this as an aim for the youngsters – it gives me a target to work towards, and makes me make the effort to get them going in an outline, and to introduce them to showjumping. They would probably go to one small showjumping competition as preparation for the Young Event Horse class, and they may also be taken round a hunter trial course.

'I don't like to put any pressure on a four-year-old. They are ridden from the field so that life is as relaxing as possible for them, and I only work them if the ground is good – I don't want them throwing splints at this stage. After the Young Event Horse class at Bramham they would be turned away again until the autumn, when they have another session of work culminating in them hunter trialling and hunting; this would continue until Christmas if they were strong and well enough.

'As five-year-olds they are brought back into work in March, with the aim of doing their first event in May. I just work on their general way of going, get them out to a couple of showjumping classes and dressage competitions, and give them maybe two or three cross-country schooling sessions before taking them to Pre-Novice competitions. Even at this stage they are ridden and competed from the field. We only go to local Pre-Novice events so there is not too much travelling involved for them; there are several local ones in the spring, and again in the autumn, which means they are usually turned away for a break in midsummer.

'I have more Advanced horses to ride now, so it is difficult to fit as much in for the youngsters as I used to – they just do what we can manage to get to, although this is probably a good thing as, again, it means they are not subjected to too much pressure. When I take a youngster across country we go round really slowly; I will often trot into the more unusual fences so it has plenty of time to work out what it has to do. At the end of their first season these five-year-olds will do some more hunting.

'As six-year-olds they are treated as one of the team and are put to the test a bit more. They would do a few Novice events in the spring, and would then go to Burgie two- or three-day event, depending on how forward they felt. After another run of Novice events and a few Intermediates I would expect them to tackle a one- or two-star three-day event in the autumn. After that you know what sort of a horse you have, and away you go – hopefully on to greater things!'

GET SMART AND TOO SMART
'Get Smart is very much the elder statesman now, and seems to know more than me about most things! As far as his flatwork goes, I just have to aim to keep him interested in what he is doing, and supple; he knows it all inside out and can do it beautifully. So I try to have some fun in his schooling sessions, playing around with different movements so that it is enjoyable for him, because I now know that when I ask him seriously to do something he will knuckle down and do it.

'Too Smart is like a much younger Get Smart,

though probably naughtier than Get Smart ever was. He had a brilliant 1994 season, winning Punchestown and Gatcombe and finishing third at Burghley. Since then he has become absolutely wild and needs serious discipline every hour of the day!,' says an exasperated Karen. 'He has got a little bit above his station and just needs sorting out to the degree that he will respect me. Otherwise he is just always looking around at everything else, and wanting to join in what everybody else is doing. He has an abundance of energy and talent, but it is essential to channel it!

'Too Smart was shortlisted with Get Smart for the World Championships in the Hague in 1994, and travelled out there even though I knew I would be riding Get Smart unless something went inexplicably wrong. However, he came back from there a far more mature horse; it was all quite an experience for him, and this sense of having "grown up" stayed with him throughout his Burghley performance later that season. Since then, nothing seems to have fazed him at all – he considers everything is just so easy! He now expects big prize givings, competitors' parades and enormous rosettes, because that is what he has got used to! I am not a great believer in grinding a horse into submission, but I have to admit that Too Smart is needing a lot of work at the moment, just to get him to remember that I am on his back for a reason – to tell him what to do! – and that I am *not* there to be taken for a ride!

'In the long term I do believe he has an exciting future. He is enormously talented, he has tremendous elasticity in his paces, and when he settles he is a real machine across country. I want to keep challenging him so he realises that the sport he is in is a serious one, and requires his concentration. I had hoped to ride Get Smart at the 1995 European Championships in Italy but an injury meant he wasn't quite fit to go. I was at least able to take Too Smart to Burghley where he finished fifth. I would then love to take them both to the Atlanta Olympics, which is possible now that there is a team and an individual competition.'

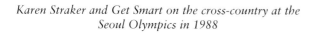

Karen Straker and Get Smart on the cross-country at the Seoul Olympics in 1988

Riding at the Olympics

■ 'At school it was always my dream to ride at an Olympic Games, but even in 1988, the year of the Seoul Olympics, I did not really expect to be considered for the team. After Badminton in that year we were long-listed, but I still didn't imagine for one moment that we would go to Seoul. For most of my early riding career I was the only rider who lived "north of the Trent", and although there is not meant to be a north/south divide you certainly do feel out on a limb being based this far up the country. In theory Ian Stark was even further away in Scotland, but in practice he moves down to the Vestey's estate in Gloucestershire each season. So I always felt that I had to work harder to get myself noticed.'

But Karen *had* been noticed, and she was chosen to ride at the Seoul Olympics alongside Ginny Elliot (then Leng), Ian Stark and Captain Mark Phillips. Karen was very obviously looked upon as the 'baby' of the team; her team-mates were older and had far more international experience than she did, and this was something she found very difficult to deal with: 'I felt very much on my own – it was a team of three, plus me. Once we were out there I couldn't worry about it too much; I just had to get on and ride to the best of my ability. The team plan was that Mark Phillips would go first, I was number two, followed by Ginny, and then Ian,' explains Karen.

In the Olympic three-day event it is the best three scores which count, and so team tactics inevitably come into play when deciding in which order the team members should ride. For the sake of team morale it is important that the first rider completes the course safely, and so an experienced and reliable combination is usually sent out first with this aim in mind; they are therefore riding very much for the team, and not for their own glory. The least experienced rider is often detailed to go second so that, depending on how they get on, the last two members of the team know whether they will have to play safe and go for a steady clear, or whether they can take a few risks in the hope of enhancing both the team's and their individual chances of a medal. As you will read in later chapters, riding to team orders and for team glory tended to be very much a British tradition. Other countries, notably Australia and New Zealand, have generally taken a more daring approach; the feeling is that the team members have earned their place by riding under their own initiative, and should be trusted to make the right decisions regarding the ability of themselves and their horses even when representing their country as a team. However, either approach can backfire on the well meaning selectors (see Chapter 8).

For the 'baby' of the team in Seoul, things did backfire when Captain Mark Phillips' horse, Cartier, tied up as he came into the ten-minute box and could not start the cross-country. Karen found that she was now the number one rider!

'The pressure was almost unbearable,' recalls Karen, 'and instead of trying to bolster my confidence the other members of the team dissolved into depression at the thought that now they would have to rely on my performance! In fact Get Smart and I were very nearly able to make our doubters eat their words, but unfortunately the news that the water jump rode most successfully if you kept to the right-hand side had not reached us. So Smart jumped boldly in on the left-hand side, and we found the hole under the water which many other riders had been warned to miss, and I was thrown off.' Lucinda Green was doing the commentary for BBC television, and for many her anguished words will be clearly remembered. As Get Smart began to stumble in the water, Lucinda was willing Karen to stay on board: 'Hang on, Karen, hang on, *hang on*!...oh, sh...sugar!'

Karen completed what was undoubtedly a wonderful performance of very determined and committed cross-country riding without further incident. Ginny and the relatively inexperienced Master Craftsman, and Ian riding Sir Wattie, both produced fast clear rounds. Under even more pressure now, Karen nevertheless rode a confident, clear showjumping round. Ian also jumped clear, which left Ginny in need of a faultless round if she wished to retain her individual silver medal position. But two mistakes meant she had to settle for bronze, the silver went to Ian Stark and gold to the ever-popular Mark Todd and Charisma; but Britain as a team also took the silver medals. When Karen is asked what stands out most in her mind from her first Olympic experience, it is, understandably, standing on the rostrum with her fellow team members, receiving her silver medal for Great Britain.

Karen's successes continued during the four year run-up to the 1992 Barcelona Olympics: team silver at the Stockholm World Equestrian Games 1990, team gold and individual bronze at the Punchestown European Championships 1991, as well as three more successful Badmintons – 6th in 1989, 9th in 1990 and 10th in 1991. With this record an Olympic team place was guaranteed, and to add to the pressure Britain was being hailed as the favourite for Olympic gold in Barcelona. It is ironic, therefore, that Karen should now dub Barcelona as 'the worst moment in my career', in spite of the fact that she and Get Smart finished 6th individually.

Karen's team-mates were the very experienced Ian Stark riding Murphy Himself, Richard Walker riding Jacana and Mary Thomson on King William. This same team had taken the gold medal at the Punchestown European Championships the previous autumn, except that Ian had ridden Glenburnie. Both the grey horses travelled out to Barcelona, but Glenburnie had suffered a virus in the build-up to the event and was not 100 per cent fit. The Brits made an excellent start by taking the lead after the dressage phase; and Karen was particularly thrilled with Get Smart who had produced the best dressage test of his career and was lying third. Looking back and considering her position she observed:

'If I had been competing as an individual I would have been looking forward to having a real crack at the cross-country course in an effort to at least maintain, and hopefully better, the position I held after the dressage. I am a great believer in going out fighting, and I would dearly have loved to have been able to make my own decisions about how to ride the course; but the selectors asked me to take the long route at two water complexes.'

Evidently Karen's past had caught up with her. Some of her worst moments have been at water: she and Smart fell at Seoul, she had had a crashing fall at the Badminton lake (see page 47), and again with Get Smart at the Punchestown European Championships she had had a stop. The selectors felt that, for the good of the team, she should play safe and hopefully have more chance of going clear. 'Smarty felt really good, and I would certainly have taken the direct route at the second water if the choice had been mine. But I had been in the team long enough to respect the selectors' wishes, and just had to bite my tongue and go out and do what was asked of me.'

Karen was the number two rider; Richard Walker had been 'first man' in Punchestown and was given the same honour at Barcelona, but British plans started to go awry even at this early stage. One British tactic is to have supporters posted around the course who will run back to the ten-minute box where the selectors are based with information as to how each fence is riding.

Unfortunately for Richard, drawn early in the running order, the only information gathered about the water crossing at fence 16 was that two riders had jumped the direct route successfully, and two had jumped the alternative. Richard wanted to take the direct route, where riders tackled the first element situated at the top of a steep bank before running down and jumping over a big hanging log into the lake. As he explained at the time: 'I knew that this particular complex would always need a fair bit of acceleration going into it, and I appreciated that it was at a point on the course when the horses would be quite tired. As I turned the corner to run up the bank I could see I was going to be on a long distance, and my first reaction was to take a check to give Jacana room to fit in another stride to get closer to the fence; but as I discovered to my infinite cost, a tired horse reacts much more quickly to a pull aid than to a forward aid. My hard-trying horse attempted to do what I asked, but having taken a pull we did not then have enough momentum to carry us up the bank and over the fence.'

Jacana stopped, and unfortunately Richard was thrown out of the saddle. With the benefit of hindsight, or if he had been drawn later in the running order, he now knows that he would have come off the corner and ridden up to the fence with everything he had. The German rider Mathius Baumann and Alabaster, the overnight dressage leaders, made the same mistake, and after that every other rider who went that way made quite sure of riding aggressively up to the fence, and worried less as to the accuracy with which they might meet it. To make a mistake at that level is a painfully public and unforgettable experience for any rider. Richard is a quiet and sensitive man, and he probably suffered more than a great many might have done. But as he observed philosophically: 'A good friend of mine said that the problem was only between the hat and the saddle, and it is a frustration and disappointment that I will have to live with for a very long time.'

Nevertheless in a team competition such as the Olympics it is the best three scores which count, so British hopes had every chance of being kept very much alive as long as the remaining team members went clear. Karen had already been told to take the alternative routes at the last two water complexes and, in spite of her personal desire to do otherwise, she went out and did all that was asked of her, finishing with a time only a few seconds slower than Ian Stark and Murphy Himself who had taken more direct routes.

Lady Luck can be very fickle about whom she chooses to smile upon. Two confident and fast clear rounds had been expected from the last two British riders, Mary Thomson and Ian Stark, but although both went clear, neither was free of problems. Mary, used to a truly Rolls Royce ride across country on the gentlemanly King William, found that he had chosen – at this, the most prestigious moment in his career – to ignore the pelham bit in which he had always run so smoothly, and she had an exhausting ride trying to balance and control him as he became ever faster and stronger. Some critics maintained that she should have left him to run on at the fences, that they were big enough to back him down and if not, that he was scopey enough to fly them; but Mary's main concern was that he would then jump himself into trouble at the combinations. Finding herself in this completely unexpected situation, she had to rethink her plans as she made her way around the course.

'The question of whether I was riding for a team or riding for individual glory did not come into it,' explained Mary. 'The way things turned out, I was riding to get us both home in one piece.' She therefore opted to ride the long route at both water complexes, and so completed a clear round but with several time faults. Nevertheless at the end of the speed and endurance phases she and William lay in fourth place.

British spirits and hopes then soared as they followed the progress of Ian Stark and the normally irrepressible Murphy Himself jumping extravagantly round the early part of the course. Almost contemptuously Murphy bounced through the one-stride combination at the first water, and powered his way on round the big Olympic track. But at the lake crossing he nearly paid the price for this attitude, suddenly realising that even he would not survive an attempt to

bounce out over the exit fence, and in changing his mind and popping in a stride he very nearly tipped up over the last element. His early exuberance and this bad mistake then began to take its toll, with the result that Ian also had to change his plans and ride a tired Murphy round the longer route at the final lake crossing before nursing him home.

At the end of the day the British team lay in silver position, one showjump behind New Zealand and five fences ahead of Australia. Although they knew that King William could be a costly showjumper, they also knew that the New Zealanders had an equally doubtful jumper in Spinning Rhombus, Andrew Nicholson's ride. However, any unsporting thoughts that might have been entertained in hoping for a New Zealand downfall and a British triumph were wasted, because on the following morning there was obviously no chance of Murphy Himself passing the final veterinary inspection: he had hit his fetlock joint on the fence at the water and was paying the price. With Richard's score now having to count, Britain's team medal chances disintegrated; the only hope was that Mary, lying fourth individually, might be in contention for an individual medal.

Richard Walker and Jacana produced one of only eight clear rounds – too late to lift the team, but hopefully it provided Richard with a happier memory to take with him from Barcelona. One fence down left Karen and Get Smart in sixth place, but things did not go so well for Mary and King William. Had they jumped clear they could have won individual silver – but William took out five fences and dropped to ninth place. If Mary felt bad, spare a thought for New Zealand's Andrew Nicholson: he had entered the showjumping arena holding the silver medal position, and left with nine fences down, his own placing having slipped to sixteenth; worse still, this score wiped out New Zealand's gold medal hopes, although at least it left them with team silver. The Australian Matt Ryan had just one fence down to take individual gold; his round also helped Australia to team gold. Germany took team bronze, while Britain finished sixth behind Belgium (fourth) and Spain (fifth).

The British arrived home to a slating by the press; it seemed to be universally assumed that had Mary and Karen taken the direct routes they would of course have jumped clear. But even if that had been the case and they had recorded the fastest rounds of the day *and* showjumped clear, Britain still would not have won a team medal; they would have finished in fourth place.

Most of the criticism was levelled at Britain's policy of 'playing safe for the sake of the team' instead of

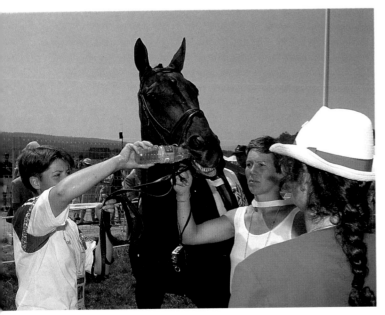

ABOVE: A crashing fall for Karen with Corriewack at Badminton's Lake fence in 1989
LEFT: Get Smart gets his after-dressage refreshment

adopting the 'do or die' approach of many of the other competing countries. As it turned out, Karen was the only rider who 'rode to team orders' and she still feels angry at what she considers to have been a missed opportunity. 'As I have said, I am the sort of person who likes to go out and have a real crack at something' explained Karen. 'I would rather go out fighting and pay the price if I make a mistake, than be told to "play safe". I remember Barcelona as the worst time of my career, and I think it was one almighty mistake on the part of the selectors to have adopted the tactics that they did.'

Since Barcelona, Karen has been fortunate to have had the opportunity to prove that she *can* perform without such restraints at international level: at the 1994 World Equestrian Games in The Hague, Karen headed the all-girl British team which rode for their lives to take team gold, and won an individual bronze herself.

Karen's team-mates were Mary Thomson with King William – the only other survivors from the Barcelona team – plus Kristina Gifford and Charlotte Bathe. With often less-than-happy team experiences behind her Karen was determined that whilst each team member would hopefully ride as if her individual life depended on it, each would also feel undeniably 'part of the team'. Having felt so much the outsider when riding as the 'baby' of the team in Seoul, the difference in terms of team spirit and support at the World Championships made it 'really the very best experience – we went out as a team, but we were all determined, as individuals, to have a serious crack at the medals.'

Britain was the only team in which every rider jumped clear across country. Further, Karen Dixon became the only rider to have won medals at every possible level: Junior and Young Riders, European and World Championships, and the Olympics.

Training at Home

■ Karen has a very relaxed attitude towards the young horses that she brings on; as she has already described, the four-year-olds are usually worked for a month or two in the early spring and turned away, then brought into work again later in the year. For example, the four-year-old Karen is shown riding here was backed in late January, turned away for two or three months, then brought into work again in preparation for the Burghley Young Event Horse class at Bramham in early June. It is hoped he will then tackle a local unaffiliated one-day event in early August. This is his first jumping session since having a break after Bramham. Explains Karen:

'At this stage the height of the fences simply does not come into it. Everything is kept small, but I generally use lines of fences with plenty of poles on the ground as placing poles or canter poles so that the horse learns to look down and see where he has got to put his feet.'

ABOVE: This particular youngster is showing his greenness by being far more focused on the photographer than on the line of fences. He steps over the first cross-pole and Karen has to work quite hard to get him to concentrate on the grid

CENTRE: At his second attempt, however, he has his mind on what he is meant to be doing and looks far more mature

BELOW: The young horse looks a little quizzically at the final element but jumps it cleanly although he can be seen to be dangling his off-fore slightly, a fault which in time you would want to improve; it is usually corrected by using 'V' poles to encourage the horse to come up cleanly in front. (See Mark Todd, Training, Chapter 6)

To end this schooling session a barrel is placed under the fence; this will help the horse to get used to fillers under poles, and as his training progresses many different fillers will be included in his jump sessions so he becomes accustomed to jumping whatever appears in front of him. Karen also uses barrels to teach a young horse to jump arrowheads and corners, and likes to include them under fences at an early stage so that he is used to them. This helps prepare him for when he is asked to jump over an upright barrel, Karen's way of introducing him to jumping corners and arrowheads

FIRST ROW: Simply The Best jumps in over the centre of the first fence but then drifts to the left

SECOND ROW: On her next approach Karen uses 'V' poles to encourage him to stay straight the whole way through

THIRD ROW: It is obvious that Simply The Best is quite suspicious of the barrels, both from the very big jump he throws over them, and the way he has not taken his eye off them even when he is in mid-air. But he is ridden quietly over them in both directions until he is confident to jump the upright barrels

FOURTH ROW (1st & 2nd right): The poles and barrels are then rearranged to form a narrow corner. Karen demonstrates the line she intends to ride, and the horse sticks to this line when she rides the fence

(Centre & second left): As his understanding and confidence increase, the corner is opened out until it is as wide as one might expect it to be at Intermediate level

(Left): 'The ideal situation is one where you have the horse contained between seat, leg and hand as you come round the corner to the fence. You show him the fence and then soften the hand forwards as you ride up to it, so that he can lower his head and neck and use himself properly over the fence. But having offered the hand forwards the horse must not take advantage of this and rush forwards – he must learn to stay in the same rhythm and balance and only change it if you, the rider, ask him to'

As the horse's confidence increases and his concentration improves the grid is added to and the jumps gradually made a little higher; Karen's main concern at this stage is that the horse stays straight and shows a good technique over the fence. She wants him to lower his head and neck as he comes to each one and to lift up cleanly in front to clear it. The value of grid-jumping is that the horse is placed at a good take-off point in front of each fence; you can therefore raise the final element to test his courage in the certain knowledge that he will arrive at it correctly, and all the rider has to do is concentrate on keeping him straight and cantering and jumping out of a good rhythm.

In the final sequence of pictures Karen rides her very talented six-year-old Simply The Best to show how she then progresses to practising arrowheads and corners. By the Thoroughbred stallion Germont, Karen bought this horse as a yearling. Although he has competed at only five Novice events he has already won two of them, including the Novice two-day event at Burgie. This means he has already accumulated 20 points (21 points and the horse upgrades to Intermediate), so he will do his first Intermediate in a few weeks' time with the aim of competing in a one-star three-day event at the end of the season. Says Karen:

'He is a very bold horse but can be very naughty. He used to have great fun going out for a hack, then bucking off the girl who was riding him and trotting home. He has a very sharp mind, and if he gets an idea into his head about wanting to do something he can be quite wicked. So I don't intend rushing him, as then he might find an excuse to be naughty!'

Karen considers him sufficiently talented probably to attempt a two-star event this year; however, since she was aiming to ride him at an event of that level next spring anyway, she is quite happy to take him slowly and do the easier level this time, especially as he is still inexperienced. For example, even though he has completed five competitions at Novice level, he has not yet had to jump a corner – which is what the practice session was going to teach him!

With Karen, the horse is always warmed up over a placing pole to a cross-pole before he is asked to jump anything more adventurous. This is progressively built up to a double of reasonable size consisting of an upright to a parallel, with the intention of concentrating on making sure he stays straight.

Before actually jumping a proper corner Karen likes the horse to feel comfortable with the idea of jumping a single upright barrel, and this is made as easy and clear to the horse as is possible to begin with; two barrels are used, with a pole placed on each side as wings to funnel the horse in.

'All my horses tend to be quite go-ey when it comes to jumping, so my aim is to teach them to *wait* in front of a fence – they must learn that I do *not* want them to come round a corner, sight the fence and rush at it. I want to teach them that they should *not* accelerate to the fence, but should stay in rhythm all the way to it so that they keep in balance all the way to the take-off point.'

SCHOOLING THE ADVANCED HORSE

Too Smart is one of Karen's Advanced horses, and is very much the 'Young Pretender' to the veteran Olympic campaigner Get Smart. Barrel, as he is known at home, is shown having his first schooling session since being turned out after Badminton.

'I start any schooling session with exercises aimed at suppling the horse, and getting him on the aids and listening to me. So I would use leg-yielding, before going on to shoulder-in and half-pass. These exercises help to loosen up the shoulders, and then to engage the hindquarters.

'Barrel is a very onward-bound horse, and at this level much of his training is about teaching him to wait for me to ask him to do things. I have to be very strict about making him work properly, and all his work is designed to help him contain and channel his limitless energy. To this end I use transitions within the pace, asking him to go forwards from working trot into medium trot or from working to medium canter, and insisting that he comes back to the previous pace as soon as he is asked.

'In all the horse's work it is important that the rider makes sure the horse always maintains the correct bend; the bend must be maintained as a curve through the body and neck. However, it is quite easy for the rider to be concentrating so hard on achieving the right amount of bend that he allows his own body to collapse inwards – his inside hip or shoulder collapses in on the circle. To make sure that I don't do this, as I ride a turn I think of looking down the horse's outside shoulder, and this immediately helps to straighten the body.'

Another movement which the horse must perfect for Intermediate and Advanced work is the rein-back. 'I have a secret instruction which I give to my horse to indicate to him that I want him to rein back,' confides Karen, 'and that is, I always teach it by lifting my seat out of the saddle. When first asked to perform this movement the horse will often hollow his back against the rider, and by raising your seat out of the saddle you are giving him less to resist against. Once he understands the movement, doing this then acts as a signal to him that, having halted, he is going to be asked to

Karen progresses from leg-yielding through shoulder-in to half-pass, all exercises which supple the horse, freeing him through the shoulders and helping him to engage his hindquarters

Barrel can be seen here working towards collected trot, when Karen rides with a very deep seat and upright body position to help engage and contain the hindquarters. She then uses her seat, legs and back to press him forwards into the medium pace

go backwards, not forwards. In the test itself I still raise my seat, but in a more subtle way!'

Karen also uses the neckstrap to help her contain the horse when making the transition from free walk to medium walk. 'As you gather up the reins the horse can easily take advantage of this and tank forwards in the walk, or even anticipate the next movement and break into trot. So at home I use the neckstrap while collecting up the reins to help restrain the horse.

'My main aim in flatwork training is very like my objective in jump training: all my horses tend to be onward bound so I am continually working on containing their energy and channelling it where *I* want it – I do not allow them to channel it where *they* want it. In all disciplines the horse must remain on the aids and be attentive to his rider,' explains Karen.

FAR LEFT ABOVE: *In many dressage tests medium trot must be performed across the diagonal of the arena; to accomplish this successfully it is important to ride the horse correctly round the turn and then to have him absolutely straight before asking him to go forwards into medium trot*

FAR LEFT: *Looking down the horse's outside shoulder helps prevent the rider's body from collapsing inwards*

ABOVE: *Karen raises her seat out of the saddle to indicate to the horse that she is going to ask for rein-back*

BELOW LEFT: *'When working in canter Barrel can become too onward bound and heavy in the hand, particularly in the medium canter. The picture shows the degree of lightness and elevation we are striving for, and even in the medium pace he must learn to carry himself like this; only then can he achieve the medium canter successfully by taking longer steps and lengthening the frame slightly, whilst maintaining the elevation and roundness'*

BELOW RIGHT: *'Coming back from medium to working canter can also induce disagreement with Barrel. To prevent him becoming too strong in my hand but at the same time to show him that I do mean him to come back to me within the pace, I pull on the neckstrap. This will very effectively check a horse, and also gives greater strength and efficiency to the rider's seat as it helps him to keep his weight deep in the saddle'*

Elaine Straker

■ Karen's mother, Elaine Straker, has gained a reputation for finding unbroken youngsters which generally succeed in more than living up to her expectations of them, and Karen is one of the few riders who has not, as yet, hit a patch when she simply does not have a top class horse to ride. First there was Running Bear, then Get Smart who has taken Karen from the Pony Club Championships to two Olympic Games, plus World and European Championships in between. And while he is still going strong she has an exceptional second string in Too Smart, closely followed by the promising grey Hot Property, and another Advanced horse Get Sharpe. And that's without considering the Intermediate and Novice horses coming up behind them. They are all of a similar stamp, not overly tall but compact and powerful, and all characterful and cheeky!

'It's more than luck,' explains Mrs Straker, 'I believe it is a gift. As a child my father always used to tell me I could have any pony I chose as long as I cared for it myself, so I started picking and choosing horses when I was very young. I prefer to buy them unbroken – there are enough problems in producing competition horses without starting off with any created by someone else.

'I have been lucky to find and work with so many wonderful horses, and combined with as talented a rider as Karen, this makes a great team. I love everything about it; I adore schooling and training the horses, and am very happy working with Karen. To have produced both the horse and the rider for two Olympics has been beyond my wildest dreams.

'I can't really say what makes me buy a certain horse – it is just a gut feeling. Both Too Smart and Get Smart came from the same place, although they are not related; in each case I saw them loose in a field and just knew I had to have them. Last year I saw a little four-year-old in a field. I chased it up and down to see how it moved, and each time it trotted back to me as if it wanted to stay with me. So I bought it; that was Small and Smart, and we will have to wait to see if I made the right decision! On yet another occasion I was looking at some horses in a yard when in a far corner I noticed a little head peeping out and staring at me. I asked about it and was told I wouldn't like it; but wherever I went, when I looked back it was watching me. So I bought what became It's Me, and was delighted to watch it competing with its new owner at the Junior Championships in 1995. Often the people selling me the horse want to know why I chose that particular one, and I can rarely give them a proper reason. Although I do like a horse to have a good eye – I like it to look at me and to challenge me.

'If the horse is broken in properly then he should progress through life with little difficulty – but too many people think they are capable of breaking in and producing competition horses, and they aren't. And, plenty of people believe they can break in and produce a horse, and very quickly rush off and compete with it; but far too many of them fail to establish the basics properly, and it will always show at some stage in the horse's life. With children, much emphasis is put on the advantages of a kindergarten education because of the head start it gives the child when it starts school proper, and it is the same for the young horse: his early handling and breaking will affect how far ahead he gets in life. You must be sure that he respects you, and you must discipline yourself to be correct and firm, but also fair with the horse at all times. A situation has to be created whereby the horse wants to work with you, and not against you. You must also be prepared to go back to the bottom of the ladder and start again if something goes wrong.

'I travel around and do a lot of teaching and I continually come across problems caused by gaps in a horse's early education – and after a certain number of years you cannot always go back and put right what has gone wrong. The most important thing to remember is that there are no short-cuts. Everything, even the simplest thing, has to be taught properly, and then performed properly.'

EARLY TRAINING WITH MRS ELAINE STRAKER

Mrs Straker takes great pleasure in backing and bringing on young horses, but she stresses that time, patience and experience are essential to do the job properly. Working with young horses can be very rewarding – but if you misjudge any stage of the training or don't know how to cope with it, then problems can quickly escalate, a state of affairs which can be disastrous for the horse's future.

Horses do have long memories, and whilst they are generally willing and co-operative as long as they understand what you want, and are being fairly and properly prepared, a lot of damage can very readily be caused to confidence and progress if the horse is given a fright or is punished unfairly; in other words when he doesn't understand what is being asked of him. All those involved with young horses should have a natural feel for the animal and for the work, and must care deeply about the long-term future of the horse with which they have been entrusted.

'People often ring and ask how long it would take me to back their horse if they were to send it here,' explains Mrs Straker, 'and you really cannot give them an answer. Every horse is different, and it is such a vital stage in a horse's life that it is absolutely wrong to rush things by setting yourself a time limit.

'Any young horse should be well handled, familiar with and trusting of people before you even start to back him. Once you have gained his confidence, one of the first and most important things to get right is to ensure that he accepts the bit – though that is probably better phrased the other way round, in that the bit must be acceptable to the horse. I do believe in using a bit with keys so that the horse is encouraged to mouth it and therefore to salivate, to keep the mouth soft and moist. We sometimes wrap horse-hair around the bit to make it soft and acceptable – but whatever you use, the horse must find it comfortable.

'The next stage is to accustom the horse to the feeling of a saddle and girth. This process is started by using a roller and girth, being sure that everything is done kindly and quietly. I will often put a crupper on as well, as this helps to secure the roller and gets him used to feeling different things on various parts of his body. Once he is quite happy about wearing this equipment then I would start lungeing. I always make sure I have an assistant so if the horse is confused or worried he can be led to begin with. He is only ever walked and trotted, as too much canter work on the lunge can overstrain young limbs.

'When I feel a horse is ready to carry side-reins I will first encourage him to find his own natural outline. If you stand back and look at any horse you will see he has a certain natural shape and stance in which he will generally hold himself. The side-reins are fitted quite loosely to begin with, to encourage him to seek a contact within this shape. I believe in quite a lot of lungeing; it is a vital stage, when the horse learns to respect you and to listen to you. As trainer, you must always be firm but polite with him, then he will begin to want to work with you. There are many constructive things you can do on the lunge, such as practising transitions up and down, trotting over poles on the ground, then poles raised on blocks.

'I am also a great advocate of long reining the young horses, because it is such a wonderful introduction to riding them. Having the two reins teaches them about being turned and halted, then going forwards into the contact again. It keeps them moving and thinking forwards, and gives them the chance to experience the sights and sounds they can expect once they are ridden

out. Ours are driven for miles all over the place: we take them through water, over bridges, anywhere we can go safely. However, you do need to know what you are doing, and the horse must be sufficiently advanced in his work and in communication with you that you can control him in long reins. It is a really terrifying experience for a horse to break loose in long reins, quite apart from the dangers involved, and it will set him back a long way.

'The process of actually backing the horse should be a very gentle, quiet affair. We always use three people, one at the horse's head, and another to help the rider get on. The rider should be legged up so that he just leans over the horse's back to begin with, and this should be done from both sides, not just from the near side, so the horse gets used to feeling weight and movement all around him. And when he is quite happy about all this, then the rider can quietly sit up on his back, still with somebody at his head and another person at his side. You can never be too careful in these early stages, and you must always be prepared to go back a stage if the horse is worried about anything. It is infinitely wiser to go back one stage voluntarily, than to make a mistake and be forced to go right back to the beginning.

'We always hack out the newly broken horse in company so that he has a "friend" from whom he can gain confidence. Then it is a case of progressing quietly through his basic flatwork training, and on to jump training when he is ready. Having established the basics of being driven forwards into a contact on the lunge and in long reins, the idea of responding to the rider's legs as the driving aid should not be that difficult for the horse to accept. But how long all this takes, and how soon you can progress to something new, depends entirely on the horse's temperament and confidence.'

Elaine Straker has had a lifetime's experience in breaking and training all kinds of horses. She had a 'wonderful childhood in which horses and ponies played an enormous part' – and she was always expected to be totally responsible for the care and education of her own horse or pony. As far as she is concerned, bringing on a young horse is every bit as rewarding as watching Get Smart compete at an Olympics. Every horse brings new surprises and challenges. Like children, some go on to achieve great things, others make a lesser mark on the world; but as any parent or guardian will tell you, those responsible for children will always strive to help each one develop its full potential, even those whose future is obviously limited compared to more talented siblings. The training of a horse should be undertaken with the same sense of duty and responsibility in order for him to realise his full potential. He is then well equipped to cope when the time comes for him to venture out into the big wide world.

4

The Olympic Philosophy: The Ivyleaze Team

Success in eventing depends very much on the strength of the partnership between individual horse and rider; however, almost as important is the back-up support available to that rider: the knowledge and advice that can be offered regarding stable management, how to progress with training, when and at what level the horse should compete, and how to overcome the inevitable problems that arise as horse and rider progress through the grades. Few riders can have had as efficient and experienced a team as Ginny Elliot: as regards her success, Ginny is the first to admit how much she owes to her mother Heather Holgate and to her trainer Dot Willis. When based at her mother's home, Ivyleaze near Badminton, Ginny enjoyed circumstances which must have been the envy of many competitors: twenty-four-hour access to the experience and expertise of both her mother and Dot, and a yard strategy where the long-term aim for every horse was an international three-day event. The training and preparation of each horse had that aim alone in view, very different indeed to the ambition of a great number of riders which is to go out and win as many one-day events as possible. Such a policy involved meticulous attention to detail, a continual search for perfection, and it paid tremendous dividends.

• *Ginny with Master Craftsman who never recorded a cross-country penalty in his career*

Ginny Elliot
COMPETITOR

■ Ginny has won two team silver and two individual bronze medals at the Los Angeles and Seoul Olympics; she has won Badminton three times, first of all on Priceless in 1985 (when she also finished third on Nightcap), on Master Craftsman in 1989, and with Welton Houdini in 1993; and she has won Burghley four times in succession. She was World Champion with Priceless in 1986, and won three successive European Champion titles, as well as two World Championship and two European Championship team medals. All this was in the course of her career as a senior rider; prior to that, in 1973, she was Junior European Champion. Ginny was awarded the MBE in 1986.

All good things come to an end however, and Ginny's marriage in 1994 to Mikey Elliot effectively closed the Ivyleaze chapter. The yard which saw so many successes is for sale, Heather is moving to a new home, and Dot has 'gone solo', teaching and training from her new home in Wiltshire. Many of her rivals may quietly breathe a sigh of relief for although Ginny continues to event, the phenomenal success achieved with the help of 'the best back-up team in the world' will be very hard to repeat.

Ginny has also proved herself to be an invaluable team member when representing Great Britain, always anxious to foster the same spirit and feeling of teamwork amongst her team-mates as was so carefully nurtured at Ivyleaze. When Master Craftsman was injured after being shortlisted for the 1992 Barcelona Olympics, Ginny accompanied the eventual team to give as much support and help as she could. Her own commitment to the team ethic was repaid by the support of her team-mates when things went so wrong for her at the World Championships in Stockholm in 1990 and at the European Championships at Achselschwang in 1993.

Two years before the Stockholm World Championships Ginny had had to make the very difficult decision to give up the ride on the powerful but extraordinarily talented Murphy Himself. He was one of the few horses Ginny chose herself, having escaped the watchful eye of Dot and Heather! In the years that followed he gave eventing enthusiasts some of the most exhilarating cross-country performances

ever witnessed. It is the mark of a true horseman or woman to want only what is best for the horse, and having been catapulted out of the saddle at Badminton when Murphy produced one of his famous leaps, Ginny began to feel that the horse really needed a stronger rider before he ended up doing himself some harm. Murphy went to Ian Stark, and in exchange Ginny accepted Griffin.

The partnership with Griffin started well when they won the Boekelo three-day event, but soon after that the horse began to reveal his limitations. When Master Craftsman was sidelined by injury, Ginny rode Griffin at the World Championships. For a rider who puts so much time and effort into the careful preparation of every horse for every competition, to be rewarded in Stockholm with a runout and a fall must have been heartbreaking. And for Ginny particularly, accustomed to the complete honesty and generous spirit of horses such as Master Craftsman and Priceless – in the whole of their career neither horse recorded a cross-country jumping penalty – it must have been soul-destroying. But she got him round, which is the number one priority when you are part of a team – and the team did take the silver medal. But it must have been with very mixed emotions that Ginny watched Ian Stark and Murphy Himself take the individual silver medal. At the time the 'swap' obviously seemed fair, and Ginny has been sufficiently sporting not to use the benefit of hindsight as any reason to begrudge the decision. Her level-headed attitude is probably tempered by her mother's reminder of 'Well, you chose him!'.

More disappointments were in store for Ginny when she again represented Britain at the 1993 European Championships. Riding Welton Houdini, with whom she had won her third Badminton earlier that year, they recorded an uncharacteristic runout on the steeplechase phase. Ginny considered that the horse had been spooked by the barrage of photographers with flashguns, but others were less charitable. For the first time in her competitive career Ginny was part of a British team which failed to complete the competition, because two other team members retired on the cross-country (see Chapter 8, Team Selection). Despite finishing 7th individually, it was a tough way to celebrate twenty years of competition success.

Ginny is still competing a few of her own horses, but she looks forward very much to starting a family and enjoying as much time as possible with her husband Mikey. They both share a love of hunting – Mikey is Joint Master of the Heythrop – and their marriage has provided him with a hunter which must be the envy of many: Master Craftsman! As the Master's horse he can spend much of his time at the front of the field, which is where most Olympic champions like to be! Ginny is also devoting more time to teaching now, and as jump co-ordinator is involved in the training of potential team members for the British squad.

THE OLYMPICS

Ginny thoroughly enjoyed both the opportunities she had to compete at the Olympic Games. 'I was lucky in that they were very good competitions for me personally and as a team member. I came away from each with exactly the same result – team silver and individual bronze. I suppose my first Olympics in Los Angeles stands out the most in my mind, but then Seoul was also extraordinary in itself; it was such a different country and culture, and in fact the language

At the 1984 Los Angeles Olympics, Ginny and Karen Stives (USA) became the first female event riders to win individual medals in the three-day event

barrier proved to be quite a problem. In Seoul we lived in the Olympic village which made you feel more involved in the Games themselves, whereas in Los Angeles the set-up was more like the usual international three-day events and was therefore more relaxed.

'Los Angeles was especially exciting for me because I became the first female event rider to win an individual medal – then about two minutes later the American Karen Stives took the silver ahead of me and became the second! We all became really over-excited and the whole trip was just the most marvellous experience. The competition itself is was highly stressful and nerve-racking, particularly as we were out there for some time, on both occasions, to help acclimatise the horses. There is a tremendous build-up of emotions, and this at a time when there isn't really very much you can be doing; you have only

one horse to ride, and just when you want to be keeping yourself really busy you find you have heaps of time on your hands and inevitably end up worrying about how it is going to go. Of the two cross-country courses I thought Los Angeles was probably the bigger, but Seoul was every bit as demanding because of the mountainous terrain. Seoul is also special to me because Master Craftsman was still a relatively inexperienced horse when he was asked to compete there, and he tried his heart out throughout.'

GINNY'S PERSONAL PHILOSOPHY

'I am very much a perfectionist, and as a team at Ivyleaze we all were, and it worked because we were all heading in the same direction. The training of an event horse must be undertaken with his long-term prospects in mind; there are no short-cuts and he must be properly and fairly prepared for each successive step in his training. The approach should always be based on the fact that prevention is better than cure; once a horse has a problem regarding some aspect of

his schooling it can be very difficult to overcome, so the art to training any horse is not to allow problems to develop. This requires patience and a thoughtful approach to all that you do.

'So, to be a successful event rider you have to be very determined, and very single-minded concerning where you are going. You must be completely honest with yourself as to where you feel you are not doing so well, and then you must be prepared to work hard to overcome these problem areas.

Thoughtful and thorough training reaps the highest rewards. Ginny and Priceless at the 1984 Los Angeles Olympics where they won individual bronze and team silver

'When I started I found the showjumping difficult, a weakness which wasn't helped by the fact that good cross-country horses don't always make good showjumpers. Dressage I have always enjoyed, so that was fun to work on; but I suppose the problem I struggled with the most was getting the time across country. I always tried to be very accurate and therefore strove for perfection at every fence; so getting round in the time was never paramount in my mind. Anyway, it should never *be* your aim if the horse is not ready to be asked to jump out of a faster rhythm. Once I have taught a horse to stay in balance and to keep his stride *round* even when he is asked to go faster, and having trained him to the point where he can nearly always take on the direct routes, then getting a good cross-country time becomes a lot easier. But it used to be quite a battle for me, and one which I only managed to overcome with a great deal of practice.

'Every rider needs financial back-up of some sort, whether from the owners or from sponsors or your own personal resources; but whilst it can be a real struggle I do believe that if you want to do something badly enough you will find a way which allows you to do it.

'I think it is a mistake to be too hungry to win; it is better to set out simply to do your best and to improve your performance each time. If you progress in this way then things *will* go right and winning will soon come naturally. Winning is important, but it should not be an over-riding goal. There is usually a certain element of good luck which contributes to your success, but I am not a great believer in bad luck – that is something we usually bring on ourselves. And it is worth remembering that we can make our own good luck by training and preparing the horse correctly.'

TEAM TRAINING

Ginny is now deeply involved in the training of potential British team riders and horses. This usually takes place during the winter training courses sponsored by the Horse Trials Support Group and the Worshipful Company of Saddlers, as well as in the concentrated team training sessions before each international championship. Explains Ginny:

'It is difficult for some of the riders I am now detailed to teach because a lot of them have competed against me in the past – it is quite hard for them to accept *my* trying to tell them what to do! However, I like to think that on the whole we have overcome this sort of embarrassment, and I have been particularly pleased that some of them have since come to me for further lessons, over and above the team training sessions. I now feel that most of them trust me and do

take on board the things I ask them to try.

'Each rider has his or her own particular style and the trainer must remember that. I don't want to change anyone's individual style as long as it is not hindering the horse, but rather I want to nurture that style in order to make it as efficient and successful as possible. There are certain faults that we all have, and these probably need sorting out and working on. I know from days of old how easy it is for small faults to creep in, and any that are allowed to develop are not going to help you leave the fences up when it really matters.'

Heather Holgate

SUCCESS BEHIND THE SCENES

■ 'Ivyleaze', the pretty house and yard just a short canter from Badminton House and its famous horse trials, has been home to Heather Holgate since 1980, although sadly she is to leave it soon. In fact it has been much more than a family home: as we have seen, it was the base from which Ginny operated the major part of her consistently successful eventing career.

Heather Holgate

Heather's commitment to the sport of three-day eventing stems from her belief that success in this field requires the complete education of the horse. 'You have to become accomplished in the three disciplines of dressage, showjumping and cross-country riding, and to succeed, your flatwork has to be in line with your jumping. You cannot ask a horse to perform a jumping exercise if he is not already working in a balanced and short enough outline on the flat' explains Heather. 'It is like having the opportunity to send your children to the best school you can, so they will receive a full and rounded education which will equip them for a successful and enjoyable life. When you train and ride an event horse successfully that is what you are giving him.'

Before Ginny was born, much of Heather's life was spent travelling and living abroad. 'Whenever I arrived in a new country, the first thing I looked out for was a horse,' recalled Heather. 'In the sort of countries we were in there were usually polo ponies. When we lived in the Philippines my father bred and sold polo ponies; with the help of a friend I had met who was very keen on dressage, we taught one of these to do advanced dressage movements – and it became one of the best polo ponies they had. When we moved back to England we lived in Devon near the Strachans.' Clarissa Strachan was a successful British event rider; after her marriage to the Dutchman Edward Bleekman, she set up a stud to breed and produce potential event horses. As well as competing themselves, the Strachans also ran a one-day event at their farm, and they were really responsible for drawing the

Holgates into the sport of eventing. When she was asked about the philosophy behind the Holgates' way of training and competing event horses, Heather offered a simple and honest answer: 'You really and truly have to love the horse, and must not abuse him in any way. Our other major stroke of luck was to have had one of the best vets in the world, Don Attenburrow. He taught us to understand exactly what was wrong with the horse. In any sphere, attention to detail can be the difference between winning and losing, life and death, and his attention to detail was second to none. We sought his advice on training techniques as well as on any physical disorders in a horse. For example when we first began to use trotting poles in our flatwork training he explained to us the degree of effort this required on the horse's part, and could advise us on how high it was safe to raise the poles to, how often the horse could undertake this sort of work, and what to beware of in terms of overdoing things.'

Heather firmly believes that event horses are trained rather than bred: horses will get to the top if properly trained, and she is saddened by the number of potentially top class horses that fall by the wayside because their basic training has been lacking in some way or other. She describes herself as a 'competitor behind the scenes: I don't want to ride competitively myself, but I want the horse and rider that I have helped prepare and train to go out and compete to the best of their ability. If we have done our job properly, and luck is on our side, then they should win.'

Heather picked up much of her equine knowledge, and her eye for a good horse, from her father, Ewart Rice. 'He was one of the greatest horsemen I had ever come across. Most of all he loved his hunting and breeding; he was not a competition rider, but he knew exactly what he was doing and why. Although he could never tell you *why* he had bought a particular horse. Like me, he usually just had a gut feeling about it which rarely let him down. To be successful in any equestrian discipline you need a horse that, when you look at him, looks back and says "Just look at me, I can do it!". Both horse and rider must want to be out there under the spotlight and winning.'

Ginny quite obviously had this quality. 'Even at three years old I remember Ginny being very obstinate and determined,' laughs Heather. 'And Sally Strachan told me that she was bossy enough to be a good competitor! But Ginny was never overly confident in herself, which I think is a good thing. You need to be determined, but being too confident is the biggest mistake a rider can make. An over-confident rider doesn't question his performance in order to improve it, and he tends not to listen to what could be useful advice. Ginny always blames herself, and looks to herself for improvement. I do think that our younger riders today have too much confidence in themselves. They need to remember that you must respect every single fence you are faced with – you haven't jumped it until you are over it.

'At Advanced level, whether or not a horse then goes on to be of true four-star championship-level calibre, and how successful it is, usually comes down to its temperament. Temperament is the most vital ingredient: it doesn't matter how talented the horse is because if it doesn't want to do the job then it is not going to be a champion. Mind you, a lot of the "I don't want to do it" is man-made, and that is why the correct basic training is so important. The right temperament is also essential in the rider. Riders must be determined, they do need a degree of talent, but more importantly they must have the desire to learn and to improve.

'The standard of riding today is not as good as it was, and we don't seem to be producing consistently successful horsemen or women any more. There are plenty of "five-minute wonders" but a true champion needs to be consistent. Too many riders cannot afford the training that they need, and in order to make a living from the sport they have to ride large strings of horses – and then it is just not possible to give every horse the time it really needs.'

GINNY'S BEST HORSES

■ Heather is often asked how she selects which horses to buy, and as she has said before, it really comes down to a gut feeling. 'Dot [Willis] tears each horse to pieces, which is an objective way of doing it, whereas I rely on something which just tells me whether I like the horse or not. When we showed Priceless to Dot her comment was that he might do nicely at Riding Club level! At this stage we already had Nightcap, who had belonged to our neighbour, so we had had plenty of opportunity to study him. Knowing that he was by Ben Faerie I took a chance on ringing Diana Scott (Ben Faerie's owner) and asking if she had anything else that might suit us, and she suggested Priceless. Despite being by the same stallion, Nightcap and Priceless were very different characters and also very different to look at. Nightcap was a good two inches bigger than Priceless, had more quality and was the most handsome, but Priceless always rode bigger than he looked, and in fact proved to be the better horse.

'Master Craftsman just had something about him that I couldn't resist. I do love big dark horses, and as soon as I saw him trot up I knew I wanted him, although he was by no means perfect. Neither Ginny nor Dot wanted to keep him as there was so much that we needed to change about him – but he was a success because he wanted to be trained. He didn't mind how many times you asked him to do something, and seemed to understand that once he got it right he would be allowed to stop. He allowed us to put into him the enormous amount of training that he needed, and was never cross or resentful. He just had the most marvellous temperament.

'We have learned so much from the different horses we have owned over the years. If you come across a problem in training you have to keep looking for a way round, and this means you quickly learn what works and what doesn't for different horses. I don't like gadgets of any sort, and so even more thought has always had to go into our training methods as there could never be any short-cuts. I suppose our general principle has always been never to put a horse in a position where he is being asked to do something which he is not really ready or able to achieve, because if he fails then you still have to reprimand him and this is a situation we would rather avoid.

'Pat Manning greatly influenced my way of training horses, and Dot was trained by Pat, and so it was through Pat that we came together as a team. Lady Hugh Russell was another tremendous influence. The sport now sadly lacks trainers of that calibre and character.'

Dot Willis

TRAINING FOR THE FUTURE

Dot Willis, trainer with a long-term strategy

■ 'It was fate,' says Dot Willis emphatically when asked how she came to help train and prepare Ginny Elliot's (née Holgate) horses; and in doing so became part of one of the eventing world's most successful stories. Dot goes on to explain her statement: 'I have always loved horses – regardless of their size or type, I just love them all. I came from a completely non-horsey background, brought up in a town where my first real contact with anything equine was looking after a show pony belonging to a friend of my father's, which was used to pull a little trap. My first "job" was looking after that pony, and then I went on to several other grooming jobs, in hunting or showjumping yards, riding out and caring for horses.

'I really do believe that if you show a certain degree of initiative and enthusiasm, then an opportunity of some sort will come your way. In my case I had begun going to evening classes in London to learn more about horse care and training; the usual lecturer was away for several weeks, and Pat Manning took his place. Pat gave me my first introduction to quality dressage, although I did not necessarily appreciate at the time just how good an introduction this was. Pat Manning worked for Robert Hall who had trained with the Spanish Riding School, and I went to Robert Hall as a working pupil; from there I went to work for Pat when she decided to set up on her own. I was her stable manager, and rode out and taught some of her working pupils.

'I worked for Pat for nine years, and during this time I tried to learn as much as possible from anyone I came into contact with. I also believe that if you want to learn from an expert in order to add their knowledge to yours to improve your own teaching and training, then you must study that person's methods at first hand; and so I attended as many lecture demonstrations and talks as possible. Having had a little bit of jumping experience when I rode at Pony Club level, I was always interested in eventing and over the years I visited various three-day events as a spectator.

'My introduction to Heather and Ginny Holgate came about when Pat became involved in the training of Juniors and Young Riders. Pat has always taught teamwork, meaning partnership between horse and rider, and also teamwork for the background people (family, helpers, grooms and so on), so when a rider came to Pat you soon became involved with the whole family. I met Ginny when she was a teenager, and hers was one of the families with which I formed a lasting friendship.

'When I left Pat's yard I spent about two years teaching freelance, and generally trying to decide exactly what I wanted to do. All the time you are working for someone you have a loyalty to that person even if you do not always agree one hundred per cent with the way they do things. I was starting to develop quite strong ideas of my own as to how I liked to see horses being cared for and trained; preparing an event horse requires an holistic approach in that you need to be aware of the background of both horse and rider, and of the feeding and stable management routine, as well as training and preparing the horse for competition. During this time I kept in touch with Heather and Ginny, and was called in quite regularly perhaps to look at a youngster they had bought, or to help get a horse going. When they moved from Devon to Ivyleaze in Gloucestershire, they asked me to join them. I was there for thirteen years and I would not have swapped one second of it!'

Dot is the first to point out what a remarkably privileged opportunity this was from a trainer's point of view. She was able to work with potential event horses, often bought as two-year-olds, right through to the height of their career. Very few riders actually keep the same horse from Pre-Novice right through to the Olympic Games, but this happened twice at Ivyleaze, with both Priceless and Master Craftsman. In particular Dot appreciated the teamwork and tremendous attention to detail which prevailed. 'I knew the people I was working with very well and that meant I was brave enough to be honest. You soon realise that things have to be talked through, and that, at worst, you may have to agree to differ. We rarely differed, but that doesn't mean that things weren't discussed in tremendous detail!'

This incredible teamwork enabled the Ivyleaze yard to produce horses capable of helping their rider to a string of successes. However, now Ginny is married, Ivyleaze is to be sold. But a positive aspect of this development is that a larger number of riders will now benefit from Dot's talent, experience and attention because she is continuing to teach on a freelance basis.

'I would like to go on with my freelance training,' explains Dot, 'and I would like to have a continuing rapport with riders who want to work with me; the pleasure is in seeing them gel and progress with the horse. I also want to continue to learn as much as possible myself; my father was always searching for new information and taking up new interests – well into his seventies he was still joining evening classes to learn new skills. I realise that this search for knowledge is quite an unusual thing to possess, but it has always been a part of my upbringing and it is why I try to learn as much as I can. And I hope that I help to provide information and answers to those with the desire to ask the questions.'

TEACHING PHILOSOPHY

■ Dot has very definite ideas about how a horse and rider should be trained: 'In my own teaching I try to get across the idea that training a horse is about a partnership – it is a two-way thing in that you should always ask the horse what he is trying to tell you before you ask him to do something. Why is he stiff, why does he find certain things difficult? If you understand the problems he is having – and although he can't tell you what they are, they will manifest themselves in the way he responds when you work with him – then you can work on removing the problem so that a resistance doesn't develop when you do ask him to work. Thus if he falls in on a corner he may be telling you that he is stiff in the shoulders, and so you can introduce an exercise such as shoulder-in to loosen him up before asking him to work correctly on the bend. If you don't bother to interpret the problem and just keep trying to make him do what you want, then his resistance to what you are asking him to do will get worse, resulting in a poor performance and possibly a very unco-operative horse.

'I want the rider to develop this feel for what the horse is telling him so that he recognises the symptoms of a bad way of going. Once you recognise the symptoms you can start to look for the cause. Horses do have feelings and they also have incredible memories. If they are taught something fairly and correctly they will retain it, but if they are not taught something clearly or are not properly prepared they will struggle to do what you ask. The horse is not to be blamed at this point because it is the responsibility of the rider and trainer to prepare and teach the horse properly.

'When you work with horses you really have to appreciate the ups otherwise you won't cope with the downs, but to appreciate them you must understand what you are trying to achieve so that you recognise when you have been successful. For example, I like to think that the riders I teach have a three-day event as their ultimate aim – although until I went to work with Heather and Ginny I simply did not appreciate that many riders do not have this aim; most are looking shorter-term than that. But if you have the three-day event as your ambition, then the one-day events are just part of your preparation rather than a goal in themselves. Winning a one-day event may not contribute in any way at all to your goal of a successful three-day event. But if at the one-day events you are consistently producing a good dressage test, and having obedient, rhythmic jumping rounds, and on each occasion are teaching the horse something new so that he has the necessary experience to cope with the three-day event, then those outings are all part of the ups.

'I get cross with riders if they are not prepared to work and try really hard because these are requirements of success in this sport, although I do accept that not every rider will get on with every horse. Some marriages don't work no matter how hard each partner tries, and the same is true of horses and riders. As you get to know the rider you are working with, you start to get a feel for how well he is suited to the horse he is on.

'As far as the horse is concerned, if you are starting with an untrained horse, or one that has just been backed, it takes at least fifteen to eighteen months to begin to know how far that horse might go. You have to bring out his natural talent, and it takes time to produce a loose-moving horse, to improve the quality and expression of his paces, and to see how he reacts at his first "parties". And after that there needs to be an assessment as to whether this particular horse and rider are going to get on together, or whether they would really be better off in a different partnership.'

TRAINING A NEW PARTNERSHIP

■ 'The first thing I hope when I meet a new partnership is that the horse is suitable for its rider, and that they are going to stay together with the aim of competing at a three-day event. I think it is relevant to ask how long the person has had the horse and to discover as much about its history as possible. Then I like to know how often the person rides the horse, its work régime, and how it is kept. All this is vitally important; for example, a lot of horses are over-fed for the amount of work they are doing, though you can't always tell this from the condition of the horse. But you don't want an over-fed horse creating more excitement and energy than it would naturally.

'I am not a believer in quick programmes, as my experience has shown me that you cannot take short-cuts. I want to keep moving forwards, to keep improving and encouraging both horse and rider, and I relate this to where they are now, and to what their aim is. The rider may think he is further down the line than he actually is, and we may discover that his intended target is unrealistic, or vice versa.

'My main aim is then to teach "feel" to the rider; he must learn to *feel* when the horse falls in on a corner, and to recognise why – why there was a loss of outline; once he recognises what went wrong and why, then he can start to prevent it happening. If he understands that, then at least as a trainer I can feel confident that, no matter how much or little he is able to ride the horse in between lessons, a part of what I have taught will carry on working for him because he will recognise and feel what is going wrong and can then work on putting it right in his own time.

'My lessons are usually structured so that horse and rider gain a certain amount of security and confidence in knowing where they are and what they are trying to achieve; but I also hope that the rider then has the desire to stretch both his own and his horse's ability so that he continues to improve. My long-term aim is to equip the rider with the knowledge and feel to improve the horse each time he rides it, and to help him improve and train any horse he may ride in the future.

'Part of my task as trainer is to assess the kind of person the rider is, and I find that people fall into three groups: those who make things happen; those who watch things happen; and those who wonder what's happened! Some riders can tell you exactly what they did to achieve a certain response from their horse; others may not even have noticed the difference in the

horse's way of going, and certainly couldn't tell you what brought it about. The first group are obviously the easiest and most rewarding to teach.'

MY HORSES, MY TEACHERS

'There is a book with the above title – the book is very good, but I think it is the title that says it all! With the benefit of hindsight you realise that you are learning all the time through the different horses that you work with. Ginny's first Olympic horse, Priceless, taught me so much because at the time I had very limited knowledge. He was five years old when I first saw him and I said he would make a nice riding club horse!

'But Priceless had three naturally elastic paces, and he was willing to do what you asked of him; he was enthusiastic and happy doing his job, although his temperament was very fragile for a horse that was not pure Thoroughbred. But from these basic qualities I learnt a great deal about how good a horse can become. At the time life was very busy, and it is only afterwards that you can reflect on how and why that horse became such a star. Priceless taught me that you have to *ask* the horse, you cannot *tell* him. He taught me that as long as you were fair, then he judged you to be OK and he was willing to co-operate and to learn.

'Master Craftsman had an absolutely Christian temperament and never questioned anything, ever; do you know he never recorded a cross-country penalty in his career. He always wanted to go forwards and to try whatever you were asking, although physically he found everything much more difficult than Priceless who was more of a natural athlete. But he was just so anxious to please and he did enjoy his job, although his technique was created rather than natural.

'All horses teach you something, and some teach you more than others – and the more horses you deal with, the more you are able to put into the next one that comes your way. There are often similarities, but no single one is ever the same as another. Moreover as a trainer you have to try to remember exactly why things went wrong – why did the horse behave in a certain way? Did you ever find out what caused the problem? – so that you can use this information either to prevent or to help overcome the same problem in another horse.'

TRAINING PRIORITIES

'As far as the trainer is concerned, every horse is at a different stage in its career. Some have been properly and fairly produced up to the stage they are at, others may have problems as a result of gaps or upsets they have had earlier in their education. But *all* training is based on the rider being fair, firm and consistent in the disciplining of the horse. You have to build on a foundation of control, impulsion and straightness. You are aiming to improve the quality of the paces, to establish an even rhythm in all paces, and to teach and develop the horse so that he can create the correct bend. Attention to detail must never be neglected.

'The maturity of the horse and rider and the nature of the partnership they form must also be taken into account; you may need to adapt or compromise your approach depending on your assessment of this.

'The trainer must also be aware of how a certain exercise affects other aspects of the horse's performance; an appreciation of this means that an exercise is always used to the overall advantage of the horse, and never in such a way as to disadvantage him. For example, I have watched many riders warming up their horses for a competition, and because they obviously don't really understand how an exercise specifically affects the horse, they will often undo with one movement, all the good they have created with another. Being aware of why you use an exercise is vital if you are to avoid this mistake.

'The good effects of the work you put into a horse can also snowball to your advantage. Thus if you can make the horse's shoulders more supple, the more powerful his quarters become; his paces become more expressive, he is more off his forehand. And once he is more balanced and controlled in his work, the less stress he puts on his front legs, which obviously works to his long-term advantage.

'It is also important to be aware of how factors outside the horse's flatwork training will affect how well he works on the flat. Thus any form of jump schooling, fastwork or cross-country riding will inevitably open out a horse's stride and push him further on to his forehand, causing his paces to become longer and flatter. After this sort of work you will therefore need to spend two or three days regaining the elevation and collection that is required for a successful dressage performance. I compare it to an accordion: jumping and fastwork open it out and flatten it, so you then need to work on lifting and closing it.'

From a rider's point of view Dot Willis' approach to training probably has to be experienced to be fully appreciated. During their enduring successes not everybody was willing to join the 'Ivyleaze fan club'; Dot, Ginny and Heather are three honest but strong personalities, and such a combination does not always

Ginny with Priceless, her first Olympic horse. Dot feels that Priceless taught her so much in her early years as a trainer

win friends. It is easy to view their obsessive attention to detail cynically, as a search for an excuse as to why they did not win, rather than seeing it as part of the learning curve on the path to perfection. They were seen by some as a formidable bunch – but when put to the test they have always proved to be open-minded and approachable.

Dot's training methods and ideas always put the horse first: attention to detail, and thoughtful and careful preparation and progress aim to ensure that he is ready and willing to do what you ask of him; in this way he rarely has to be chastised. There is a Chinese proverb in which Dot sincerely believes, one which can be applied to people as well as horses: 'Go back we cannot, stand still we dare not, go forwards we must.' I doubt a young horse exists that would not benefit from her approach.

Judging the Potential Three-Day Eventer

■ Competitions for potential performance horses have been a part of the continental scene for many years, and it is only more recently that they have become popular in the United Kingdom. The most popular class for the young eventer is the Pet Plan Burghley Young Event Horse competition for four- and five-year-olds. The horses are judged on their performance throughout a simple dressage test, a course of showjumps and on conformation. The ten highest-scoring horses are then seen at the gallop and are also judged on presence, or 'star quality'. Qualifiers are held all over the country and the final takes place at the Burghley three-day event in September. Dot Willis is often asked to help judge these classes, and she comments here on what she is looking for in the potential three-day eventer:

'I am looking for a loose-limbed horse which moves with a light step, not a laboured one, and that looks unrestricted in the shoulders. Schooling exercises can help free up the shoulders, but if you can *start* without any restriction then you will end up with much greater variation and expression in each pace. A good training system will help you get your four variations in pace in trot and canter out of any horse, but the horse that is naturally free in his shoulders will give you a much greater difference between the paces. The horse should also be sound in terms of the regularity and evenness of its steps. Some unevenness is rider-induced, however, and so although I would mark it down, I would not ask such a partnership to stop unless the horse was definitely uncomfortable.

'Ideally the horse should move straight when viewed from the front; if he does swing a leg one way or the other I don't mind too much as *long* as it is straight when the foot actually touches the ground. I don't mind if a horse is small as long as he has big movement.

'I like to see a horse with a naturally active hock – in order for the foot to travel cleanly over the ground there has to be a certain degree of bend in the hock. Some horses compensate for lack of bend in the hock by bending through the fetlock, and you have to watch for the difference because the one that bends through the fetlock will not produce a good jumping canter – that *has* to come from the hock.

'I like to see a horse with a reasonable amount of rhythm and balance, although having said that you can improve the paces, and the trot in particular, through schooling; so if the horse had a bit of a short step in trot I wouldn't mind too much. However, it must have what I call a "jumping stride" in canter; it should be active, and not too long and flat as a natural step.

'With the horse that is restricted or stiff the judge has to try to decide whether it is so because of the rider. It can be difficult to tell, but sometimes it is obviously rider-induced, particularly if the horse is out of balance – this is often a result of the rider hurrying the horse. The walk should have a good size overstep, as this is usually a sign that it can gallop. But equally, a *very* big overstep will make it difficult to shorten and collect the horse for dressage.

'When considering the horse and rider in profile I look to see if the rider is sitting in the middle of the horse so as to get an idea of how the length of front compares to the length of back. Only the conformation judge sees the horse untacked and, therefore, his true proportions.

'When judging the jumping, the horse should give you the impression that he wants to go forwards willingly. Even if he is having a look at the fence as he comes in, and is going forwards a bit of his own accord and a bit because his rider is telling him to, that

---

Dot comments: 'Watching this particular horse work, I am not too worried that he is showing the wrong bend – meaning that he bends to the outside instead of to the inside on curved lines – because that is a result of his training rather than an in-built problem that the horse himself has. He appears to be lame in trot, although this may have happened as a result of him knocking into himself while he was working in, something which can easily occur if the rider allows the horse to be bent to the outside in canter. I tend to assume that any horse presented to me is sound, but you often see horses that are anything but that. So you do have to look for unlevelness or irregularity in the step; there are degrees of both, and some is rider-induced, so I would only stop the rider if the horse appeared to be uncomfortable'

'A mistake such as this in the jumping, which was due to the rider bringing the horse in on a bad stride, would not be held against the horse; but what the judge will look for is the horse's attitude at the next fence – has he put the mistake behind him, is he still confident to jump, and does he try harder over the fence as a result of hitting the previous one?'

'The grey horse is much more established in his outline; he does not show as much movement as the first horse, but that could be improved with training. At the moment he is not working with enough impulsion but again, that is something that will come with further training. He keeps an even rhythm and takes level steps of a good length; he is a little on the forehand, which I would expect, at this stage of his training. He has a disappointing canter from a jumping point of view in that he bends the fetlock rather than the hock; again, the activity of the hock can be improved with training, but if a horse is naturally active in the hock then eventually you get better expression in the paces'

'Unfortunately he showed a very poor attitude to his jumping; you would forgive the "look-before-I-leap" type of jump typical of a novice, but not a horse like this which was saying "no" before it even came off the turn to the fence – the first thing the judge wants to see is that the horse wants to get to the other side. Nor does this one have any conscience about hitting fences, either; he has obviously learnt that these fall down and it doesn't bother him at all!'

'This horse is a nice type, but he is very lazy in the stifle; he looks super in front but behind there is no activity at all, and you need activity in the stifle and the hock if the horse is going to perform properly. However, he showed a good attitude and promising technique in the jumping'

is fine, as long as he is not busy going backwards or sideways on the way to the fence. The four-year-old horses *should* look quite green because they shouldn't have done very much. I really do believe that the more you do to the under-five significantly reduces the amount you will do once that horse is over twelve. The horse should have a jumping canter, and natural athleticism. I don't mind if he has a bit too much *joie de vivre* or is a bit humpy or bucky, as long as he isn't nappy. The canter must have life to it; it should travel upwards as well as forwards over the ground. After all, a very small jump is quite simply a canter stride with elevation.

'The horse must have a good fold in his forearms and knees. You can improve straightness, the bascule, the confidence and the balance with training, but the desire to go forwards must be there from day one.

'The next priority is that the horse is confident in himself and his rider. He must be bold and wanting to go somewhere, even if it is at a different speed to what the rider wants; he must *want* to get to the other side! If the horse loses confidence, or is generally sour or uninterested in going over a fence, then that is much harder to put right. Looking at a young horse, I don't mind if he is a bit crooked or too fast through the air as long as he wants to go to the jump with confidence, regardless of whether the rider is playing an active or a passive role.

'The horse's temperament is hard to judge within the confines of a competition, but a willing temperament certainly does help from an obedience point of view. But equally, obedience only exists if the horse trusts his rider.

'The interesting thing about the Young Event Horse classes is that you see each horse "in the raw", as there hasn't been time for the rider to manufacture too much in his way of going – if the horse looks good, it is usually because it *is* a potentially good horse, rather than a mediocre horse that has been intensely schooled to produce a half-decent performance.

'The rider who takes on the training of a young horse takes on a very big responsibility, and he should take time to do the job properly. In eventing, it is rare for any horse not to be *able*, physically, to jump the height and width of the fences involved; the reason most horses fail to move up through the grades is because they have been allowed to get stiffer with training, or have not been kept straight and correct in their work, or have lost confidence in the training they are being given. You can sometimes give confidence to a young horse by hunting him, ideally over hilly country with lots of ditches rather than over flat terrain with very big fences. But it can be *very* difficult to restore confidence to the horse that has got to Advanced level and *then* had a fright.

'Thus the rider's aim should be to make sure the horse always has the confidence to keep doing what you are asking him to do. If you teach him to jump straight and correctly in the beginning then that foundation stays with him throughout his career. As time goes on, any faults in the foundation training that the horse has received will show; and if the foundations crumble, then everything else goes with it and you have to rebuild from scratch. Thus the rider should aim to cover as many examples and situations as possible so that the foundations are laid securely and broadly; with this proviso the horse should be able to cope with whatever he is asked to do in life. The trainer owes that much to every horse that comes into his care.

'As a trainer I am looking for education, not the spectacular. To me there is no joy in being able to boast that my pupil got round nearest to the optimum time. My ideal is to say that my pupil has completed twelve three-day events without a cross-country fault. And that is how the rider should view the training of his horse: he should be aiming for long-term results.'

THE POTENTIAL OLYMPIC HORSE

■ 'If you look at the Olympic Games as one of the top championships in the sport, it has to be said that not every rider is capable of riding at that level, and not every horse is capable of winning at that level; but I am quite sure that with correct training, far more horses could compete at that level. There are certain basic attributes that your potential Olympic horse should possess: first, his natural way of going must be loose and supple; he must have three adequate paces, which cannot afford to be naturally stiff or restricted – you can loosen him up and improve his balance, but you want to start with as much natural ability as possible.

'The horse must be very enthusiastic about his job, and must be naturally forward-thinking. You can make a horse faster through his fitness programme, but what you are looking for is a horse which is always wanting to generate a forward gear. We want to make the horse more of an athlete, to become more "elastic" and to create more expression in his paces, and this is easier if you start with a horse that can "dance" to begin with.

'Temperament is very difficult to assess when you first see a horse. The attributes we have mentioned are apparent straightaway, but you can't really be sure of a horse's temperament until you have worked with him for several months: some horses, like people, rise to a challenge, whilst others may be overwhelmed; some have nerves which they don't show in a tense manner, so you may not realise when they are worried.

'Finally, the event horse you buy must want to get over the fence you put him at; the jockey may be a wonderful technician and prepare and place him just right at his fences but the horse must, from day one, want to get over the fence. The Pet Plan Burghley Young Event Horse classes are good for assessing this because it is obvious which horses want to get over the fence – they may not do it perfectly, but you can tell if the intention is there, and this is most important; a horse's technique can usually be improved with work and time, but his attitude may be impossible to alter.

'I am always wary of spooky horses as they tend to be very "looky" jumpers – although on paper it is easy to look for perfection, and some spooky horses lose their lookiness as they gain in confidence and education; with a brave rider they may go on to the highest level. After all, you don't have to jump every direct route in order to win an Olympic medal.'

THE LONG-TERM VIEW

■ Anyone who has experienced the Ivyleaze approach will appreciate that the training programme was built on the assumption of a horse and rider partnership being together for some time, the long-term aim being success at a three-day event. Thus the régime of which Ginny was a part allowed both her and the horses that were lucky enough to come into the yard to fulfil their maximum potential. Such a policy takes great self-discipline and also a certain amount of confidence – the sort of confidence that means you will choose to wait until a horse is as well prepared as possible before asking him to compete.

One of the problems in the sport of horse trials today is that many riders make it their career and so need to make money from it in order to live. However, prize money in eventing has always been low and so they have to derive their income in some other way. Few are lucky enough to secure long-term sponsorship, and most rely on the income derived from keeping other people's horses in their yard, schooling and competing them on the owners' behalf. Another option is

to buy and sell event horses. However, both these avenues put pressure on the rider to go out and win points: if he can keep winning then surely the owner will leave the horse with him, and if he can pick up points on a horse he is bringing on then he will get a better price for it when it is sold. Very often the result is that the horse's training is not long term, but is based on pushing it into competition as soon as possible and getting placed. This can mean that a great deal of the steady preparatory work is rushed, the work which helps to build up confidence and physique and so prepare the horse for the future; the horse may succeed for a certain length of time, but once it upgrades to Advanced the deficiencies in its basic training and upbringing will start to show. It is highly likely that the true potential of many good horses is lost in this way.

The most important ingredient for success in a horse's education, therefore, and the one that every rider should grasp from the Ivyleaze approach, is the need to think in the long term. A great many horses would be grateful for such an attitude.

5
The Olympic Experience

The one thing that comes over loud and clear when speaking to Olympic competitiors is that the Olympics are different to any other competition. Olympic gold is seen as the pinnacle of any sporting career, and is recognized as such the world over. And on a more personal level, from the competitors' point of view, there is the added excitement of training and living amongst the world's top athletes. Having said that, competitors' attitudes have changed slightly with regard to what they expect from a competition: riders from eventing's golden era such as Bertie Hill and Richard Meade still see it as paramount that the sport remains in the Games. But some of today's riders such as Andrew Nicholson and Bruce Davidson are beginning to question the price to be paid in terms of the hot, hard conditions which seem to prevail at Olympic sites. As Andrew Nicholson concluded 'To previous generations the Olympics were all-important. Today's riders would probably rather compete where the conditions are appropriate, but then we also have to think of future generations: do we have the right to deny them their Olympic opportunities? That is what would happen if the sport left the Olympic movement in search of more suitable venues.'

• *Munich 1972: Richard Meade remains the only British rider to win an individual Olympic gold medal. The team also won gold*

Matt Ryan

OLYMPIC GOLD MEDALLIST

■ Matt Ryan's success at the Barcelona Olympics appeared to come as a surprise to everyone but himself, although he is the first to admit that the rest of the world had not taken too much notice of him until he rode at Badminton for the first time in the May of that Olympic year. Riding Kibah Tic Toc, a horse that he had brought over from Australia with him to England in 1989, he produced an exceptional cross-country round in what proved to be some of the wettest conditions Badminton had experienced for many years. Later that year the 28-year-old Australian went on to ride the then 15-year-old Kibah Tic Toc to take team and individual gold medals in Barcelona – but he had been knocking at the door of top class competition for some time.

'I was long-listed for the Seoul Olympics in 1988,' explains Matt, 'and at the time I had two possible rides. The one I personally preferred did not have such a good competition record as the other horse, but I kept pushing all the good points about my favourite horse to the selectors, and telling them I wasn't sure that the other horse was really quite up to it. But my favourite horse went lame, and I was not selected on the second horse! That taught me never to run a horse down to anybody, because I am sure if I had not been biased towards the first horse I would have been picked on the second one; but like a fool I had been continually planting doubts about that horse in the selectors' minds. I went as reserve rider, but it was still a high price to pay.'

Matt then hoped he would be picked to represent Australia for the World Equestrian Games in 1990, but Kibah Tic Toc wasn't fully fit. However, Matt found himself at the Games grooming for the rest of his family: his brother Heath finished 21st in the three-day event, his father was competing in the carriage driving, and Heath's wife rode in the dressage.

With the 1992 Barcelona Olympics in his sights, Matt rode at Badminton in the May of that year in order to qualify for the Olympics, and to show the selectors that he and Tic Toc were worthy of a team place. Their fast, clear cross-country round left them in third place with just the showjumping to come; but five fences down dropped them from third to eighth place.

Matt was angry with himself; he had overdone things in the practice ring, then found himself in the main show-jumping arena on a very tired horse. Explains Matt:

'The problem goes back to when I rode at Saumur in 1990. I was fifth after the cross-country, and as we warmed up for the final showjumping phase, Tic Toc was jumping brilliantly. The person training me at the time suggested that the best tactic was to ride the horse really deeply into the practice fence to make him hit it, which would just remind him to pick his feet up when we went in to jump his round. Tic Toc was so genuine and honest that the more I tried to make him hit the fence, the harder he tried to clear it. When I did finally get him to hit it, I had obviously tired him out because he went into the final phase and had five fences down.

'I thought I had learnt my lesson; but on the last day at Badminton I just couldn't believe our luck to be lying in third position and got carried away with my warm-ing-up again, though for a different reason. This time Tic Toc was rushing into his fences, although in fairness he was clearing them. But I went into "schooling mode" and kept checking him to make him listen to me on the way to the fence and not to rush. Again, I eventually got him doing what I wanted, but by then he was tired. I should have let him go into the ring while he was still feeling fresh and sharp – it may not have looked a very tidy round, but I am sure it would have been a more successful one.'

The performance was still good enough to get them into the team for Barcelona; Matt felt he was harshly marked in the dressage to finish up in eighteenth place, but there was no time to waste worrying about it. Then on cross-country day he asked to be kept informed of everything that was happening on the course, even if it was chaos out there.

'Before I ride across country I do get very, very tense and am sometimes physically sick, but once I set off I am completely focussed on what I am doing. Whilst I ride very positively, I do find it helps to be aware of what might go wrong; and this is not negative think-ing, it is good preparation. If I am aware of *how* things can go wrong at a fence, then if I sense even a hint of

Matt and Kibah Tic Toc competing at Badminton in 1994

that happening I am prepared for it and can counter it. Cross-country is my strongest phase and so if I hear that a course is causing lots of trouble, instead of making me nervous it gives me confidence, because I know I have a chance then of moving up the places if I make a good job of it. Andrew Nicholson, who had had a worse dressage score than me, was the provisional leader when I set off, so I was determined to give it everything I had – I knew I could take the lead if I got it right. We had a hairy moment at the first water complex: the fence on top of the bank above the lake had been causing some problems so I rode it really strongly – but the stronger and longer the stride you are on, the harder it is to see a good stride; we arrived a long way off the fence, so Tic Toc chipped in a little stride. It was an uncomfortable moment! – but although some people said that as a team the Australians were lucky to survive such moments, I would argue that it was our style and technique that allowed us to survive, not luck.'

Matt's cross-country round was the fastest of the day and took him into the lead, ahead of Andrew Nicholson for New Zealand, and Herbert Blocker for Germany. The team situation was that New Zealand had one showjump fence in hand over Britain to retain gold, while Australia was a further five fences behind in bronze position, and the Germans were fourth.

At the final veterinary inspection on the morning of the showjumping phase, Great Britain had lost one team member – Murphy Himself, who was lame – and had thus dropped to sixth place. New Zealand was now leading with six fences in hand over Australia, and Germany had moved up to bronze position. Matt still held his individual lead, which meant that he would be the very last competitor to jump. Although he maintains he felt pretty calm about it all, it is hard to believe that there were no doubts in his mind after his Badminton disaster in this phase; but he knew he had improved his showjumping with the help of Vicky Roycroft (whose father-in-law Bill Roycroft had been in the last Australian gold medal-winning team thirty-two years before in Rome) and, having convinced himself that this was 'just another event', Matt rode confidently into the ring. It was perhaps fortunate that he had not witnessed the demise of the New Zealand team's hold on gold as a result of Andrew Nicholson's heartbreaking round on Spinning Rhombus: nine fences down saw them plummet from second to sixteenth position, and with them went their team's gold medal.

Somehow Matt and Kibah Tic Toc kept their cool to produce a flowing round – they were clear until the last fence, and they could afford to let this fall – and the gold was theirs! Amidst the tumultuous applause Matt finally became aware that Australia had also won team gold.

Looking back at what was the experience of a lifetime, Matt says that the worst part about it was that he had tried so hard to convince himself that this was just another event at which he was competing, that when he won, it still felt like 'just another event' – he couldn't bring himself to accept that he had just won Olympic gold!

'It was almost an anti-climax! The first feeling was just of tremendous relief that both myself and the horse had come back in one piece. We had gone out and done the job we were there for, we had done it well, and had both come back safe and well. I know from the video that I spoke to Princess Anne when I was presented with my medals, but I can't remember any of it, and I certainly don't know what I said! It's only as time goes by that you experience the exhilaration and delight, and the realisation of what you have achieved. I probably get a bigger kick out of watching the videos of what happened than I do of trying to remember what it was actually like while it was happening. Certain things stand out in my mind, but not the event as a whole.

'During the build-up to the event we attended several lectures with the other Australian athletes, and one of these was given by a sports psychologist. He seemed a very nice sort of chap, and I got to know him quite well as he spent a lot of time chatting to me over the next few days. I rang my parents one night and mentioned this fellow to them; I think my exact words were, "He can't have much work to do because he spends all his time chatting to me!" I was completely oblivious to the fact that our selectors had obviously filled him in on my showjumping record to date, and he had been instructed to work on keeping me calm and building up my confidence. It shows how good he was at his job – I just thought he was being friendly!'

Winning both team and individual gold medals at the Olympics might well satisfy the ambition of a good number of riders, but Matt wants more. 'My aim in life is to continue to represent Australia and to win gold medals,' he says emphatically. Obviously he has concerns about the heat and humidity problems in Atlanta, the site of the 1996 Olympics, but because adjustments will be made to the speeds and distances involved on cross-country day, he is confident that it should still be an enjoyable and successful event. 'Initially I felt we should not run at Atlanta, but now I can see that if we *don't*, then we risk the sport of three-day eventing being dropped from the Olympic Games' he concludes.

With selection for the European Championships in mind (in 1995 the Championships were opened up to allow non-European countries to take part to give riders another opportunity to qualify for the 1996 Olympics) Matt entered the eighteen-year-old Tic Toc for Badminton, where they had their best-ever result. The old horse produced the dressage performance of a lifetime to put him in second place behind Britain's William Fox-Pitt and Chaka. An exhilarating cross-country ride, which included bouncing out of the Sigma Hollow instead of taking a stride, saw them finish 25 seconds inside the time and able to hold on to their second place; William Fox-Pitt held his pole position, and America's Bruce Davidson was lying third. Tension increased the following morning when Chaka was eliminated at the final veterinary inspection; suddenly Matt was in the lead, but without even the luxury of a fence in hand over the fiercely competitive and highly experienced Bruce Davidson. Lady Luck had smiled once on Matt to put him in the lead, but she wasn't going to oblige twice; coming in last to showjump, Matt knew he had to go clear. Kibah Tic Toc jumped his heart out, but at the gate, which proved to be the bogey fence of the showjumping phase, he just got a fraction too close and had it down. The groan from the crowd must have made it almost impossible for Matt to hold his concentration and nerve to finish the course, but that was their only mistake and they finished a well deserved second, behind the veteran Bruce Davidson.

YARD SET-UP AND GENERAL ROUTINE FOR THE RYANS

■ Matt and his English wife, Nikki, have their base at the East Lockinge Stud in Oxfordshire. Their facilities include a large American barn complex plus outdoor stabling, an indoor school, and paddocks for grazing and schooling. They also have easy access to the local hills, and gallops for fastwork. Most of the seventeen horses in the yard belong to owners who pay a livery fee to have their horse cared for, schooled and competed by Matt and his staff. Matt takes his responsibilities towards his owners very seriously and makes sure that he personally rides every horse at least every other day; this means riding up to eleven horses each day!

Fellow Australian Felicity Crib does much of the schooling of the horses he can't ride on a particular day, helped by yard manager Heather Cummings and a young Italian rider who, although he 'still has a lot to learn', Matt considers to be quite talented. Rachel, Matt's travelling head groom, accompanies Matt to most of the big events and is also responsible for riding some fastwork and lungeing any horses that need it. Depending upon the time of year, there are usually two or three working pupils.

Nikki takes charge of the surprisingly large amount of paperwork that running a big yard creates: entries, bills, vaccinations, passports and so on for all the different horses, answering owners' questions, and keeping each one informed as to where his or her horse is entered. She also supplies an enormous picnic at every event for the owners, their families and friends. Indeed she sets a wonderful example to all riders as to how they should treat their owners: people like to feel appreciated, and Nikki's picnics and relaxed, friendly manner certainly make them feel well looked after. It obviously worked for Matt; he met Nikki while she was sharing a house with a friend in Dauntsey, Wiltshire, where Matt was based for a while. As Nikki recalls, 'My house mate was very "horsey", and one night when it was my turn to cook, she announced that someone called Matt Ryan was coming round, so would I cook for him as well!'

Although Matt lacks a main sponsor, he is helped and supported by a number of companies whose products he endorses. They include IT Professional Systems who produce computer software for accountancy firms; Wintec Saddles; Joseph Liddy (an Australian company producing horse-care products); Hydrophane champion gloves and Tipperary body protectors; the Horseland range of skull caps; and Bluntstone Boots, another Australian company. Riders are finding increasingly that they have to use their initiative to market themselves as a worthwhile investment for a wide range of different companies. It is not always enough just to be good on horseback – you have to be good with people, too.

Matt's Barcelona partner, Kibah Tic Toc, was gracefully retired shortly after his Badminton success. Ideally Matt would have liked his swansong to have been the 1995 European Championships but decided against asking any more of this wonderful horse. There are very few event horses that compete beyond the age of fifteen or sixteen, but Matt attributes Tic

Matt and Tic Toc at the Barcelona Olympics

RIGHT: The Ryans enjoying one of Nikki's
splendid picnics

Toc's longevity to the fact that he hasn't had to compete him too rigorously; Barcelona was only the fifth three-day event that the horse had done, and because at present the nucleus of Australian riders is relatively small, no one has to run a horse excessively in order to impress the selectors.

Matt confidently predicts that he should have five or six really good Advanced horses up and running for the 1996 season, and he is hopeful that at least one of them would be considered good enough for a team place. Of his possible Olympic rides Matt had particularly liked Regal Style: a tough, wiry Australian Thoroughbred, he was the right type to cope best with the conditions in Atlanta. However, life as a professional event rider can be tough: you have to make a living and you rarely own the horses you ride, and in the summer of 1995 Regal Style was sold to America. As Matt explained, 'Nikki and I part-owned Regal Style and whilst I rated him very highly we were offered an extremely good price for him. We needed a new lorry, and without a main sponsor, the decision had to be a commercial one.'

Matt is certainly not the only event rider who has found himself in this difficult position; unfortunately money *does* make the world go round. On the bright side as regards Atlanta, however, as reigning Olympic champion he automatically has a place in the individual competition. In Atlanta the competition is split, for the first time, into individuals and teams, and this does pose another difficult question for riders selected to compete in both competitions: do you save your best horse for a chance of personal glory as an individual, or does national pride persuade you to ride that one in the team competition?!

Mary King

MAKING IT TO THE TOP

King William tackles the showjumping phase – always a nerve-racking time for everyone involved with him!

■ The story of Mary King's (née Thomson) rise to the top in the eventing world, crowned by a win at Badminton in 1992, team gold medals at the World Championships in 1994 and the 1995 Open Europeans as well as the individual bronze, reads very much like a fairy story: born into a completely un-horsey family, Mary begged rides on anything until she was finally loaned the local vicar's pony. She took on any number of odd jobs – a butcher's round, cleaning campsite loos and gardening – so she could keep two horses to compete, and a third to bring on to sell in order to swell the funds. Finally she managed to secure sponsorship, first from the Carphone Group and then from Gill Robinson, whose friendship, loyalty and

support has been unwavering and who is still the owner of most of Mary's horses. More recently, additional sponsorship has been given by Frizzell Countryside Insurance. In 1995 Mary married David King, finally rewarding his patient courtship of twelve years. David has always supported Mary in her endeavours, and is a part-owner of both King William and Star Appeal. His 'stag night' was spent in Ireland so that he could watch Mary compete at Punchestown, and Star Appeal gave them an early wedding present by winning the three-day event.

But to refer to Mary's climb to the top as a fairytale does not do justice to Mary herself. All her successes and achievements have been hard won and are a tribute to her character as much as to her talent as a rider; she is rarely seen without a smile on her face, always appearing to be thoroughly enjoying herself. She and her horses are immaculately turned out and, most important of all, she always has time to spare for anyone: whether it is a fellow competitor seeking advice or a child wanting an autograph, no one is made to feel unwelcome or a nuisance. Before setting up her own yard, Mary worked for Sheila Willcox for two-and-a-half years. Sheila was Britain's first consistently successful lady event rider, winning Badminton three times, in 1957 and 1958 on High and Mighty, and the following year on Airs and Graces. A tough employer she may have been, but Mary learnt a great deal, particularly regarding the training of young horses.

Mary rode at Badminton for the first time in 1985, riding Diver's Rock; they finished seventh, and were shortlisted for the European Championships that year. But it was not to be Mary's year, as Diver's Rock developed navicular and had to be put down. For some years after that Mary seemed to be for ever knocking at the door but never quite getting in, being consistently placed but with the big wins seeming to elude her. Then in 1989 she was second at Badminton on King Boris, and in 1990 they won the British Open Championship at Gatcombe. The following year she retained this title on the young King William, and at long last was selected, with William, to be a member of a British team, riding at the European Championships held at Punchestown in 1991.

At Punchestown, William galloped confidently from fence to fence and looked all set to finish within the time and take the lead. But at the penultimate fence, a big drop into water, he jumped in so boldly that his legs buckled underneath him and Mary was thrown off. They completed the course, but Mary had injured her knee and could not showjump on the final day. Nevertheless the team went on to win the gold medal.

At Badminton in 1992 Mary was determined to get it right. She knew the selectors liked William but she had to prove that they could survive the big occasion without mishap (at William's first Badminton in 1991 he had slipped up on the flat between two fences). And William more than proved his ability by winning the world's most prestigious three-day event. For all that it was a hard-won victory: although William led from day one, it was his showjumping which had tended to let him down in the past – at his last two three-day events he had knocked down three showjumps – so although Mary went into the showjumping phase with one fence in hand over Ginny Leng, with William's record this was a very narrow margin. For those spectating who knew the horse and his record, the sus-

pense was almost unbearable, and William inspired no real confidence when his first reaction on entering the arena was to shy at the ornamental fountain! But although he rattled a few poles, his nerve held until the final double where he knocked the first element. The groan from the crowd convinced Mary that they must have faulted at both elements, but as she went through the finish the cheers told her that they had won.

This victory earned Mary and William a place in the British team for the 1992 Barcelona Olympics; they were detailed to go third in the team's order of running. William's dressage was not until quite late on the first day, but even so the atmosphere was highly charged with excitement. At Badminton there is usually an expectant but respectful hush as each rider enters the arena, but in Barcelona the enthusiastic crowd greeted each rider with cheers and waves. William performed a very good test but was much stronger and more tense than Mary would have liked. After the dressage phase she lay fourth individually behind the German rider Matthius Bauman and her fellow team members Ian Stark and Karen Dixon, and the British team was in the lead. Knowing William's ability across country Mary was looking forward to attacking the course, because a fast clear could well lift her up through the places.

By the time Mary's turn came she already knew that Richard Walker and Jacana had had a refusal and a fall, and that Karen Dixon had achieved a good clear although she had been instructed to take some of the longer routes. On the steeplechase, however, Mary soon became aware that, for the first time in his life, William was trying to use his strength and power against her; he was jumping beautifully out of his stride but was continually trying to accelerate away from his fences. He settled for her again on Phase C, but on the narrow early stretch of the cross-country course he became increasingly strong, and seemed to be trying to bolt away from the crowds which flanked him on each side, cheering and waving. And Mary was finding it harder and harder to hold him; the course was twisty in places and the ground very hard, and she was worried about him slipping up on the flat.

Her problems increased as she realised she would not be able to jump the direct route at the first water complex safely. As she explained: 'Although I could hold William on the approach to the fences, as soon as I released the rein to allow him to jump, he took hold of it and accelerated forwards. I simply did not feel it was safe to jump a combination into water with a horse that was continually running through my hand and therefore making up too much ground with each stride. I hoped that by the time we reached the second water he would have started to settle, but he just scorched down the hill towards the first element. There was no way I could contain him so as to jump it safely, and so again I had to opt for the alternative. The further we progressed the harder William pulled, and I had to resort to swinging him from side to side to get him back enough in front of his fences. The finish was a very welcome sight!'

Mary's round meant that she maintained fourth place, and with a good clear round from Ian Stark and Murphy Himself as well, the team was lying second behind New Zealand with high hopes of overtaking them in the final showjumping phase. Both teams had potentially weak links as regards this phase, namely King William and Spinning Rhombus, but the British were quietly confident that William would outperform his New Zealand rival. By the following morning, however, things were looking very different; sadly, Murphy Himself failed the final horse inspection and so Richard Walker's score had to count, and with it the prospect of a team medal faded away. Although William was far more tractable and ridable in the showjumping than he had been on the cross-country the previous day, he was too tense to be really round in his canter, and so lift his shoulders which he needs to do in order to jump cleanly. In short, he had five showjumps down and fell to ninth place. Karen Dixon finished sixth, as did the British team. As Mary recalls: 'My immediate thoughts as we left the showjumping arena were how lucky we had been at Badminton. And then, in a funny way, I still couldn't help but feel really pleased with William. He had completed an Olympic competition and was ninth in the world!'

The following year Mary and William were not included in the British team sent out to the European Championships in Achselschwang; however, they found favour a year later when they were selected to go to the 1994 World Championships in the Hague. There was some muted criticism regarding the choice of King William but, having failed to complete the team competition at the European Championships (see Chapter 8) Britain still needed to qualify for the 1996 Atlanta Olympics. William might prove to be a disappointment in the final phase, but you could almost guarantee that he would go fast and clear on the cross-country, and that he would pass the final inspection.

King William took an early and unbeatable lead in the dressage, 7.8 penalties ahead of nearest rival and fellow team-mate Karen Dixon on Get Smart, and the British team headed the field at the start of speed and endurance day. William went first for the team, and it was a shock to everybody when suddenly he showed signs of real tiredness towards the end of the course.

Mary nursed him home clear, but it was a warning to all concerned that the heat and humidity would take their toll. Later William was found to be partly dehydrated, and after that the British horses were stomach-tubed with fluids in the ten-minute box.

On the final day, Britain had five fences in hand over the French team. This seemingly generous margin would not, however, have done very much to settle Mary's nerves, because she knew that William could go in there and do anything, from jumping clear to knocking the lot down. The pressure was made greater by the fact that she was lying second individually and was therefore the last of the British riders to jump. The others had done their best; Kristina Gifford had jumped clear, but both Charlotte Bathe and Karen Dixon had knocked the final fence so William had three fences in hand if they were to keep the team gold. He started well enough, although observers who knew him well would have noted nervously that he was jumping left-handed, a sure sign that his nerves were close to bubbling over. He knocked two elements of the treble, and there were still too many fences left for Mary to relax for a moment; but the water fence seemed to help get him high in the air again, and he came home without a further mistake. He had done more than enough to secure the team gold but not quite enough to reward Mary with an individual medal; for the British, individual bronze went to Karen Dixon, a thoroughly deserved reward for a solid, reliable performance.

The 1995 European Championships saw a British challenge spearheaded by Mary and William. They went into the showjumping phase just 0.2 penalties behind the leader, but two fences down was still good enough to secure gold for Britain and bronze for Mary: her first individual medal. King William is a horse that you cannot help but admire, and he has a huge fan club; but for his rider his supreme ability in the dressage and cross-country phases must be somewhat tempered by the uncertainty of what he will do in the showjumping. For Mary, the pressure has been partly eased by the emergence at Advanced level of her prodigious talent Star Appeal, who was fourth at Burghley in 1994, and won Punchestown in 1995. Not that William has been demoted by his arrival, as Mary continues to work on solving his problems in the showjumping arena; these do seem to be as a result of the tension he experiences at three-day events, because he has produced some super rounds at one-day events. In an unguarded moment after Barcelona Mary once said that she hoped she would never have to ride him in a three-day event again: she is now convinced, however, that King William's finest hour could still be to come.

LIFE AS AN OLYMPIC ATHLETE

■ 'The honour I felt at being asked to represent my country at the Olympic Games is something that will never leave me' says Mary, 'and I have never felt as patriotic as I did when we all went out to Barcelona. And what is extra special about the Olympics is that you find yourself amongst so many other people who have worked hard to make it to the top of their particular sport. I was really looking forward to the whole experience, although a great many people told me not to get overexcited, that it wasn't that different. But I loved every aspect of it – even arriving at Badminton for the team concentration was exciting, especially as Badminton has such a special aura anyway. It was the start of our becoming a team, and as time went on it came home to us more and more that it really was going to happen: we were going to the Olympics!

'We were given all kinds of clothing and tack by the Olympic team sponsors, including some wonderfully lightweight show jackets from Bernard Weatherill. All the horses were measured up for new dressage saddles from an Italian company, and although we knew they wouldn't be ready for the Olympics themselves, we were all looking forward to using them. Sadly the company went into receivership and the saddles never did arrive. In fact, in spite of all the equipment you are given, riders do get very attached to certain things they have always used, so you are not made to use anything new that you don't wish to at the competition itself. But it was all part of the general buzz and excitement that started the countdown to when we actually left for the Olympics.

'The Olympic village was a purpose-built complex which would later become a holiday centre. We lived in self-contained apartments with three double bedrooms, a lounge and kitchen area, and two bathrooms. But we did not have to worry about catering for ourselves; I love my food, and the Olympic canteen was beyond even the wildest imagination. Every nation was catered for, with every kind of food, and you could have as much of whatever you wanted, whenever you wanted it. There were huge refrigerated displays of every kind of fresh fruit, freezers full of ice-cream, and rows and rows of cold drinks and yoghurts. You all sat together at long tables – one morning I had breakfast with Linford Christie! That is what is so wonderful about the Olympics: competing there puts everybody on the same level. Outside the main canteen there were fast-food places such as MacDonald's and Pizza Hut, and everywhere you walked there were free cold drinks dispensers. Everything was free, and it was all open twenty-four hours a day.

'Most competitions finished between twelve and two because of the heat, and everybody headed for the beach. It was amazing – everywhere you looked there were fit, tanned, well muscled bodies. We used to try and guess what people did by the size and shape of their muscles! And it was made even better by the fact that there were about three males to every female!'

Mary remains enthusiastic about the whole experience, in spite of the hostile reception the team received when it returned home (see Chapter 3, Karen Dixon). As Mary said, 'It was very disappointing not winning any medals but personally I take things as they come, and you can't expect to win all the time. I don't think there is any particular thing any of us could or should have done differently. The problems we faced were quite unexpected, and they occurred on the day, and each rider had to deal with them as they arose. As far as I'm concerned it was someone else's turn to win. You can only ever win at the expense of someone else, and sometimes you have to accept that *you* are that someone else. We have shown what we are capable of since then, but winning does require luck and in Barcelona we were unlucky.

'It has always been my ambition to ride at an Olympics and I thought Barcelona might have satisfied it; but it hasn't! I desperately want to ride at the next Olympics – *and* win a medal!

'King Kong seemed to be the most suitable of my horses in terms of being the type best able to cope with the climate in Atlanta, but sadly he injured his tendon at Burghley in 1995 and there is some doubt as to whether he will be able to event again. There is the possibility that one competitor may be able to take two horses because there is now a team and an individual competition. What happened to William in the Hague frightened me a bit, and for a while I thought he wouldn't be the sort to cope with Atlanta. However, I now know that he wasn't as fit or as lean as he could have been. At Badminton in 1995 I had him much lighter and fitter and he wasn't worried by the heat at all. A year ago I would have ruled him out of competing in Atlanta, but now I do believe he would be a good team member; he is such a sound, strong horse, and – touching wood! – his cross-country is almost guaranteed.

'William has also proved since Barcelona that as long as he remains quiet, relaxed and soft, he can showjump very well. It does just seem to be the tension he experiences at Badminton – which in 1995 spilled over into the dressage and upset his performance. Despite this he has

Gatcombe 1995: Mary looked set to win the Open Championship title when, only a few fences later, King William made a rare cross-country mistake – he overjumped a very straightforward fence and unseated Mary

helped Britain to both World and European gold. Recently I have been taking him to Lars Sederholm who has had some good ideas for us to try. One of these has been to put him back in his snaffle for the showjumping, and to use a neckstrap to help slow him down, rather than the rein contact. I used to ride him in a continental gag, but he could be very "rubbery" in this; you could slow him down, but it was difficult to drive his quarters up under him and he would evade you by bending too much through the neck, or swinging his quarters. I tried the snaffle and neckstrap for the first time at an Advanced one-day event and he jumped extremely well. Although he feels quite strong in the hand, when you check him with the neckstrap he still seems to keep coming through from behind. I felt brave enough to use it at Gatcombe and then at the Europeans.'

Mary Gordon-Watson

CORNISHMAN'S OLYMPIC YEARS

■ To many people the slight, shy girl astride the big rangy horse must have seemed a very mis-matched pair, but together Mary Gordon-Watson and Cornishman V scored a great many victories both on home ground and internationally, including the 1969 European Championships, team gold at Burghley 1971, and team gold at the 1972 Munich Olympics. Added to that was another Olympic team gold when Cornishman was ridden – at short notice and in atrocious conditions – at the 1968 Mexico Olympics (see Richard Meade). Much of Mary's success with Cornishman, and her continuing love of dressage, was due to Sergeant Ben Jones of the King's Troop. Ben Jones rode at the 1964 Tokyo Olympics where he finished ninth behind Richard Meade, and was in the gold-medal-winning team at the Mexico Olympics where he finished fifth individually.

'I first met Ben when he came to teach at our Pony Club camp,' recalls Mary. 'I was fourteen and riding a 13.1hh Connemara pony which, as far as I was concerned, had no mouth at all and just kept galloping off with me. Ben thought she was a good enough pony to persevere with and helped me with her when he came to stay prior to the Tokyo Olympics. For two weeks he made me ride her in trot on the same circle in the field. He explained that the pony had to learn to submit to me and that the easiest way to achieve this was through repetitive exercises. The pony was a real fighter and it took a whole fortnight to get the result, but after that she never looked back, and I rode her in all the Pony Club teams. By then I had complete faith in Ben's training and so when I was riding Cornishman I went back to him. We had upgraded to Advanced very quickly – Cornishman was a Novice when he won Tidworth three-day event, but his £35 prize money upgraded him to Advanced – and so we had missed out on all the "inbetween" training.

'Ben was a perfectionist, and would battle on for hour after hour until he got the result he wanted. He expected the horse to be very obedient, and he achieved this through repetition rather than through the use of force, although he was a very dominant rider. He worked all his horses very, very low, and behind the vertical, so that you would say they were overbent, but this is how he kept them supple and submissive. When he asked them to come up and work in a more advanced

outline they always came up very correctly and remained light in front. With Cornishman, he concentrated very much on the discipline of the horse, drilling us through loads and loads of school exercises to achieve suppleness, obedience and responsiveness. He also introduced me to the benefits of lateral work.

'He had very strong ideas about how things ought to be done, and was very scathing about riders who forced their horses' heads into an outline when they were not working through properly from behind. I well remember him watching some of the British pure dressage riders when the sport first became popular here – he said he had never seen so much rubbish!

'When Ben started eventing he rarely had especially good horses, but he always seemed to get a very good response from them. He often led the dressage on the little hog-maned gun horses from the King's Troop. But when he had the opportunity actually to compete on my horse, Cornishman, things did not go very well at all. I had broken my leg and Cornishman was offered to the selectors as a team horse. Ben rode him first but he had not really had enough time to mould him to his way of doing things. When they went into the dressage arena at Burghley Cornishman rebelled and fought him the whole way. Ben's way of training meant that he had to have the horse on his terms, and there had not been time to achieve that with my horse. Richard Meade had the ride on him and Ben rode The Poacher.

'Ben never really achieved the same acclaim as the other riders of his era, partly because of his work commitment to the army, and also because he did not own any horses; he was reliant on being offered rides by people such as the Allhusens and the Whiteleys. He did have an amazing talent; his life could have been so much richer if he had enjoyed better health and had a little more money.'

The sport has changed enormously since Mary first entered it, as a very young rider amongst mainly male competitors. There were far fewer competitions, and riders did not have a great number of suitable horses to choose from; the whole scene was really very amateur compared to how the sport today. Mary has this to say on current standards:

'At the top level the standard of dressage is pretty high. Riders get so much practice in competition now,

Mary Gordon-Watson and Cornishman V on their way to fourth place individually and team gold in Munich 1972

and the sport has become so much more competitive, that they have to take their dressage training very, very seriously; more seriously than when I competed. And something that most top riders have grasped is the technique of actually riding a good test.

'More competition horses today are naturally good movers and this is a great advantage. No matter how hard the dressage judge tries not to be biased towards this type when the standard is very high, the naturally good mover is going to beat a less good mover that has been trained to the same standard. Warmblood horses are becoming more fashionable in eventing as they begin to prove that they can cope with the cross-country. Riders of non-warmbloods are finding they have to work harder and train their horses to a higher standard to keep up and so the overall standard improves.

'But at Novice and Intermediate levels I don't think riders put enough work into making sure that the horse is taught the basics, and that he is working correctly.

Too many horses are forced into an outline. If the dressage training is lacking then the showjumping and cross-country will suffer at some point.'

Going back to Mary's own career, she explains how she came to ride the talented but difficult Cornishman: 'We came across Cornishman by mistake, really' explains Mary. 'Father wanted a hunter, and so went off to a farm sale in Cornwall; he came back with this barely broken four-year-old which we all thought was totally unsuitable for him – though you couldn't help but admire the horse; he was very impressive. I was still at school and happily playing around on ponies, but Cornishman was soon to become my first horse. Father hunted and point-to-pointed him, but then I needed a horse on which to take my Pony Club A test and Cornishman was the only one available; he stood 17hh and took some getting used to after a pony! We didn't seem to have lessons in those days, you just went out and got on with it, and I think we only ever possessed one showjump to school over. Cornishman was a big, unruly horse with a huge stride, but he did show great potential and he had terrific natural ability across country. He was potentially a good dressage horse because he moved well, but up until this time – he was seven – he had neve been schooled properly.

'I had always wanted to event, and Cornishman was my chance to have a go. Tidworth three-day event was only his third horse trials, and he won it. After that I thought we had better take it all a bit more seriously and so we had some dressage lessons from Ben Jones. In our first season, when I was eighteen and Cornishman was eight, we suddenly found ourselves at Advanced level. I had a great deal of help from some wonderful people all of whom kept me pointed in the right direction: Ben Jones continued to help with our dressage, Major Derek Allhusen advised me on fitness and general training, and Dick Stilwell helped with our jumping.

'After our win at Tidworth Cornishman missed the rest of that season; he had started coughing and had to be hobdayed. We were allowed to ride at Badminton the following year but *hors concours* as we weren't qualified; however the selectors wanted to see him there. I didn't really have him fit enough, and after an awkward jump at the third from last I fell off him. The following year, shortly before the Mexico Olympics, I broke my leg. The selectors then approached my father and asked if they could have the horse, originally for Ben Jones to ride. Surprisingly Ben didn't really hit it off with Cornishman and I thought he would be sent back to us; however, Ben was put on The Poacher and Richard Meade rode Cornishman. I think father felt very honoured to be asked to lend the horse, but it was still quite a difficult decision – he wasn't just any horse, he was our only horse! I was able to go out and watch him in Mexico, and it was a strange experience because I didn't really feel involved; yet it was very exciting.

'The following year I was back with him again and we won the European Championships, and then the World Championships the year after. We were in the British team from 1969 until 1972, and at the following European and World Championships we were fourth individually at both. By the time of the next Olympics, Munich in 1972, Cornishman was thirteen and during that Olympic year, and the previous year as a twelve-year-old, I think he was at his very best. Because he was such a big horse and had missed out on any early training, it took until then to make a complete athlete of him. In fact at Badminton in 1972 he had the one and only fall of his career, and I thought it would be held against him; but we were still chosen to go to Munich. To win the team gold there was really very thrilling. We were not favourites to win, and the build-up to it all had

been quite difficult. Debbie West was in the team until literally the last minute when Baccarat went lame, and Bridget Parker was chosen as her replacement at the expense of Lorna Clark [née Sutherland], which was a great disappointment for Lorna. So the "human side" was quite difficult to cope with.

'The competition itself was great, particularly as Cornishman was a very adaptable horse. It was a continental-style steeplechase course which was different, but fun. I was one of the first to go and started at about 7.30am, so it was very lonely on the roads and tracks; and I do remember being stung on the bottom by a bee in the ten-minute box, which affected me for about a week!

'The cross-country course rode really well, even though three of our four team members had a stop at what turned out to be the bogey fence on the course; but it didn't seem to matter. The personal thrill for me was jumping a clear round in the final phase to finish fourth overall. We won the team gold, and Richard Meade won the individual gold medal. Cornishman was extremely naughty in the parade, fly bucking all over the place, so he had obviously thoroughly enjoyed himself too!

'He completed his last three-day event the year after, in America, and then went hunting until he was twenty-seven. So he had a very active life, and his overall mileage must have been considerable. For all his success, however, he was by no means perfect: for example he was always very keen to go home, and this made him extremely nappy when we first had him. All in all he was quite an individual – he didn't like being caught, particularly by anyone male, and he couldn't be ridden out in company. He was very fast, but he must have had some pony blood in him somewhere; I was never a very accurate rider and he could put in an extremely short stride to get us out of trouble if he had to. But having said that, he wasn't stupid, and if we were completely wrong then he would stop.

'He was sired by quite a decent racehorse called Golden Surprise which produced some good point-to-pointers. His dam was called Polly and described as a bit of a nutter; she had raced over banks. Apparently Cornishman wasn't handled at all until he was two, and his first close experience with man was when he was caught to be gelded. He woke up from this and galloped off, jumping from field to field, and couldn't be caught for days!'

Mary continued to compete, but on other people's horses, and was a successful point-to-point rider. Racing has always been a great love, and as well as now being a dressage and hunter judge, Mary is also a member of the Jockey Club.

Richard Meade

A GOLDEN TALENT

■ Great Britain is renowned for consistently producing top class event horses and riders, but for all that she has still only produced one individual Olympic gold medallist, and that was Richard Meade. At the 1972 Munich Olympics, riding Derek Allhusen's Laurieston, Richard headed the British team effort which also resulted in the team gold medal. Richard rode in four Olympic Games, each time on a different horse, in Tokyo 1964 finishing 8th individually riding Barberry, 4th and team gold in Mexico 1968 riding Cornishman V, 4th individually in Montreal 1976 on Jacob Jones, as well as the ultimate success in Munich on Laurieston – team and individual gold. Just how elusive a gold medal can be is further illustrated by the fact that only two event riders in the

Richard Meade and Speculator at the Whitbread Barrels Fence, Badminton 1982

history of the Olympic three-day event have won two gold medals, the most recent being New Zealander Mark Todd in 1984 and 1988.

There is no denying that the Olympic movement has, in recent years, lost some of its golden image. Overly influenced by commercialism and politics it is easy to become cynical about the glories of Olympic gold. But speaking to Richard Meade rekindles much of your faith in what the Olympics should be all about: patriotism, sportsmanship and teamwork. As the images and emotions of his many Olympic experiences flicker through his mind, Richard Meade alights on the Mexico Games of 1968 as the one that really stands out in his memory. And that is a good measure both of the man and the Olympic ideal, for it was not at these Games that Richard enjoyed his personal triumph; many a lesser sportsman would surely have had the memory of an individual gold etched most firmly on the mind!

'Mexico was the most wonderful setting for an Olympic Games,' recalls Richard. 'We were high in the mountains, so high that some athletes needed oxygen, and the scenery was absolutely beautiful. We had quite a bit of time out there before the competition started which meant we got to know everybody very well – it was a very happy preparation for us. The British team enjoyed a tremendous spirit, and great determination to succeed as a team. The previous Olympics in Tokyo had been disastrous for us; we had led after the dressage but then two team horses, Mike Bullen's and James Templer's, were eliminated, which wiped out the British team. So although we had won the European Championships the year before Mexico, as far as an Olympic Games was concerned we were coming from behind, and there was a tremendous ambition to win.

'The general disorganisation meant that chaos reigned supreme for much of the time, although when things did happen they happened with enormous enthusiasm and flair. As a rider, the conditions on speed and endurance day made it the most challenging event I have ever ridden in. Four-and-a-half inches of rain fell in one-and-a-half hours during the actual event. Two riders from every team had already got round before the worst of the rain – for us it was Derek Allhusen and Jane Holderness-Roddam – but Ben Jones and I had to contend with a completely flooded course.'

The challenge facing Richard Meade was made even greater because the horse he was riding, Cornishman, was not his usual partner.

'Cornishman was well known to me through his successes with his usual rider Mary Gordon-Watson,' explains Richard. 'The selectors were concerned that

Mary wasn't experienced enough to cope with what would be very tough conditions in Mexico, but the difficult decision was made for them when Mary broke her leg shortly before the Games. Ben Jones was originally going to have the ride as he had worked with Mary on improving the horse's dressage for some time and so knew him well. But then Martin Whiteley's The Poacher was also made available to the team, so I was put on Cornishman and Ben rode The Poacher. I had jumped one cross-country fence on the horse in front of the selectors before leaving for Mexico, and in total had about two-and-a-half weeks to get to know him before the event started. We had all thought we would do some cross-country schooling once we were in Mexico but the practice fences were vast – and having seen several competitors have crashing falls over them, we decided not to jump them at all.

'I did regard Cornishman as a very talented horse; he was nine at the time and still hadn't realised his full potential. He proved quite difficult to ride in the dressage, however – he didn't like being schooled in the heat, and in the test he was quite lazy so it was hard work keeping him moving forwards energetically. But he really was a lovely type of horse and since Mary had done well enough with him for him to be considered an Olympic horse, I had no qualms about accepting the ride on him.

'The cross-country course in Mexico wasn't huge – the effects of competing at a high altitude had been taken into account – but it certainly wasn't an easy course, and the conditions produced by the torrential rain made riding it a matter of survival. When we set off the rain was so fierce that I was very concerned as to whether or not Cornishman could see the fences; I had to peer out from under the peak of my hat, but the horse had no such protection against the elements. The first fence was a bright, painted viaduct bridge, but the next was a post and rail with a ditch under, set in a fence line. I had no idea whether or not the horse could see it, and all I could do was hold him together with hand and leg and hope for the best – but he jumped it beautifully. But as we progressed around the course the true extent to which the ground conditions had deteriorated became apparent.

'The last but one fence involved jumping from a ledge on the river bank, over the river to land on a ledge the other side. As I approached this fence I could see that the river had burst its banks and that water was swirling over the take-off ledge. There was about a yard of bank still visible and I just rode at that hoping it wouldn't be submerged before we got there; luckily Cornishman saw what to do and sailed over. By the time Ben Jones rode the course, however, the whole ledge was under water, although some brushwood had been stuck into the mud to show the riders where to take off and hopefully to encourage the horses up into the air – otherwise they would just have fallen over the edge into the river. I was very lucky, because the competitor following me did just that!

'You then turned back on yourself and had to cross the river again to finish the course. Earlier in the day it had been possible either to jump or ford this water fence, but although the course hadn't actually flooded when our second rider Jane Holderness-Roddam and Our Nobby went round, the ground had got very boggy. Jane had planned to jump the water where possible, which Our Nobby did beautifully, only to become completely bogged down on landing and falling each time. After that the team tactics were to ford those particular water jumps. By the time I was to ride, the river had swollen so much and the current had become so strong that some competitors were swept off course down the river. I negotiated this last hazard successfully by entering by the red flag and being swept towards the white flag where we did manage to get out.

'Looking back, I think the ground conditions certainly affected the individual placings – notably the first three horses all went before the rain – but as far as the teams were concerned it was fairly even because two riders from each team went before the worst of it, and two went afterwards. Cornishman recorded the fastest time of all those who went after the rain started.

'At each of the Olympic Games I rode at I made the most of the opportunity, and we stayed out for the whole of the Games and joined in all the celebrations. The Olympics have become so big now that athletes are encouraged to leave as soon as their event is over. But I always stayed on and explored more of the country once the Games were over. At the Mexican Games there was a very intimate atmosphere because the event was still relatively small and everybody got to know everyone else. But by Munich, which were the biggest Games to date, the feeling of unwieldiness was apparent and the atmosphere was far more serious, especially during the opening ceremony which was almost sombre; although as time went on everyone became more relaxed. Tragically the murder of the Israeli athletes destroyed that fragile atmosphere and completely overshadowed what could have been a very enjoyable Olympics.

'Nevertheless, the excitement and the feeling of privilege and patriotism was very strong at each of the Olympics I rode at. I remember travelling in a taxi late one night with Ben Jones. Ben was so proud of his medal, and so frightened of losing it that he wore it under his shirt the whole time. Our taxi driver, who was

very like Manuel out of *Fawlty Towers*, could barely contain his excitement when he discovered we were gold medallists, and when Ben Jones said "Here, do you want to see a gold medal?" he turned round and stared in amazement, and only just avoided crashing into the car in front!

'Since then the Games have grown ever bigger, and sometimes the vast infrastructure seems in danger of swallowing up the spirit of the Games themselves. Even so, it would be very sad if, as a sport, we were ever to leave the Olympic movement. It is very easy for a sport to become insular, isolated and introspective. The Olympics not only brings all the equestrian disciplines together, even more importantly it puts the riders in contact with other athletes. It is a very inspiring event to be involved in, and it brings the sport into a much broader focus – particularly if we win medals! I was lucky enough to live through some of the halcyon days of the sport and there can be no doubt that the Olympics gave us far greater exposure than if we had just had a World and European Championships.

'I do believe that a lot of other countries have caught up with Britain; they are breeding better horses, or are buying young horses from Britain and Ireland – which is fair enough, since we buy showjumpers and dressage horses from the Continent. There has been much talk about Britain's lack of eventing success compared with her golden era in the fifties and sixties, but when it comes to an Olympics or any kind of international championships, your country's success comes down to just four riders. It doesn't matter how broad the base of the sport is: at the Olympics you must have four very good riders with four top class horses. The riders must be extremely good horsemen or women and must be very capable technically.

'In theory, because of the Junior and Young Rider systems we should be consistently producing riders capable of making it to the top; in practice, however, very few actually do make it. If you really want to get to the very top of the sport you have to be completely single-minded and that means you cannot afford to sell your best horses, you must keep one for yourself. But even then it isn't that simple; there are an awful lot of riders who are very good up to a certain level but when it comes to the big occasion they crack under the strain. I was lucky enough always to feel happy competing under pressure because I knew that at that level there would always be other riders who would not be able to cope, and their mistakes could help me to win. And it is people blessed with that characteristic who need to be in the team – the showjumper David Broome is a very good example of a man who really excelled under pressure.'

Mark Todd

DOUBLE OLYMPIC GOLD MEDALLIST

■ Mark Todd is the man who makes things equestrian look effortless, whether it is winning Olympic gold medals or Badminton on a horse he barely knows. Even when things go wrong he handles the situation with enviably controlled ease; at the 1995 Badminton Horse Trials his stirrup leather broke early on the course, but Mark completed clear without it. Two years before, Just an Ace turned a somersault at the first element of the Quarry fence and rolled over him; his reply to the doctor who was trying to see if he was injured was to vault onto his horse and continue on his way. He appears to be the complete athlete, always at one with the horse he is riding. He has opted to be an event rider, but whatever the sport he chose, you get the impression that Mr Todd would have been highly successful at it.

Mark won individual gold medals at the 1984 Los Angeles and the 1988 Seoul Olympics, riding the little horse Charisma. He won Badminton at his first attempt in 1980 riding Southern Comfort, and again in 1994 riding Horton Point; this was a chance ride for Mark as the horse's usual jockey, Lynne Bevan, had broken her collar bone – Mark sat on the horse for the first time the day before the event, in which he was drawn first to go! Mark has also won Burghley three times, finishing first and second in 1987 on Wilton Fair and Charisma.

Mark was born and brought up on a farm in New Zealand and started eventing through the Pony Club. There are not that many competitions throughout the country so most keen competitors combine eventing with showjumping throughout the year. This certainly paid

LEFT: Here's where it all starts – Mark Todd and Charisma at the first horse inspection, Seoul 1988. It ended with a second Olympic gold medal

TOP RIGHT: Los Angeles 1984: Mark and Charisma about to win their first individual gold medal

RIGHT: Mark Todd, double Olympic gold medallist (1984 and 1988) with daughter Lauren

dividends for Mark because he also represented New Zealand in the showjumping team at the Barcelona Olympics. He explains how his involvement in eventing grew; 'I had a horse called Top Hunter which got to grade A showjumping but was not really good enough then to succeed at that level. I turned his attentions to eventing and rode him in one of the three-day events in New Zealand; from there I went to the 1978 World Championships in Kentucky, but this was only my second three-day event and I was eliminated on the cross-country! I sold that horse to somebody in England and they offered me a job riding over here. So I came over with one horse, and went on to win Badminton on Southern Comfort the following year, 1980, at our first attempt.

'My partnership with Charisma did not begin until 1983. I was still based mainly in New Zealand at the time, but had again come over to England to ride

Felix Too at Badminton that year. While I was here I had a call from New Zealand asking if I wanted to take on the ride on Charisma. I knew a bit about the horse – he had been to the New Zealand Pony Club Championships a couple of times, and had done a Novice three-day event; he was now an Intermediate horse and a grade B showjumper, and was working at medium-level dressage. But to me he still looked like a fat hairy pony! Charisma won the five events I rode him at in New Zealand, and he also won the three-day event there. He did ride like a much bigger horse and he was a very good mover, but it wasn't until after the New Zealand three-day event that I began to realise what a class horse he was. He came over to England in the spring of 1984 and a lot of people thought I was mad to bother to take him to Badminton – but by then I knew that he really was a bit special. He finished second, which was a big confidence booster for me in the run-up to the 1984 Los Angeles Olympics.

'Riding at the Olympics is very different and also very special. It is a unique occasion in that you are just one amongst thousands of other athletes, all of whom are at the top of their chosen sport, and each one is out there to try and win a gold medal. As a competition it is probably not as big as Badminton but it is unique.

'I think we were sixth after the dressage and then went clear, inside the time, across country. On the last day we were in second place behind America's Karen Stives [now Reuter]; we jumped a clear round and she had a fence down. That was our first Olympic gold medal.

'Winning in Los Angeles had a huge impact on my career, and back home in New Zealand it certainly made a difference to the profile that the sport of eventing was given; suddenly everyone knew who I was and what eventing was. Mine was also the first medal for New Zealand of the Olympic Games, which all added to the impact that winning it created. But although from a status or celebrity point of view it made a big difference to me personally, financially it unfortunately had very little effect on my circumstances at all.

'Charisma was twelve years old when he won in Los Angeles and I certainly did not think he would be going to the next Olympics in Seoul. I just assumed he would have retired by then, and hoped that I would have another horse good enough to go. But as time went on he felt better and better; at Burghley in 1987 he felt fantastic and was very close to winning. His only fault was that he could be an unreliable showjumper, and two fences down that day relegated him to second place behind my other horse Wilton Fair. I decided then to miss Badminton the following spring and to aim him specifically at the Seoul Olympics, with the proviso that if at any stage he felt as if he wasn't up to it we would call it a day there and then.

'In the spring of 1988 we concentrated on getting him really fit – and at one point I very nearly gave in and rang Badminton to see if we could still enter because he felt on top of the world. I had planned to give him just two runs at one-day events before taking him out to Seoul, and at the first he was appalling! He was just so above himself – he blew up in the dressage, had five showjumps down and ran away with me on the cross-country! He was given a severe amount of work between that and Gatcombe, which was his only other run, and he duly won that for me.

'From the moment we arrived in Seoul everything felt right, and I just had a really good feeling about everything. Charisma led the dressage by a good margin, and many commentators felt he deserved an even higher mark than the one he was awarded. He achieved the fastest time across country and made it all feel very easy – he was well within himself. Going into the showjumping he had three fences in hand, and just had the one down.'

You see, he even makes winning two gold medals sound easy! Mark and Charisma became only the second partnership in the history of the Olympics to achieve this feat; the first was the Dutch rider Charles Pahud de Mortanges and Marcroix who won the individual gold medals in 1928 and 1932.

Like his rider, Charisma was a superb athlete. As Mark explains: 'Although he was small, he was perfectly proportioned; he was also extremely strong and had really good limbs. He was fast, tough and sound, and equally importantly, he had a very good temperament and loved to perform…he was very well named. The only chink in his armour was, as I have said, his showjumping, when he could be careless. Towards the end of his career, though, unless there was a decent crowd he didn't bother to perform!'

Charisma was retired after his second Olympic win, and returned to New Zealand. Mark rides him occasionally when he goes back there, and still can't hold him! In 1994 they were asked to give a dressage display at the main three-day event; in spite of being roughed off in the field and only ridden from time to time, Charisma gave as good a performance as any fit and competing three-day eventer.

Charisma was by the Thoroughbred Tira Mink, out of a mare called Planet who was ⅞ Thoroughbred and ⅛ Percheron. A full sister of Charisma's played high goal polo in England with Johnny Kidd. Mark did once ride a horse very closely related to Charisma called Night Life but he considered that it wasn't in the same league. As he says, Charisma was 'a bit of a freak'.

At the Barcelona Olympics Mark rode the big grey, Welton Greylag, on which he had won Burghley. This scopey horse did not have as easy a temperament as Charisma, although undoubtedly he had great ability. Sadly his full potential was never fulfilled because he pulled a ligament on the steeplechase phase of the Olympic three-day event and had to be retired. Mark is confident that had he been able to continue he would definitely have had a winning chance. Greylag was retired from three-day eventing after that and concentrated on pure dressage; but his second career was also tragically shortlived as in 1995 he had to be put down after an attack of colic.

Looking ahead to the next Olympic opportunity, Mark admits a degree of circumspection in that each successive Olympics seems to be staged in an even hotter climate: 'I am not really looking forward to the competition because although I am confident it will be safe for the horses, you can't get away from the fact that it will be very uncomfortable for everybody, both horses and humans. But it is the Olympics, and not to go, and not try to win, would be unthinkable!' So says the man who has twice tried and been ultimately successful.

Andrew Nicholson

KIWI INVADER

■ Andrew Nicholson has represented New Zealand at the Los Angeles and Barcelona Olympics, winning team silver at the latter. In 1995 he had his greatest personal success to date, when he won Burghley with Buckley Province. He is as well known in England as he is in his native New Zealand, because home for Andrew, his wife Jayne and daughters Rebecca and Melissa, is Somerset, England. Over the five years from 1990 to the end of 1994 Andrew was the leading points winner at British events, an achievement that leads some competitors to keep encouraging him to return to New Zealand! That aside, he is popular and admired amongst his fellow competitors, named by even the maestro Mark Todd as one of the riders he most admires; one proud owner of a British gold medal team horse at the World Championships even announced that the best thing about the championship was not winning a gold medal but 'getting two big smackers on the cheek from Andrew Nicholson'! On the other hand, as one of the few with the courage to speak out when he believes something is wrong, certain horse trials officials are less fond of him.

Andrew is disarmingly modest about his ability and achievements: 'My brother and I, and a guy called Warwick Robinson, all learnt to ride on a donkey – and then Warwick Robinson went on to become New Zealand's leading flat race jockey! I moved on to one of my brother's ponies, but never learnt to canter because it used to throw me off as soon as we started to trot! And when I got as far as jumping I *always* used to fall off because I was so surprised at actually getting over the fence! We rode everywhere bareback, and as we lived on a dairy farm we could just gallop all over the place. Next door were the Pony Club grounds – I didn't enjoy the Pony Club much, but we used to go along just to see what the other kids were getting up to.

'While I was still at school I started helping out with racehorses, riding about twenty yearlings round the track early each morning for a local trainer. I had ridden horses from when I was about fourteen, and did a lot of showjumping as well as the Pony Club one-day events. I rode at the main New Zealand three-day event when I was seventeen on two Advanced horses that I owned. Both were placed, and both were longlisted for the New Zealand team for some major

championship that never seemed to happen.

'I came over to England that same year to work for the National Hunt trainer Derek Kent, with the idea of trying to do some more eventing. I brought a five-year-old horse over with me which I sold at the end of the first season. When he arrived in England he had never even been cross-country schooling, but it never occurred to me that he wouldn't make a good event horse; I remember the people who gave me a lift to my first event asked where I had taken him schooling, and when I said "nowhere" they all burst out laughing! But by the end of that season he was Intermediate, and I sold him to Holland where he was selected for their Young Rider team.

'For a few years I travelled back to New Zealand each year having sold a horse, and returned the following season with another one. I met my wife Jayne at an event, and when Jenny Fountain offered her another horse to ride she persuaded her to let me ride it instead; soon after that I decided to settle over here. In about 1986, after several years of renting yards which we kept outgrowing, Jayne and I bought the farm in Somerset.

'We have between ten and fifteen horses of our own which we buy as four- or five-year-olds, and about the same number of horses owned by other people which I ride. I am very lucky in that most of my owners don't want to sell their horses – it really is gratifying to know that a horse will stay with you. I like eventing at all levels, but having said that, although you *can* get a great deal of enjoyment when you persuade a good ride out of a novice, riding at that level can get a bit depressing because you will never exactly set the world alight. It's nice to have the older horses, you know them really well and can have a crack at the major competitions with them. You can make a mistake on a novice and look really stupid, but you can make the same mistake on an experienced horse and he will cover it up for you. You never quite know what a novice might do next.'

Andrew's English wife, Jayne, was a keen event rider herself, representing Britain at Young Rider level. Despite what must now be a hectic schedule of organising the yard, travelling to events and looking after their two little girls, Jayne gives the impression of being the calm amidst the storm; always outwardly relaxed, good humoured and polite no matter how busy the timetable. Jayne met Andrew at an event while she was still competing herself. 'At the time, Andrew was only in England for the eventing season and would then return to New Zealand. I had quite a lot of horses to ride and, when Jenny Fountain offered me another, I suggested that perhaps Andrew could compete it for her.' Jayne admits that this seemingly selfless gesture had good reason: 'I knew that Andrew would stay in England then!' It was a move that helped Andrew establish himself over here. Jenny bought him several more horses which gave him the security to set up his own yard with Jayne. They bought their Somerset farm in 1986 and, with a yard of twenty-five horses and two children, Jayne no longer has time to compete herself.

It takes some organising to ensure that each horse is entered for the appropriate events. Jayne and Andrew buy a bunch of young horses each year which Andrew trains and competes to then sell on. As Jayne says, 'Because they are all for sale we never know how many horses we will actually have to ride for the whole season. But we try to work it so that if one is sold or upgrades, then one of the youngsters is brought in and takes its place. The working pupils who train with us often bring their own horses, but these are usually quite young and inexperienced so their training and competing fits in well with our own youngsters.

'February is the worst time of year – the weather is dreadful, all the horses are fit and raring to go but there is nowhere to take them. Once the eventing season starts, everything seems to work much better.'

Despite the vast number of horses that Andrew competes at all levels, Jayne seems to manage not to worry too much. 'The trouble with being in the yard and knowing all the horses is that I do worry about him on some, more than on others! But generally my feeling is that he is a very good rider, and is experienced enough to take the least possible risks. I worry far more about the children, because they are an unknown quantity and don't understand the risks. We don't push them to ride; they have an old pony, and sometimes he is flavour of the month, sometimes he isn't. At the moment they prefer the tortoise!'

OLYMPIC EXPERIENCES

■ 'My first Olympics, in Los Angeles in 1984, was very, very exciting. At that stage I hadn't done many three-day events and had never been to anything like it; and it was the first time that New Zealand had sent a three-day event team to the Olympics. By the time Barcelona came round in 1992 it was all a bit more serious; we all knew more by then and so more was expected of us. The team aspect of the Olympic Games makes it very special, and the fact that you are there amongst so many famous athletes; the man of the moment in Los Angeles was Carl Lewis, and in Barcelona Linford Christie.

'In Los Angeles I was riding a very young horse called Kahlua which I sold soon afterwards. We went clear across country, but were quite slow. Mark Todd was the main man, the rest of us were there for a cup of tea and a look-around! But the team finished fifth, so we were happy, and Mark won the gold medal so he was delighted.

'As I said, in Barcelona it was all a bit more serious, although I didn't know I was actually going to be in the team until after the trot-up. We went out with five horses and riders and I had a feeling I was going to be reserve. This time we knew what we were out there to do, and we knew we could do it well. All the same, I certainly did not expect to be in the position I was – second individually – after the cross-country. I thought Mark or Blyth would be up at the top, and I would be chasing along behind. But Mark had had to retire Welton Greylag before the cross-country, and Blyth fought back from a poor dressage mark to pull up to fourth. So it was all pretty exciting.

'Spinning Rhombus had had three showjumps down at the Stockholm World Championships in 1990 when we won the team gold, and the New Zealand Federation had said I needed to concentrate on his showjumping if I wanted to be picked for the team again. I went to lots of people for help, and I think that was the worst thing I could have done. Even as a novice he was quite a poor showjumper and we were all trying to make him into something that he could never be. At the practice fence in Barcelona he was barely getting off the ground. I was being given a lot of advice from a great many people, and ended up in a muddle over it. The horse was jumping really badly outside and so that worries you even more, and then it just went from bad to worse. I couldn't believe we had so many fences down – nine! The worst thing was letting the team down; we lost the team gold, although we still held on to the silver.

'After Barcelona we altered our approach to Spinning Rhombus' problem; he was hardly jumped at all at home, and his attitude and the results improved considerably. However, I couldn't have gone to Barcelona on that strategy because the federation would not have been prepared to select the horse. Spinning Rhombus has always been very good to me. His owner, Rosemary Barlow, bought him originally as a Pony Club horse for her daughter, so you can't really complain about his performance! He retired after Badminton in 1995; he had completed fifteen international three-day events, and had gone fast at all of them. At Badminton, where I retired him on the cross-country phase, he was telling me that he had had enough.'

THOUGHTS ON ATLANTA

Looking ahead to Atlanta, Andrew hopes to take Jägermeister to compete there. This relatively young horse coped well with the 1994 World Championship course in the Hague, his only mistake – repeated almost to perfection by fellow New Zealander Mark Todd – being to fall over the step coming out of the water, depositing Andrew on the floor. Andrew also has Cartoon and Buckley Province (his Burghley winner) who are both ideal types, good gallopers but also very nippy and light on their feet.

Andrew is concerned about the prospect of competing in Atlanta: 'I am not really worried for myself because if things start to go wrong I know I will pull up, but it could turn out to be a very sad day for the sport of eventing. Personally I am not a great fan of sitting through competitors' briefings and being told how hot and humid it is going to be, and that we should all ride accordingly – to my mind we should not be competing in those countries in the first place.

Andrew with his wife, Jayne, and their two daughters

Three-day events should be held where the climate is suitable for the sport.

'If we pulled out of the Olympics I don't think it would make any difference to the sport itself; I feel that this generation of riders would rather compete in a country where the climate was suitable. But then the next generation of riders will miss the opportunity to ride at an Olympics, and if you asked them which they would rather have had, they will probably say they would have liked to have gone to the Olympics.'

Bruce Davidson

OLYMPIC GOLD MEDALLIST

■ Bruce Davidson's first Olympic experience came in Munich in 1972. 'The hostage situation was very sad, and overshadowed what should have been the experience of a lifetime. The team had three older and more experienced riders and I was very much the new boy. But it was a great team to be on for my first Olympics, and the others helped me tremendously. I had only been in the sport two years and was riding an older, and quite difficult horse, Plain Sailing – but everyone pulled together to help me. The facilities at Munich were the best the world had ever seen at that stage, and as a star-struck twenty-two-year-old it was a very impressive beginning. We won the team silver and I finished eighth individually.

'At the 1976 Montreal Games I rode Irish Cap and the whole team was less experienced than at Munich. The facilities once again were spectacular, but once again we were isolated from the rest of the Olympic venue. In Munich the equestrian events were held outside the Olympic site but we lived in the Olympic village. At Montreal we had our own equestrian village. There was more pressure on me because I had won a World Championship in between (Burghley 1974); on top of that, I had just become a father so I dreamt of winning a gold medal for my son! And we did win the team gold [Bruce was tenth individually]. At the 1984 Los Angeles Games we had a pretty experienced team, and each of us was quite independent. The facilities were phenomenal and an extra day was included as we had to 'move out' to the cross-country course which was at a separate location. We won the team gold and I finished thirteenth individually.

'By contrast, at Seoul in 1988 we had a really very inexperienced team – three girls going for the first time and myself – and we were caught out by our inexperience. I did not go to Barcelona, but I hope very much to compete in Atlanta, preferably in both the team and the individual competitions. I have enjoyed each of the Olympics I have ridden at. At my first one I was riding a fantastic cross-country horse – holding him was a harder job than jumping the jumps! But having grown up with horses and spent many a long day in the hunting field, I have learnt from experience that it is no fun doing anything on an animal you have any doubts about. I have never gone to an Olympics on an animal I have doubted; you need to know your horse and to know your own capabilities, and then you enjoy yourself.'

Karen O'Connor

RIDING AT THE SEOUL OLYMPICS

■ Karen's first Olympic experience in Seoul was not a great success from a results point of view, although the thrill of being there lives with her still:

'Everyone had told me what a thrill it would be to go to an Olympic Games, but it is impossible to appreciate that fully until you are part of it. Nothing compares to the excitement and the emotions you feel, especially during the opening ceremony. I think the actual competition is harder than anything else you ever do because of the distractions of being part of the Olympics. More than ever you want it to be your best performance, and sometimes that can beat you. Prior to Seoul all the team horses had to go into quarantine for thirty days, and this time was spent at Bruce Davidson's yard in Pennsylvania. It was thirty days of temperatures in the nineties, and the ground became like rock which meant it was difficult to give the horse enough work without risk of injury; because of this they didn't get the preparation they needed. My horse, The Optimist, hadn't run across country since the Kentucky trial in the spring. I went to Seoul as the reserve rider and was only named for the team when another horse went lame during its fastwork. Travelling out as a reserve rider makes it even harder to focus on the competition as you never actually believe you are going to be taking part. Because of the hard ground, The Optimist was out of practice when he arrived in Seoul and he was the sort of horse who got very strong and wooden if he was a bit rusty. I have probably gone down in history as one of the few riders to fall three times on the cross-country! Today's rules mean you are now eliminated after two falls.

'However, I learnt a lot from the experience. I now know that it is no good wrapping your horse in cotton wool before a major championship. You have to keep going with his training and competitions, and if in so doing you make the team then that is a bonus; but being selected should not be allowed to become the be-all and end-all of your schedule because an over-protected horse can end up being an under-prepared horse.

'I would love the opportunity to ride at Atlanta and, although Biko is a very big horse, he is bred to race and has a big gallop. When you first look at him you would say he is too heavy for running in very hot,

hard conditions, but when you see him gallop and jump you think differently. He is not a small wiry Thoroughbred, but he has other qualities that would help him. If he were not a full Thoroughbred I would stay away from Atlanta, as I hope riders of non-Thoroughbred horses will, but he has the quality and the ability to do it.'

6
Training: The Way of Champions

To succeed in the sport of eventing, the potential Olympic champion not only needs to be a talented rider, but must also have a talent for training horses. Whereas in racing, for example, the champion jockey needs only to show his skill as a race rider, the event rider has to have the ability both to train his horse at home, and to ride it successfully in competition. This chapter give an insight into how some of the world's best riders prepare and train their horses to compete at the highest level.

• Bruce Davidson and Eagle Lion under the watchful eye of Captain Mark Phillips

Flatwork Training with Matt Ryan

■ Matt Ryan firmly believes that the horse's flatwork training has a huge influence on how successful his jumping is, and that flatwork also plays an important role in the fittening programme.

'My horses do very little roadwork; I believe in getting them fit by working them on the flat in the school and doing fastwork – galloping – rather than short sessions of schooling and lots of hacking out. I look on flatwork as being the equivalent of gym work to an athlete: it builds and tones muscle, improves heart and lung capacity, and supples and strengthens the body. And on top of all that it leaves you with a more obedient and ridable horse. So my horses do a lot of flatwork schooling on the indoor surface that we have, usually four or five days a week. Their usual routine would be to have an easy day after a competition and then to be schooled on the flat or over jumps for most of the rest of the week, apart from the days they do their fastwork.

'Some people worry that the horse will become stale if it is given this amount of schooling, but that is up to the rider. Of course, if you just plod round in circles day after day then both horse and rider *will* become fed up. I train my horses to as high a level on the flat as possible – far higher than they ever need, even for top level eventing. They learn canter pirouettes, flying changes, passage and piaffe, and this means that there is plenty of variety in our day-to-day schooling sessions.

'My brother, Heath, has been the most influential flatwork trainer I have had. He spent a couple of years training in Germany, and then had six months with Numeiro Olivera, and six months with Bertie Hill. At the 1994 World Championships Heath was dressage trainer to the Australian three-day event team. Whilst I am open-minded about other trainers' ideas, no one has really inspired me as much as my brother.'

Although advanced dressage movements such as passage and piaffe are not called for in horse trials dressage, Matt does teach his horses these movements; it improves their performance in the dressage phase, and the better their flatwork the easier they are to ride to a fence

A TYPICAL FLATWORK SESSION

■In the accompanying photographs Matt is riding a nine-year-old Advanced mare, Lady Jane Gray.

'When I first come into the school I work the horse in walk, using as many lateral exercises as possible. Shoulder-in is a very useful suppling exercise: for the older horses it helps them to loosen up before being asked to do anything more demanding, and for the younger horses it is also an exercise in obedience, in listening and responding to the hand and leg aids. Control and accuracy, on the flat and over fences, all comes down to the horse moving away from, and around your leg.

'Still in walk, I then go on to ride half-passes; again, this is a lateral movement teaching obedience as the horse has to move away from your outside leg, while bending round your inside leg. It supples him and also engages his hindquarters, so it is an invaluable exercise.

'I then progress to trot and canter, incorporating the same lateral movements in each of these new paces. Then I just play around between the different movements and paces: shoulder-in in trot, then forward into medium trot, back to a ten-metre circle in a more collected trot, canter half-pass, counter canter, and so on. This particular horse finds canter half-pass to the left difficult; like many horses she works better on the left rein than the right. The big question in canter half-pass is asking the outside hind to come across and underneath the horse; in the half-pass to the right it is the left hind that has this task, and she finds this easier than trying to do the same thing with the right hind in canter half-pass to the left. So with this horse I do more work on the rein she finds difficult, with the aim of strengthening and suppling her on that rein.

'In general, I work my horses quite low and deep. My interpretation of roundness is more to do with a feeling than with a picture of a particular outline. I want to feel the horse stretching down through the rein and going forwards into the hand – then he will start to swing through his back, which is what you want. One of the problems of competing in England is that because there are so many competitions, the horse is worked in a "competition outline" for most of the time – that is, the outline that the dressage judge likes. I personally do not think the horse works as well in that kind of outline; as I said, the best feeling I get from a horse is when he is working lower and deeper than a dressage judge likes to see. But you have to adapt if you want to earn sensible dressage marks, and so during the schooling session I gradually ask the horse to work a little higher in front.

'I nearly always use sitting trot as opposed to rising

when I am schooling the horse at home because the sitting position is a far more effective one to be in. Some people worry that this is a strain on the horse's back, but your weight is still on his back whether you are stood in the stirrups or sat in the saddle. It is much more likely that the rider finds sitting trot uncomfortable, and if he is bouncing around in the saddle then that will be uncomfortable for the horse, too – but it is up to the rider to improve his seat and position so that this doesn't happen. You need an effective, deep and independent seat for jumping as well as for flatwork. If you can't cope with sitting trot how are you going to stay secure and in balance with the horse over fences?

'During the schooling session I bring the horse back to walk after ten or fifteen minutes of trot and canter work. I use the walk pace to re-establish the horse's balance and engagement. Walk half-pass and walk pirouettes help to achieve this before going on to do more in the other paces, or to work on a specific problem.

'This particular mare has a lovely big canter but finds it very difficult to shorten and collect herself, so in canter I would concentrate on shortening her stride whilst still making sure it has enough energy and lift to it. Improving her canter in this way will help not only her flatwork but also her jumping. If you are coming into a combination with a short distance you need to keep the canter short but with enough energy and power to ensure you clear the fences. This mare has an amazing jump when she is able to just bowl along and power over things, but she needs to learn to create a big jump from a collected pace, and not rely on sheer pace to give her the power to clear the fence.

'I canter her in tight circles to encourage her to "sit" on the inside hind leg; this engages her hindquarters and will help her to shorten her stride without sacrificing the impulsion that must be contained within that shorter stride.'

During any training session Matt expects his horses to give him their complete attention. 'I have no sympathy for the horse becoming distracted by anything – he has to learn that when I am on his back he listens to me. I do not want to have my chances of winning an event spoilt because the horse was distracted by a spectator waving an umbrella, or a car door slamming. My horse must keep his attention on what I am telling him to do, no matter what is going on around him. This is just as

important for the jumping phases: the horse must be listening to *me* and focussed on the approaching fence, not on the fence judge's car, or the banner beside the jump. So any inattentiveness is swiftly disciplined.'

Preparation and practice are generally believed to be the key to success, but whilst every rider may know this, some lack the discipline or knowledge to carry it through. Matt is fiercely competitive, and he has the self-discipline to strive constantly for better performances from himself and his horses. He is prepared to take calculated risks; for example, he will use the opportunity when he is competing a novice horse to see if it will tackle every direct route on the course, even at risk of a refusal or run-out, because his main aim is not to win Novice events, it is to produce a horse that is capable of helping him win gold medals. And if you don't ask the question, you don't know *how* capable or courageous the horse is. And Matt always rides to win; he doesn't understand the mentality of those who say they will go quietly round X number of events and will *then* try to win. As he points out, we all make plenty of mistakes which cause us to lose anyway, so what is the point of setting out without even the intention of trying to win? To win you have to put yourself at risk, and just like everything else, it takes practice – you have to practise winning.

Dressage Training

MARY KING

■ The dressage marks obtained by Mary's horses are the envy of many of her fellow competitors. Most attribute her consistently high standard to her natural ability and feel for training her horses, and certainly anyone who watches them work soon appreciates that they do look very impressive in all paces and movements. As far as Mary is concerned, however, there is no great secret to training horses well on the flat: it comes down to the trainer having a clear idea in his mind as to what he is trying to achieve, also to consistency in approach to the horse's work, to self-discipline and finally patience.

Mary has always had the determination and self-discipline to resolve a problem, however long it takes. There have been occasions when a routine schooling session has turned into a battle of wills lasting many hours – but eventually the horse has accepted what he is being asked to do. For example, a young novice horse that Mary was training one afternoon refused to remain in trot for a full twenty-metre circle. He would get part of the way round and was then obviously determined to rid himself of his rider, to the extent that he would throw himself to the ground in an effort to lose Mary. Three hours later, however, he realised he was not going to win that particular game and did what had been asked of him. King Kong, second at Burghley in 1994, often had very firm ideas about what he wanted to be doing, even when upgraded to Intermediate; there were several occasions when Mary went to her trainer, Ferdi Eilberg, for a dressage lesson, only to find that King Kong was so excitable, all they could do was keep him cantering in large circles! So it does not necessarily come easily; the rider has to be determined to see the job through, and never be content to accept second best.

Mary is very sure in her own mind as to what she is aiming for when training her horses on the flat: 'Dressage training is all about developing the ability and obedience of the horse. The ultimate aim is that the horse remains calm, willing and confident throughout all his work, no matter how difficult it is. The understanding between horse and rider should be such that the horse appears to be performing his work of his own accord,' explains Mary. And those who have seen King William soar majestically round the Badminton cross-country course can appreciate that, in his case, this principle applies to his cross-country jumping as well. Mary

goes on to explain her basic training principles:

'One of my first aims with the younger horses is to get them working steadily on the bit; this means that they accept the bit and the contact, and do not alter their outline in an attempt to evade the contact. I like the horse's neck to be arched so that the poll is the highest point, but the height of the neck is dictated by the horse's level of training. Thus a horse such as my novice, King Henry, would work with a much lower headcarriage than, say, King William. This is because the horse can only elevate his front end, and therefore his headcarriage, correctly once he has learnt to carry more of his weight on his hocks; only then is he truly working off his forehand. The younger horse will not have the balance or the muscle development to carry a very great percentage of his weight on his hocks, so his overall outline is inevitably longer and lower. As he learns to come off his forehand and work in self-carriage, when he is carrying his weight on his hocks and is not reliant on the rider's hand for support, the outline becomes progressively more compact and elevated.

'I want the horse to maintain a light, even and consistent contact, never offering any resistance to and be attentive enough to respond to the very lightest aid. His paces should feel and look free, regular and supple, and he should work with his nose held vertically, or slightly in front of the vertical.

'In theory, teaching all this is very simple: the rider must insist that the horse stays consistently straight on straight lines, and bends correctly on curved lines. He should work towards achieving an immediate reaction from the horse in response to his aids so that all transitions are instant and smooth, but not abrupt. He must always be consistent in what he asks of the horse, and in his reaction to the horse; mine are rewarded with a pat or with my voice when they are working correctly, and reprimanded or corrected when they are not. In this way they learn clearly and quickly the difference between right and wrong.'

Mary would school her novice horses for several days in succession, as she feels this more effectively consolidates anything they have learnt. The Advanced horses would probably be schooled on the flat once a week, and perhaps have a quick 'tune-up' the day before an event. Once a horse has been trained to Advanced level

LEFT: Working on a twenty-metre circle, Mary asks William to go from collected to medium and back to collected trot. This encourages the horse to engage his hindquarters and to put more expression into the pace

RIGHT: Mary practises coming out of the corner and putting William straight into shoulder-in

the emphasis in his flatwork training changes: he no longer needs to be taught what to do, as is the case with the younger horses, rather the rider attempts to perfect and enhance the work and the movements that he now knows so well.

Finding yourself in the same section at an Advanced one-day event as King William and Mary could be a dispiriting experience because they consistently acquire for themselves an impressive lead. In the past their rivals have enjoyed a certain breathing space because William's showjumping has, on occasion – especially at three-day events – let him down, but he is fast improving in this area. If Mary can finally crack this problem, which seems to be the result of tense nervousness on William's part, they could become almost unbeatable! Here, Mary describes how she works on ensuring that her horses consistently gain an early lead in competitions:

'William knows all his work inside out as far as the movements are concerned and how he should be performing them. So in his work at home I concentrate on making sure he stays really soft and supple through his body; this is especially important as the horse gets older [King William was born in 1984 and upgraded to Advanced when he was only six, so he has been working at this level for a long time] – he must stay soft and supple and equally manoevrable on both reins. My aim now is to try and create as much flair and expression in the horse's work as possible. Plenty of horses can perform an adequate Advanced dressage test, but you will only get really good marks if the horse can be made to work as impressively as possible, with maximum flair and expression; you achieve this by continually striving to encourage the horse to work in even greater self-carriage, giving as much elevation and life to his work as possible.

'To help bring the trot to life I work on transitions within the pace, usually on a circle so that the inside hindleg is made to come further under the horse. On a twenty-metre circle I will come back to a very collected trot, making sure the hindquarters are really working under the horse and that he is not simply shortening his stride. I would then send him forwards for four or five strides of extended trot before collecting the pace once again and repeating the exercise.

'William finds forward and extended work far easier than the collected paces so a greater percentage of his work is performed in the collected pace (the exercise can be ridden in canter as well). When I bring him back from his extended work into the collected pace I concentrate on trying to retain the same energy and elasticity in the collected pace that he offered in the extended pace; the more active the hind end, the better the horse can carry himself in front and the more impressive his work looks. In this sort of exercise it is important that the rider keeps the leg on during the downward transition, straightens his back and deepens the seat. The rider should always think first with the leg – the transition must not be solely reliant on the hand.

'Although at home William is sensitive to the leg, at Advanced level the rider has to wear spurs during the dressage test and so I do still occasionally ride him in spurs so that he accepts them during a competition; but with him I only ever wear very short spurs. Some horses don't move away from the leg so easily: for example Star Appeal doesn't find the extended work as easy as William does, and so he is always ridden in spurs; this gives me a back-up aid to the leg if he doesn't go forwards from the leg straightaway.

'At a competition the atmosphere tends to lift the horse's natural way of going and usually results in his paces looking more impressive anyway. At home I make sure I always ride the paces in a very strong and forward way because his natural paces are more likely to be a bit flat when he is schooling at home. But it is important not to make the mistake of letting him work in a flat, hurried way; at home you need to create the lift first by using exercises such as shoulder-in and half-pass. Then when you ride the horse forwards there will be enough lift and energy in the pace so that he goes upwards and forwards, and doesn't just scuttle along getting flatter and faster.

'I try to discipline myself and the horse to be very accurate at home, especially in movements such as shoulder-in when it is very easy to get the angle wrong. The shoulder-in encourages the horse to place his inside hindleg further underneath him so that it is carrying both his own weight and that of the rider, and it acts as an early introduction to the ultimate aim of working in self-carriage. When teaching the movement to a young horse I always start by coming off a ten-metre circle, as this dictates to the horse the correct bend that he needs to hold through the shoulder-in. The horse should be working into the outside rein, with his weight off the inside rein and inside shoulder. With the older horses it acts as a suppling and engaging exercise, as well as being a specific movement that they must perform in their dressage test.

'I make the more advanced horses ride through the

LEFT: *When schooling William at home in half-pass Mary starts by allowing him to work with his shoulders in advance of his quarters as this encourages him to really step forwards and across...Then you ask the quarters to come across in line with the shoulders, the aim being not to lose too much of the really good forward movement that you had before*

BELOW: *Riding counter canter through the short corner is a greater test of the horse than is required in competition. Demanding more of the horse at home will make his competition work seem easier*

corner of the school and go straight into the shoulder-in movement without wasting two or three strides getting there, and I am very strict about this. When I mark out an arena in the field at home I always put the quarter markers closer to the corners than they should be so that when I come round the turn I am obliged to go straight into the shoulder-in movement.

'A horse will generally find it harder working on one rein than the other – William has always found the right bend more difficult than the left – and so when schooling on the rein the horse finds hardest, I always exaggerate the bend to help open up the stiffer side. Then at a competition when you ask for slightly less, the horse will find it easier and will offer it to you without resistance. If he is used to offering more bend and more engagement at home, then he will find the amount required of him in competition very easy in comparison.

'The half-pass is another suppling and engaging exercise, which I teach to the younger horses once their shoulder-in work is well established. The correct way for the half-pass to be performed is for the horse to be working on two tracks, with a slight bend through his body towards the direction in which he is travelling. The head, neck and shoulders travel very slightly in advance of the hindquarters; the outside foreleg crosses over and in front of the inside foreleg, and the outside hind crosses over and in front of the inside hind.

'To teach the movement to a younger horse I would come out of a ten-metre circle and go into shoulder-in as the horse started to travel down the long side of the school. Then I use my outside leg to ask him to move his quarters across the diagonal, and I use my inside leg to maintain the forward movement, as the horse must move forwards and sideways. A less experienced horse will find it easier to work with his forehand well in advance of his hindquarters to begin with, and as long as he gets the idea of maintaining his outline and rhythm then that does not matter initially. As he becomes accustomed to the movement and to keeping his balance throughout its execution, I would start to ask him to bring his quarters across more and more until they were parallel to the long side of the arena; the aim is not to lose too much of the really good forward movement that you had before.

'To improve the canter and the horse's overall suppleness and balance I do a lot of canter lateral work such as shoulder-in and half-pass in that pace; it frees the shoulders and activates the hindquarters, as well as helping to keep the horse supple and correctly bent through his body.

'Counter canter is another movement required in the Advanced dressage test, and I practise this at home with the same principles that I apply to most of the horse's flatwork: demand more at home than you need to ask for in the competition itself. So for example with the counter canter I ride through much tighter corners than would be asked for in the test; then at a competition, when the horse may be a little bit tense and harder to ride, he finds the work easier than if he had not had more demanded of him at home.' Thus Mary might start by cantering some ten-metre circles, then cross the diagonal and ride counter canter through the two short corners of the arena. This is tighter than would ever be required in a test, when usually either a loop or a three-loop serpentine is called for.

'Straightness is something else which must never be overlooked in all the horse's work. To this end I often practise the turn down the centre line, the halt and the move-off, to make sure the horse will stay straight when he doesn't have a straight edge to work alongside, and that he comes back to halt relaxed and square. And when you move off from halt, again it is very important that the horse moves forwards and off your leg immediately and goes straight until you ask him to track right or left. If you can't hold a straight line down the centre line you are unlikely to get a square halt, and equally unlikely to get a square move-off, so it is very important to work on this.'

As the horse canters down the centre line he must be straight through his quarters and shoulders, although a very slight bend of the head and neck is allowed over the leading foreleg.

Watching Mary demonstrate these finer points on a horse like King William, it is easy to think that any rider should be able to put these things into practice and produce a stunning test. But there can be no short-cuts; the fact that a horse has got to Advanced level in eventing is no guarantee that he has actually been properly and correctly schooled right from the beginning. How often do you hear a rider say that the horse is a brilliant jumper but his dressage lets him down? Whilst it is true that some horses find dressage work naturally easier than others, the key to how successful they will ultimately be in this work comes down to their basic schooling and their introduction to flatwork. The principles and theory are certainly not beyond any competent rider, but where Mary has been very lucky is in the fact that she generally buys her horses quite young, and if they are good enough, they stay with her until they reach the top. Many international riders have to run a large yard of horses in order to make a living, and will often only take the ride on someone else's horse when it has reached Intermediate or Advanced level. Any shortcomings in its early training are therefore much harder – and sometimes impossible – to correct fully.

ABOVE LEFT: At the first attempt Mary felt that William's hindquarters were a fraction to the left. She explained that as the horse makes the turn down the centre line it is easy for him not to move his quarters across so that they are directly behind his shoulders, but to trail them round the turn and let them swing in.

CENTRE & RIGHT: To correct this the next time, Mary thinks of riding a very slight shoulder-in as she makes the turn and comes down the centre line. Moving the shoulders over very slightly pushes the quarters to where they should be; if you tried to correct it just by pushing the quarters over more, it is easy for the horse to then let them swing out too far the other way

During the canter-to-halt transition the rider must be aware of first making sure the horse is straight, because any crookedness will be accentuated as the downward transition is made; then straighten the back and keep the leg on so that the horse remains balanced and off his forehand as he comes down to halt

PUTTING IT ALL INTO PRACTICE: GATCOMBE 1995

■ At the 1995 British Open Championships at Gatcombe Mary had entered her three longlisted horses, King William, King Kong and Star Appeal. It was their last event before the final trial to be held at Thirlestane Castle in Scotland, after which the British team would be shortlisted for the 1995 European Championships. Here, Mary explains how she tried to get the very best from each of her horses in the dressage phase:

'William is the best established of all my horses on the flat, but his temperament is such that he can get quite tense at competitions which then spoils his work. Instead of being relaxed and allowing me to really ride out the movements, he tends to come up too high in front and I have to ride him more quietly so as not to add to his tenseness.

'As soon as we arrived at Gatcombe William was led out in hand and allowed to graze near the main dressage arena to help him get used to the atmosphere. He then stayed on the lorry until about two hours before his test. I rode him round to warm him up and then worked him in a long low outline, trying to get an idea of how he was feeling in terms of how settled he might be. He felt calm and relaxed so I then put him through some of the test movements, feeling for any signs of stiffness on either rein or in any particular movement. He felt sufficiently settled that I was happy to put him back in the lorry and get on him about half an hour before his test. Unfortunately everywhere had got a lot busier by then, besides which the Pony Club mounted games were in full swing which proved a bit much for William! I usually make a point of working him near the arena so that I can be sure of having his attention and being able to ride the movements as well as possible in spite of the atmosphere – but the mounted games were just too much to expect him to accept and so I kept him away, and just hoped they would have stopped by the time I went in.

'As usual when he is excited William had come up too high through his neck, so I tried to ride him in a very round outline so that he was actually overbent in the hope that he wouldn't feel the need to come up quite as high once I wanted him to go in the correct outline. At this point you don't want to blow the horse's mind by asking for too much in the way of different movements, but in this sort of situation I do need to be sure that William is listening to me. So I went through a few transitions and did some extended trot, making sure he was firing forwards off my leg as soon as I asked, and that he then came back to me calmly when the movement was finished. The mounted games were just finishing as we walked towards the arena but I still got Annie, my headgirl, to walk by his head, shielding him from the excitement in the ring in the hope he would not become distracted by it. However, he still "grew" by a few inches once we were in the arena.

'It was very hot and there were lots of brightly coloured sunshades in amongst the spectators. Once

William is tense he becomes hyper-aware of what is around him, and the crowds add to his tenseness – whereas if he comes into the arena calm he barely notices the spectators. But as he worked through his test he gradually relaxed, and produced some very good work to finish equal second after this phase.

'Apple [Star Appeal] did his test much later in the day. I would have loved to have been able to swap his time with William's – it would have been quiet and relaxing for William, whereas Apple, who lacks William's natural flair and is a little bit lazy, would have

benefited from performing when the atmosphere was buzzing.

'He had a walk around during the morning to stretch his legs and then I got on him about an hour and a half before his test. I know that Apple will always be calm and well behaved, so his warm-up generally concentrates on putting more activity and expression into his work. He usually feels quite stiff when he starts off and not very active behind, so I work on engaging the hindquarters and keeping him as light as possible in front. If he is at all hesitant about moving away from my leg then he gets either a tap with the whip or a good kick from my leg to wake him up to what is being asked. I use changes of direction and serpentines to keep him stepping under with his inside hindleg and supple through his body. Once he feels softer, looser and more engaged I put him back on the lorry until about twenty minutes before his test.

'When he comes out again he always feels much better straightaway as a result of having loosened up in his earlier work. I then go through some of the movements in the test, exaggerating what I want from him so that

when I ask for a bit less in the arena he finds it easier to give it to me. So in shoulder-in I would ask for more angle than is needed, and in half-pass I would make sure he was really stepping across, allowing the shoulders to lead more than is correct in order to get the maximum sideways and forwards movement from him. Because he is a stiffer horse naturally than William or Conker, and lacks some of their self-carriage, he finds lateral work easier in canter than in trot. So I do most of his warm-up in canter first, so that when I ask for the same movements in trot he finds them easier than if I had battled with him in trot to begin with. The advantage of a horse like Apple is that you can ride him as hard as you like in the arena without any risk of making him explode. At Gatcombe he performed a very calm, accurate test.

'Conker [King Kong] is a real monkey – I never fully trust him because he is quite capable of working in a lovely relaxed manner during your warm-up, and will then go into the arena and think that it's funny to explode! He is naughty but very, very talented and his talent is part of his problem: he finds his work very easy and doesn't have to try or to think very hard in order to perform well, so he likes to amuse himself by turning his energy and attention into misbehaving. In the spring when the ground is good I often lunge all the horses once they are at an event, but when the ground gets very hard I am reluctant to use this as part of their working in. However with Conker I did feel it was better to work him initially on the lunge because he settles more quickly when he has only got himself to fight against, than if I am on board trying to calm him down. So he had half an hour on the lunge, starting with the side-reins fitted long and low on the saddle, then with them higher and shorter for the last ten minutes or so. I change the rein every five or ten minutes as well. He then went back on the lorry until twenty minutes before his test.

'Before his test I worked him inside the boards in the practice arena as this helps to keep his concentration, and I was positive and dominant in all I did with him because he has to learn to give in to his rider. I rode him very deep into the corners of the arena, and kept his circles small so that he really had to work to do what you wanted. He felt really quite wicked, but actually coped very well once he got into the arena – until his extended canter when he could contain himself no longer and rushed forwards with his head in the air!

'I have also found that it helps all my horses to turn them out the night before their dressage test. I don't think this does them any harm as long as they are not going across country that day; certainly they all seem far more relaxed and happy the next day than if they had been stabled.'

Cross-Country Training

ANDREW NICHOLSON

■I drove home having spent an afternoon watching Andrew Nicholson and his co-riders giving some youngsters their first cross-country schooling session with decidedly mixed feelings, not sure whether this particular Kiwi was completely mad or whether the more sedate approach taken by most of us meant that we were completely neurotic! Andrew was riding a stallion called Samuel, one of his working pupils was on his own novice, a grey which had done a few events, while his French rider Thibault and New Zealand rider Dan were on the other two very green five-year-olds.

They warmed up over some rails and a ditch, the younger horses being allowed to follow the more experienced grey, but then the schooling session developed into something resembling a cross between a team chase and a musical ride; as soon as any one rider felt his horse was sufficiently confident to go first, he would set off over a series of fences with the rest following behind. At a complex such as the water which could be crossed in a number of different ways, once the horses had got the general idea of jumping in, each took his own route; so very soon they were criss-crossing the water complex from all directions.

The horses were given little time to worry about what they were doing; they were expected to pick up the canter from wherever they had stopped and take on whatever fence their rider put them at. Amazingly they all seemed to do just that, with no apparent indication of worry or doubt. In fact the only one to show any concern at all was Andrew when, having asked if this was the way most other people schooled their youngsters, I had to reply, 'Well, not quite – they tend to build up the questions gradually, not ask them all at once!'. Nevertheless Andrew's approach resulted in an atmosphere of relaxed good fun, and it certainly seemed to work for his horses.

In reality the Nicholson way is not quite as simple and 'gung ho' as it looked; there was method in the madness! Each rider was more than capable of bringing his young horse into every fence confidently and on a good stride; and although they might have done relatively little jumping at home, Andrew's first priority with all his youngsters is to teach them that they must get to the other side. Having instilled that principle, his theory is that if you look after the horse and don't let him make a mistake

that frightens him, he should have no reason to think about stopping at something new. The session was not without its unnerving moments, however: Thibault's horse sat down in the water the first time it attempted the bigger of the drops in, and Dan's little chestnut turned a complete somersault over a ditch and palisade. Both were unhurt, and what is more they went on to be placed in their first few Novice events.

Andrew explained that if they had had the time, these particular horses would have done a bit more jumping at home before coming cross-country schooling; however, they had been broken in late, in January, and since they were already five and the aim was to event them in that same season, they just had to keep going with them. 'Normally we start them off as four-year-olds,' explained Andrew. 'They would be backed in the autumn and do a bit of dressage, and then once the older competition horses were turned away for their rest at the end of the season, we would have more time to concentrate on them. They would get plenty of gridwork and cantering to small fences through the winter, and would then be well prepared for cross-country schooling in the spring.

'These five-year-olds have come into the system later than usual, however, and the only jumping they have done is over some small uprights and oxers; they've cantered through some small combinations, too. They haven't done any gridwork quite simply because it is too time-consuming at this point in the season. It's not an ideal system, but as they belong to us we were keen to get them started this year, to see what we'd got. How I introduce them to cross-country schooling also depends on the time available. The ones that are started earlier in the spring I would always ride myself for their first session; the boys would be warming them up and I would take them round one at a time. But when time is short it is easier to take them round in a group. I don't worry about the fact that they might want a lead from another horse to begin with; often it doesn't matter if the lead horse doesn't even jump the fence – just having a horse in front helps the young ones to think forwards and to go forwards. By the end of the session they will each have taken the lead somewhere.

'Young horses vary a great deal as to how quickly they adapt to cross-country. Some take to it straightaway and know how to land in water or jump up and down

Andrew talked about Samuel's technique and attitude, pointing out qualities that he would look for in a horse's style, and those he would avoid or hope to correct: 'I like the way Samuel is lowering his head, neck and wither on the approach to his fences; a horse will learn a lot more if he is prepared to look where he is going, rather than jumping in hollow and blind. But the rider must keep the lower leg on so that the horse keeps going – he can look, but he must keep going. Also, if the horse is allowed to stretch his head and neck down, as Samuel does, then he will land more comfortably and in better balance than if he keeps his head and neck high'

After warming up over a few small rails, Andrew pops the young stallion over the ditch – Samuel finds it all great fun and throws a few bucks which, at this stage, Andrew is happy to ignore. 'Letting the horse hump his back and give a buck and a squeal is all part of showing him that cross-country should be fun, so I don't correct it at this point. Maybe I should, as it can be really annoying later on when you are at a competition if they think it's okay to let fly all over the place!' However, when the other horses left Samuel during this session, his bucks got a bit more serious. In this case Andrew would use a different tactic: 'I wouldn't let him carry on like that until he put me on the floor. If a horse is playing around too much I will quite often just turn him to a jump so suddenly he has to concentrate and get his act together'

117

TOP ROW (l to r): 'At the sunken road on this course Samuel copes well, and looks down and works out what he has got to do'

MIDDLE ROW (l to r): 'The little chestnut horse that Dan was riding, however, had his eye fixed on the rail on the far side of the sunken road right from the start, and quite simply cantered straight off the edge of the bank, oblivious to the drop, and ran straight into the step up the other side. He is a very brave horse nevertheless, and kept going and jumped very happily over the rail. It may be that he simply didn't see the sunken road, or he may have thought he had to jump across it'

BOTTOM (r to l): 'Some horses are quicker than others to work out how to tackle different questions. The grey horse was the only one of this bunch who had been across country before and yet he found it quite difficult to work out what to do with his legs at steps and banks. But then, the reason you school a horse is to teach him what to do and with a little practice the grey was soon hopping confidently up and down the different levels'

'The bay horse ended up making quite a mistake in the water; he started off by jumping in very big and bold, too bold really for this type of drop (far right). It obviously gave him a bit of a fright because when he came round to do a similar size drop the other side, faced with the water again he jumped in with his front legs but chickened out with his hind legs and ended up sitting down in it! However, we managed to restore his confidence by bringing him in over a smaller drop; he had learnt from his mistake and came in with a more sensible jump'

banks, and others can make a complete mess of it the first time; but as long as these have time to build up their confidence and are given the chance to school over cross-country courses so that they can learn what they have to do, they can still become good horses. If I have several very green horses to school myself I will usually go round first on a more experienced horse so that I have a good ride – I then get on the youngster and try to ride him with the same confidence, and it usually works.

'The number one priority at this stage is that they get to the other side of the fence. The way they do it is the second thing to worry about. It is also very important that the rider should try never to put the horse in a situation where he can stop, and that means using your head about what you ask him to jump. At home we keep everything very small so he can be pushed over from a standstill if necessary. There is nothing wrong with showing the horse the jump before you approach it, because everything should be geared to gaining his confidence, and not giving him an excuse to stop. At home we even trot our youngsters over poles and fillers on the ground when we first start them off. I always ride the young horses over their first fences, and then when I feel they have a good attitude one of the boys will carry on with them. If at any point they feel as if they are losing confidence or are just not going very well I will ride them again.

'When I go cross-country schooling I never ever jump just one fence and stop, especially if the horse is lacking confidence; once he has got into the swing of things and jumped a few fences in succession, then you can stop and rest. But to keep pulling up is the worst thing you can do. Young horses which are very bold often make the sort of mistake shown in the picture sequence at a complex like this or at water, because they think they have to jump right over it. But a horse has to learn to work out what to do at different obstacles, and the decision he makes is partly influenced by the way the rider brings him in to the obstacle: if he is being ridden strongly forwards on a long stride he is quite likely to assume he has to try and jump across whatever is in front of him. But if his rider collects and balances him, he has more time to work the problem out, and he will also know that he can't physically clear the obstacle from that sort of pace, and will hopefully work out what is expected of him. But the rider has quite a responsibility to his horse in this respect.

'The little chestnut is the horse that tipped up with Dan at the ditch and palisade, and he is a case in point. I suspect he had his head up and simply didn't see the ditch – dropped his front feet in it but was brave enough to try and jump it still, and ended up turning a somersault instead. Because at home he had been taught that he must get to the other side, that was his first priority

today, even when it all went horribly wrong. However, the rider must learn to protect a horse like this – when Dan saw how wrong they were, he really should have pulled him up and not let him still try and jump; but the word "stop" isn't in the vocabulary of this particular horse or rider so they paid the price. Once we knew they were unhurt I gave them a lead over a couple more fences and then we called it a day, and luckily the horse's confidence wasn't affected: a week later he jumped clear rounds at his first Novice, and two weeks after that he was placed at Hartpury Novice. I think he will be a very good horse – I know for sure that he is very brave!

'The bay horse also found some of the banks and steps quite difficult – he was a bit hesitant and tried to step up or down them, one leg at a time, rather than jump them. Thibault, his rider, had to be very positive with seat, legs and stick to send him forwards so that he jumped off and out; it was important that he didn't allow him to fiddle his way down. It is quite interesting that this particular horse is one that bucks badly – he threw me off the first time I sat on him, and when he dropped Thibault in the water during this session he flybucked back at him, and narrowly missed kicking him.

'Horses that buck are often quite difficult to ride forwards to a fence because they are always thinking and looking backwards to their rider, rather than forwards to the fence; their attention is more focussed on what the rider is doing to them, than on the jump ahead. It is therefore up to the rider to do something to focus the horse's attention on the fence. Letting this horse have a lead until he really got going helped him, because it made him concentrate on the horse in front and so think forwards, rather than backwards at his rider.'

All the horses used in this schooling session tended to dangle their front legs as they jumped, a slackness in technique which clearly indicated how inexperienced they were and what little jumping they had done. 'That is why it is very important not to get in front of the movement, particularly when schooling a young horse,' says Andrew. He has quite definite views on a horse's early training:

'I think a lot of people are a bit hard on their young horses at home; if their jump is not technically perfect they keep schooling them through different grids trying to get them to snap up in front or flick up behind, but I don't think you can beat competing them for sharpening up their technique and attitude. My horses always seem to improve more quickly once I start competing them than they do from heaps of schooling at home. And it does prove it, really, when you consider how these youngsters jumped during their first schooling session – certainly there was plenty to find wrong with the way they tackled some things, and many riders would have considered them much too green to go out and compete, but they all went out and jumped clear rounds at Novice level soon after, so it didn't take them too long to sort themselves out.'

Andrew finds the attitude and expectations of many riders towards young horses really very frustrating: 'My horses tend to pick up points quickly, but if someone comes to try one out because they want a novice with a few points they usually say that my horses are too green for them. In fact it's not that the horse is too green, it's that the rider isn't good enough to help the young horse. It can be very disheartening having someone try a youngster out who isn't really up to the job. And if I have been away with the older horses there isn't always time to ride

it again and restore its confidence before I have to compete it again; the person who tried it out has probably dropped it in the bottom of a few fences and then stood it right off the next one, and I find myself on a very confused young horse. It isn't the horse's fault – and usually its ability is proven by the fact that I keep on competing it until it is "experienced" enough for any rider to get on it and be given a reasonable ride.'

Andrew went on to describe what he looks for in a horse's attitude and natural technique: 'What I really like is a horse that canters down to every new fence as if he has seen it all before – but these are pretty rare! You do get some which are naturals across country; they are confident and work out quickly what to do at each new obstacle – but then their very boldness can sometimes make them careless, particularly in the showjumping.'

'If a horse does want to have a look at the fence, which most of them do, you should then only need to give it a kick or a squeeze, or click to it, to send it forwards over the fence. I don't like the ones that come back at you when you ask them to go on. The most important thing, in all the horse's training, is that when you tell them to go, they go. It is the same as working them on the flat: when you put the leg on and ask them to move forwards, they must go forwards immediately.

'Equally, however, you don't want a horse that rushes its fences, because if it is happy to rush at cross-country fences then it is almost bound to rush its showjumps and be careless. If I have a horse that is naturally very bold I would not cross-country school it very often because I find this sort generally ends up being too brave in its approach to everything – then I

end up protecting it all the time because I am worried that it isn't going to look after itself. If I am schooling a horse that rushes at a fence, I would usually turn it away in a circle rather than pull it up in front of the fence. If you pull it up in front of the fence it tends to be a bit confused, and when you come in next time it will often break back to trot; then you have to send it strongly forwards again, and this rather defeats the object of the horse learning to stay in a rhythm and wait for the rider to send it up to the fence. So I turn away in a circle, but then turn back into the fence quite sharply so the horse doesn't have too much of a run up to it.

'It is a difficult problem to sort out if it happens to be a young horse with a lot of talent over a fence; these get brave and start to rush, but because they are talented they always get over the fence without touching it. They never get a fright, and very often as their confidence increases so does their speed. So the bold, clean jumper is harder to· correct than the horse that backs off its fences. The wary horse that backs off is easier because the rider can afford to keep moving him forwards right up to the fence; and if you can press the horse up to the fence he usually makes a better shape over it.

'As the horse moves up through the grades, usually you find little reason to cross-country school it.

However, if a horse has not had a run for some time, and particularly if it is quite a young Advanced horse, then I would school it over a few fences and through some water just to check its confidence. And I would also school a horse that has had a bad fall, or one that is maybe just starting to feel as if it is lacking a bit of confidence. And obviously, horses at this level would go on their own without a lead from another horse.

'During the winter months we build corners and coffins with showjump poles and water trays, but I do find that no matter how much of that you do at home it is never the same as jumping the real thing. I never used to be a big fan of cross-country schooling – when I left New Zealand there were very few places where you could have done any cross-country and it was standard practice to do lots of showjumping and then go eventing. Now, however, I use schooling courses quite frequently although I treat a schooling session like a competition: the horse is warmed up, then I set off and jump several fences in a row – and I am sure this pays off. Even the little chestnut that fell in this schooling session still had enough confidence to go quite soon after to a Novice event where he jumped straight through both waters and a coffin. A schooling session teaches them what cross-country is all about, then when they see another course they trust you to give it a go.'

ABOVE LEFT: All the horses in this schooling session tended to dangle their front legs as they jumped, indicating how inexperienced they were

BELOW: Not every rider has the experience or technique to ride a young horse successfully. Here Andrew persuades a very inexperienced horse to take on an imposing fence in its second Novice event. They went on to be placed

CROSS-COUNTRY TEACHING

■ 'I enjoy teaching cross-country as long as there is sufficient time to do it justice; but quite simply if you are rushed you can't offer value for money. I usually manage to fit in one clinic a year! In fact a lot of the art of cross-country riding is quite difficult to teach; for example, at a clinic I held in the winter there were two riders who had never gone across country although they had showjumped a lot, and they were worried that they would hold the others back because the rest had all done some eventing. But of the whole class they were the only two who could ride their horses on a level stride to a fence, and that ability stood out a mile! Cross-country riding requires the same technique as showjumping: you need to be able to produce a short, powerful canter, and that is the same for a great many cross-country fences. These two riders found everything in the cross-country clinic easy. The other riders still needed to learn how to ride their horses on an even stride, but they wouldn't have thanked me if I had spent the lesson teaching them something as basic as that, and had not allowed them to jump until they had mastered it! But that was really what was needed.

'I can never understand riders who say they love cross-country but hate showjumping – in fact they are usually the ones who can't keep a level stride on the approach to a fence. And a great many people also have quite the wrong idea about going fast: riding the correct cross-country speed shouldn't feel fast, and if it does it is because the horse isn't balanced or in a rhythm. If the horse is balanced and is in a good, level rhythm then you don't have to waste time setting him up in front of each fence, and you are also able to ride the most economical route between fences.

'Most riders inevitably develop their own technique, which they may have to adjust slightly depending on the horse they are riding; but whatever your style, I do feel there are certain basic rules in cross-country riding which really must be obeyed. For example coffins, and very upright fences such as gates, or something like a hayrack which has a false groundline, must be treated with an awful lot of respect in terms of the speed with which you approach – you don't want to be on a backward stride, but equally none of these is the type of fence where you want to be trying to make up three or four seconds on your time; save that for the spread fences. The golden rule is to have the horse balanced and in front of your leg, not for you to be in front of the horse!

'The other basic rule is always to be in touch with the horse with your legs and your hands, not by pulling on the horse's mouth, but neither should there be loops in the reins when riding across country: you must keep a contact with the horse's mouth. You may get away with loopy reins on a schoolmaster or an Advanced horse, but if the novice horse trips on landing or hits a fence, if you have contact with him through your hands and legs then you have a much better chance of either staying on board, or keeping the horse on its feet.

'The other thing that many riders get themselves in a muddle about is seeing a stride. I have bad days, too, and find myself missing at fences left, right and centre. When that happens you should go back to the basic premise of not trying to see a stride, but trying to *feel* for the horse's stride; feel for an even rhythm and treat the jump as something that just happens to get in the way. I have seen riders put up a very classy performance and yet they say they cannot see a stride – but they ride on a level, even stride the whole time.

'You often hear riders saying they "can't see a stride but they know when they are going to be wrong". Well, if you know you are coming in wrong, then you have the beginnings of being able to see a stride – otherwise you wouldn't know you were wrong. But you then need to train yourself to *do* something when you *are* on a bad stride! I would rather the rider did anything – turn around and face the other way, even! – as long as he does something. That way, at least you are learning; you may do the wrong thing, but at least the mistake will teach you what not to do, whereas doing nothing will teach you nothing. I really believe that you must make mistakes in order to learn, and that applies to horses as well as riders. The rider's usual reaction when he thinks he is wrong is to fire the horse into the jump – but usually the horse will then go flat and that just runs you into trouble more quickly. Often if you just sit and hold the horse for another stride or two, suddenly you will see what you need to do, either hold for two more short strides or press the horse forwards for one longer one.'

Thoughts on Training

RICHARD MEADE

■ 'For me, the cross-country was the central feature of the sport, and I took a horse's cross-country training in its overall preparation very seriously. Hunting has always helped in this respect, and I hunted both Barberry and Jacob Jones. The latter was not the most courageous of horses, always rather cautious and suspicious about ditches, and hunting made a world of difference to his confidence and approach. I had eight or nine days hunting on Laurieston which proved the perfect way for us to get to know each other. It is terribly important to ensure that a horse enjoys his cross-country because there is no pleasure at all in eventing one which doesn't, and hunting certainly helps to instil enjoyment and confidence.

'My approach when training any horse has always been that you have to work at every aspect of the competition. The training routine has to incorporate everything, from the roads and tracks, steeplechase and cross-country, to the showjumping and dressage, and the way you ride the horse must be consistent throughout all his work. Thus it is most important to care about the way the horse goes all the time, which means throughout his training and the build-up to anything that he is asked to do.

'Going back to basics, it is terribly important that the horse accepts the bit, and always works on the bit; the basic principle of the horse being contained and controlled between hand and leg is the foundation of everything that he does. It should be an accepted part of the horse's life, and an automatic part of the way you ride him.

'The horse must be trained to be athletic in all his work. At gallop you must be able to lengthen and shorten his pace instantly, and he must be trained to be as responsive as possible. The horse must be comfortable in what he is doing, and be able to carry out his daily work in an athletic manner.

'I heard the trainer of a top football team once make the comment that, because a footballer is only one part of a team, it was important to concentrate on improving the individual's particular strengths – so if he is a good goal-kicker, then that is what his training should concentrate on. With an event horse the complete opposite is true, and your priority must be to work continually to minimise his weaknesses – then his strengths will look after themselves.

'The most important thing in training the horse is to build up his confidence. He must be confident in you so that he is happy in his work, and happy to work with you in all that you ask of him. That does not mean being particularly soft or passive, it means getting through the resistances in a fair but firm way, so that the horse understands and respects you.'

Richard enjoyed his major successes on a number of horses: 'Cornishman was probably the best horse I have ever ridden, although all horses are very different and special in their own way. But he really was a brilliant horse, and went on to even more consistent successes with Mary Gordon-Watson, including another team gold at the Munich Olympics. You could gallop him into a fence and if you were coming in a bit strong he could balance himself in front of it and still jump it well; for a big horse he could put in a very short stride to get you out of trouble. He was a charming horse, very talented and a real thinker. When I rode him, in terms of his career, it was still early days and he was yet to reach his peak.'

Barberry was another of Richard's horses: he rode him at his first Olympics in Tokyo in 1964 where they finished eighth, they won individual silver at the 1966 World Championships, and team gold at the 1967 Europeans.

'Barberry was another wonderful horse, and I have a very soft spot for him because he taught me such a tremendous amount; he was very sensitive and so I had to learn to ride with feeling, which stood me in good stead for any other horse I ever rode. He wasn't as easy as some – you couldn't afford to make mistakes with him, although of course I did in the beginning. But I really do believe that every rider needs one good horse to take him to the top. Once you get there, other good horses tend to come your way, and you will have learnt a lot from your first horse which then helps you to produce other top class horses. But you need one really good horse to get you going. Mine was Barberry, Lucinda Green had Be Fair, and Ginny Elliot [née Holgate] had Dubonnet and then Priceless – whoever you look at, they all started with one good horse – you can't make it on your own.

'And I have been fortunate enough to ride some

wonderful horses. The Poacher, whom Ben Jones rode in Mexico, was a fantastic horse and a real trier although he didn't have the scope or the class of Cornishman, and Laurieston [on whom Richard won individual and team gold in Munich in 1972] was another, though very difficult. He could be really naughty but was truly brilliant once his energies were channelled. In Munich I remember saying to somebody on the day before the start of the three-day event that I wished the Olympics were a year later. Laurieston was only eight, and I felt that he needed another year to produce his full potential. He could be very difficult in the dressage as he was always trying to find a way of getting away from you. He was very energetic and a great character, which is why I was very fond of him. I knew he had this brilliance and scope across country, but it all needed channelling.'

THE SPORT TODAY

When Richard Meade was eventing there were far fewer riders competing for team places; the sport had a relatively narrow base. Where riders were fortunate was in the fact that there were quite a lot of people willing to buy, but not compete, really good horses, and the ride on such horses went to the likes of Richard Meade.

'Today the rider usually buys his own horse and then goes looking for sponsorship of some sort. If he finds a sponsor they usually back both the rider and the horse and so a good horse is unlikely to be made available to another rider if that is what the selectors wished. There is no doubt that in the past, we have won medals because the right horses were put with the right riders, but because of the modern structure of the sport such a policy would not work today. There is now a broader base of competitors trying to get to the top, and if they are to be selected for a team it will be on the horse they usually ride.

'Today's cross-country courses have become more technical and have made people ride and think more technically, but I do believe that something has been lost along the way...to say we no longer have true horsemen is perhaps too strong a criticism, but we do have a lot of technically correct, trained riders who are not necessarily experienced horsemen. They are technically good while they are dealing with conditions and situations which they have been trained to deal with, but they are not necessarily so good at reacting to an unexpected situation in a spontaneous

way. The ability to do this is the mark of the feel and intuition that the very best horsemen possess.

'It is not a coincidence that the New Zealand and Australian riders who have become so successful have usually been brought up with horses. They have had to break in and ride perhaps difficult youngsters, and they have not always had time to wait until a horse is beautifully prepared before going out and competing in public.

'When I walked the course for the European Championships in Achselschwang where the conditions were very deep and heavy, I commented to Stephen Hadley that it should suit the British riders as they would have dealt with such conditions out hunting – but one of the team riders looked horrified and said he hadn't hunted and had never ridden in ground like that before. I compared this to how I felt when I rode at my very first Badminton in 1963, when it was held as a one-day event because the ground conditions were so bad. The more it rained the more confident I felt because I knew how to handle the conditions, while a lot of my rivals didn't. It was the same in Mexico with the floods – it was a challenge to ride and help my horse through adverse conditions.

'The other thing that has changed is that although the courses are more technical, they are much better built, and present a far more imposing obstacle to the horse. However, the distances in combinations are nearly always "right", so as long as the horse is bold and jumps in all right, he should then be able to look after himself. I think both these changes allow riders to get away with quite a bit more than we would have been able to. In our day the fences were trappier and built with very small timber, and there were nearly always a few dead upright fences sited down a hill – these required great accuracy and balance otherwise you would fall. So although riders may feel that today's courses are more technical, I suspect they are actually fairer to the horse than they used to be.

'Looking ahead to Atlanta, I do think it is a great pity that three-day events have to be run in such excessively hot and humid conditions, but a great deal of good will come out of the research that has had to be undertaken into the care and welfare of horses in these conditions. As long as the welfare of the horse is safeguarded then I am glad that a modified three-day event will still be held – it would be a far greater pity for riders to lose the opportunity to compete at an Olympic Games.'

Richard Meade on Kilcashel at Lawson's Leap, Locko Open Championships 1982

Jump Training

MATT RYAN

■ One of the most talked-about aspects of Matt Ryan's Olympic performance was the remarkable improvement in his and Kibah Tic Toc's showjumping: at Badminton a few months earlier they had had five fences down; at Barcelona, when there was so much more at stake, they finished with just one error. Matt, who was only too well aware of one reason why the showjumping had been a problem previously – doing too much in the practice arena beforehand – was less surprised at the result, particularly as he had made some significant changes to his technique. Moreover he has been applying these new methods to the jump training of all his horses.

Matt describes Kibah Tic Toc as a scopey but careless jumper when it comes to showjumping; but with help from Vicky Roycroft he feels they found a technique which brought out the best in Tic Toc. As he explains:

'If a horse knocks showjumping poles down with its front legs, it is tempting to try and "hold" it off the fence. Most riders think that this will give it more room

and time in which to get its front end up and clear of the top pole, but it can make the situation worse. Vicky taught me to approach the fence in a more positive, but shorter canter, and then to ride deeper to the base of the fence. It took a lot of getting used to, but she has been proved right – riding Tic Toc deep to the fence and challenging him with the front rail makes him snap up his front end, rather than diving forwards over the fence, which is how he was having them down before.

'I try to ride all my horses like this now, particularly when we are jump training them at home – I keep the canter as short and collected as possible, and I try to ride them deeper to the fence. At an event I would only deviate from this approach if I felt that the horse wasn't responding well to it.

'To perform well over fences and on the flat I believe you need to instil three things into the horse's way of going, and into his rider's mind: confidence, forwardness and roundness. But to begin with, when you are training a young horse, the most important thing is

ensuring he is confident and familiar with his fences.'

Matt cites ditches as an example of how important it is to instil in the horse right from the start that there is nothing to fear:

'Most horses have a natural fear of ditches – as far as they are concerned these are dangerous dark holes with monsters lurking in the bottom. A lot of people are taught to chase a horse over a ditch; they think that if they come in with enough pace and hold the horse's head up, then he won't see the ditch until it is too late. This approach is wrong because the horse never learns to overcome his fear of ditches, and once he starts jumping round the bigger tracks, those ditches are wide enough for the horse to see them from a long way out. You're not going to kid him into jumping over them with his head in the air.

'With a young horse, my approach is to find a small ditch which is shallow enough for him to walk into. I walk him up to it and let him lower his head and look in it. If he spins round, then he is turned back to look at it again. As soon as he faces the ditch I *stop* hassling him, as his reward for being brave and facing the hidden

monster! I then encourage him to go up to it – if he takes a few more steps forwards, I again stop using the leg, as his reward for facing up to danger. If you are patient and follow this approach he will usually end up walking over it himself quite willingly. The idea is that as soon as he goes in the wrong direction – that is, turns away from the ditch – you use leg and voice to get after him; but once he is going in the right direction, be less aggressive with the leg so that you are not hassling him – this is his reward. I use this same approach when introducing the horse to small drops and steps down.

'At an event you obviously don't risk allowing the horse to stop and have a look, but sit down and ride him strongly forwards to the fence; if he has been introduced properly to a ditch at home, then he should let you ride him forwards to it. And as the young horse becomes more confident and more familiar with what is required of him, you can put him under more pressure by using bigger fences and combinations and suchlike.

'In general I think it is very important to relate your training at home as closely as possible to the questions you will be asked at a competition, be it for the

---

Matt described Tic Toc as a scopey but careless jumper. Although he uses his head and neck to make a nice round shape over the fence, he doesn't snap up his front legs any more than he has to.
To make the horse jump more cleanly in front, Matt always tries to ride him deep into his fences, thereby challenging him with the front rail to make him use himself more

showjumping or the cross-country. So, for example, I don't do very much gridwork, or if I do then I would set the grid up so that I approach it in canter. At an event you have to be able to canter down to a combination or a single fence and feel confident that you will meet it on a good stride; jumping through grids from trot doesn't teach you this. One of the hardest things to get right when jumping is the ability to see a good stride to a fence, and this is a skill that can only be acquired through practice. With a young horse I would use grid-work to begin with, because to meet a fence well you have to be able to lengthen and shorten the stride, and this takes time with a young horse. But once he has that ability I would almost always canter him to his fences when training at home, apart from his initial warm-up over a cross-pole.

'I concentrate on accuracy and on obedience, and I practise this by using different angles, arrowheads and corners to teach the horse to stay straight and to jump on the line I have put him on. The grey mare pictured, Lady Jane Gray, is a very scopey jumper but prefers to run on at her fences and use her pace to clear them, rather than letting me ride her up to the base and using a better technique and contained impulsion to jump them. She tends to jump very big so as not to hit the fence, but is still a bit dangly with her front legs. She needs to be shorter and bouncier on the approach to the fence so that she learns to snap up in front and to spring up off her hindquarters to clear the fence rather than throwing a huge jump from further out. I always warm up over a cross-pole, but even here I insist that she trots right up to the base of the fence before taking off. I expect her to continue to listen to me once we have landed and to pull up when I ask her, not to go bounding off getting carried away with her own enthusiasm.

'I build the cross-pole up to an upright of about 3ft 9in (1.3m), still approaching in trot and still riding her up to the base to make her use herself properly over the fence. In between the fences I try to get her as round and soft as possible, emphasising to her the need to be short and bouncy during this work. She must wait and listen to me on the approach to the fence so that her energy is contained, and she can then be ridden up to the base and can just pop it from there.

'Once she is warmed up and concentrating I progress to the angles and arrowheads that I like to practise over. We start over a narrow fence with a barrel on end underneath the pole; this gives her the idea of focussing on a relatively narrow target and shows her that the barrel is part of the jump, because later that is what she will be expected to jump for the arrowhead.

'We then make an arrowhead using the barrel with poles angled off it as arms. To start with I jump over the

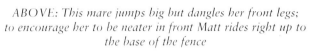

ABOVE: *This mare jumps big but dangles her front legs; to encourage her to be neater in front Matt rides right up to the base of the fence*

LEFT: *Jumping a narrow fence with a single barrel beneath the pole: an introduction to jumping arrowhead-type fences*

BELOW (left and centre): *First jumping the arrowhead with the arms guiding the mare in*
BELOW: *Jumping the arrowhead, a test of accuracy and confidence*

point of the "V" so that the poles guide her in; then I turn and jump it the other way, as a true arrowhead, insisting that she stays on the line I have put her on. It is important to ride positively forwards to arrowhead fences as it is easier to hold the horse on a line when he is going forwards into your hand; if you have to check him you may lose the straightness of the shoulders and hindquarters. We gradually move the arms of the arrowhead in, making it narrower and more of a challenge. Then I might jump across this fence, as it now forms a corner if it is jumped from the side. I start by jumping the corner centrally when it is harder for the horse to run out, but gradually I ride a line nearer and nearer to the barrel, with the ultimate aim of holding a line over the barrel, or the point of the corner, without the horse even thinking about ducking out to the side.

'The majority of riders have to work continually to improve their ability to ride the horse up to a fence so that they meet it on a good distance. Lines of fences set at specific distances apart help the rider to practise this – he or she knows how many strides he is meant to fit in between the fences, and gradually he will find that as he lands over the first fence he will start to see what he has to do to meet the next fence well. There are still plenty of people who say that you should leave the horse to sort himself out, because that is what he will have to do on the occasions that you make a mistake and get it wrong. But we all make more than enough mistakes for the horse to have to cope with at the best of times, and it will not do his confidence or his performance any good if you *keep* leaving him to get in a muddle. If as a general rule you can help him as much

as possible, then on the day you *do* make a mistake he will hopefully have the confidence and the agility to get himself out of it somehow. When you ride across country it is probably even harder to see a good stride because the horse's stride is generally longer and so there is less room or time to make any adjustment in front of the fence.

'However, as much as the rider must practise his being able to see a good stride, when he is actually riding in competition it is not the number one priority; the overriding priority at any event is to get over the fence somehow. You can get so wrapped up in looking for your stride that you forget to ride the horse forwards to the fence, and a stop is a lot worse than the untidy jump that may be the result of a bad stride to the fence. But when it comes to combination fences the rider must at least be aware of trying to ride the distance that has been set for him; so if it is a long distance between the two fences, then you need to come in on a stronger stride so that you get a big jump in and the horse is able to cover sufficient ground to get to the next element. And if it is a tight distance, you obviously approach the fence in a much shorter, more collected canter.

'When schooling at home I jump mainly through lines of fences, playing with the distances between them so that I learn how to ride a long distance or a short distance on each horse. I also use angled fences to a large degree. In order to go within the time across country it is often necessary to jump fences at an angle. A good cross-country time is not about galloping fast between fences, it is about riding the shortest possible route

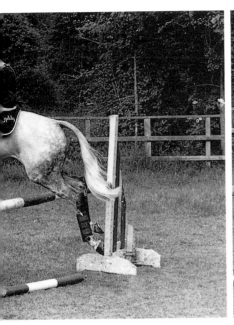

around the course. This involves being confident enough to jump the direct routes, and also to jump some of the fences at an angle to give you a better line which can shave seconds off the time.

'I don't jump school the older horses much; once they have got to Advanced level you know they can jump, and you want to keep them fresh and sharp. Tic Toc is not a very clean showjumper so I jump him only once a week. He would jump something pretty big to give him plenty to think about, and then I would concentrate on jumping over angled fences, narrow fences and corners, always insisting on straightness and accuracy.'

ABOVE: Jumping a corner centrally, when it is harder for the horse to run out; the nearer to the barrel, or the point of the corner, the greater the temptation to run out

BELOW: Kibah Tic Toc jumping a wide corner near to the point, with not a thought of ducking out!

SAVERNAKE FOREST ONE-DAY EVENT

In the accompanying photographs Matt is riding Regal Style in the Advanced class at Savernake Forest horse trial.

■ 'This fence involved a bounce of logs followed by three strides running downhill to an arrowhead. The logs were pretty big but the distance was fair. I felt the important thing with this fence was that you got on your line – the line that would take you through the bounce and straight to the arrowhead – as early as possible, and then kept your eye focussed on the final element of the combination. I am very conscious now of getting on a good line to a fence, and particularly to a combination, as early as possible, and then keeping my eye fixed on the final element.

'I felt my approach to the bounce was slightly too tentative; you can't really over-ride a bounce as solid and fair as this one, and I could easily have come in with a stronger approach. This horse has a super technique and has jumped in very well – the fact that we could have jumped in a bit more strongly only shows in the way he is having to stretch slightly

more to clear the second element of the bounce.

'When riding through a combination fence it is very important to get the upper body back quickly as the horse lands over each element, so that you are in a strong position to ride him forwards and to hold him on your line. As the distance to the arrowhead here was already set up for you – a good three strides – it allowed you to ride positively forwards to the fence. It is always easier to hold a line if you are riding the horse forwards rather than fighting with him or having to check him because you are nervous about him running out. It's a bit like riding a bike, the slower you are going the more likely you are to wobble. If you are pressing the horse forwards up to the fence you are far more likely to keep him straight; you don't want to give him time to consider the option of running out.

'For the three strides between the bounce and the arrowhead you can see that I have sat deep in the saddle and have kept my upper body very upright. I consider this to be the safest and most effective position on the approach to a cross-country fence, unlike the crouched, forward position favoured by many showjumpers. My position may not look as pretty, and it does mean you are sitting very much on the horse's back, but it puts you in a stronger, safer position either to drive the horse forwards or to keep your weight back far enough if something goes wrong, if he hits the fence or pecks on landing.'

Mark Todd

HORSEMAN SUPREME

■ Mark is based for most of the year in England having just bought a new yard in the Cotswolds. Mark and Carolyn Todd's 'real' home is a 500-acre livestock farm in Cambridge, New Zealand, which is managed for them during their many long absences. Trips home are usually for a couple of months during the winter; the older of his two children, Lauren, particularly enjoys these holidays. They are also an opportunity for Mark to be more involved in his horse-breeding enterprise over there; in the main these are potential racehorses, although there are plans to go into competition horse breeding.

The various yards where the Todds have been based in Britain have previously been rented rather than bought, and inevitably this has meant several changes of location; but with each move they seem to keep landing on their feet. Like most full-time event riders in Britain, Mark relies on the support of owners and sponsorship to enable him to continue eventing. There can be anything up to twenty-six horses in work at any one time, including three or four belonging to students working at the yard. Mark actually competes about fifteen event horses, and at the time of going to press was without a main sponsor.

On most days Mark will ride between four and eight horses; he also does a lot of teaching, either of his working pupils or for other event riders hoping to benefit from his advice and experience. Two members of the staff are sufficiently experienced and have the right aptitude to undertake some of the schooling work, particularly of the novices. Mark schools all the older horses himself, and does nearly all the canter work.

Mark Todd proudly displays the gold medals he won at the 1988 Seoul Olympics, while Charisma wonders what all the fuss is about – it's all in a day's work for a world class eventer!

LESLIE LAW JUMP TRAINING
WITH MARK TODD

■ The more you see of top riders training at home the more obvious it becomes as to just how vital a role flatwork training plays in the success or otherwise of a horse's jump training. Mark Todd is shown here giving British event rider Leslie Law some help with his jumping, but the session starts with a critical look at the horse's way of going on the flat. Leslie is riding Perryfields George, a very talented six-year-old which has rapidly upgraded to Advanced. In spite of his competition success, however, he is obviously still very young and inexperienced, and is hardest to ride in the showjumping phase not least because he is a big horse to keep contained and balanced in the confines of the showjumping arena. He is also very laid back, which means that his technique in canter and as he jumps is not always sufficiently active or engaged.

To start with Mark instructed Leslie to work on shortening and engaging the trot: he wanted to see the horse taking more of its weight on the hindquarters so that it carried itself more. This can be achieved by frequent use of half-halts, leg-yielding and shoulder-in to make sure the horse does actually increase the engagement and impulsion in trot, and doesn't simply shorten its frame. Mark also stressed the importance of keeping the horse as round as possible all the time so that its back stays round. Mark explained how dressage judging can sometimes adversely affect the way riders work their horses: 'In the past riders have been penalised in the dressage if the horse's poll hasn't formed the highest point of the neck. But in this outline the horse can often still be stiff through his back because he is being made to carry his neck unnaturally high in order to meet the requisite of being "poll high" in his carriage. Fortunately it is becoming more accepted for the neck to appear rounder and the poll to be slightly lower than the highest point of the neck.

'If the poll and neck are high then the back is almost bound to be stiff, but for the horse to jump well the back must be round; so it is very important to work the horse in as round an outline as possible. Many horses which earned high dressage marks throughout their careers by being very straight and high in the neck, but then their showjumping usually lets them down. When the horse is stronger and more advanced in his general

way of going to the degree that he starts working up through his shoulders, then his neck can be higher in front. But if you ask for this outline from day one you will end up with a horse that does not work through its back properly.'

Leslie then tried the same approach in canter, keeping the horse as round as possible and then using half-halts to shorten and engage him. As Mark explained, it is the same principle that you use when you need to shorten a horse so as to meet a fence properly: he must be taught to 'sit down' on his hocks and lighten his

front end. The objective of all work on the flat is to engage the hindquarters more effectively, and in canter to encourage the hindleg to come further underneath the body. Exercises to this end include riding a 10m circle where the canter is slowed as much as possible, almost to a pirouette canter, before the horse is allowed to go forwards again. Flexing him to the right when he is in canter left, and vice versa, also causes the inside hindleg to step further under the horse and to carry more weight. Another exercise which is frequently used in a warm-up session is canter to halt to rein-back, and then forwards into canter again. This can be repeated every ten or twenty steps and again helps to teach the horse to 'sit' more on his hocks.

Even when warming up in trot over a place pole to a small fence, the horse must not be allowed to increase his pace on the way to the fence

A spread fence with the back rail much lower than the front rail encourages the horse to lower his head and neck and to bring his shoulders up and forwards

Leslie's jumping session started by trotting to a place pole in front of a small upright fence. Mark's jumping arena is interesting in that his lines of fences include small fillers, frames and wall blocks rather than just lines of plain poles, as used by most riders for gridwork. At this early stage in the lesson Mark emphasised to Leslie how important it is to ensure the horse does not change pace on his way to the fence, and if necessary to half-halt a few strides from the place pole to check and rebalance him.

Leslie then trotted George to a higher upright, concentrating on keeping the trot round and on using half-halts to make sure his back end was engaged, as Mark felt he was getting too long just in front of the fence. He advised Leslie to practise the half-halt on the way round the arena, and to be sure that he got a definite reaction from the horse; it was no use using the aid if the horse ignored it. Over the trot pole he wanted Leslie to allow forwards with the hands – as Leslie is shown doing – but to keep his upper body upright and still so that his bodyweight was not thrown forwards onto the horse's shoulders.

Next Leslie cantered George to a larger spread fence where the back rail was significantly lower than the front rail; this encourages the horse to lower his head and neck, and to draw his shoulders up and then forwards. Mark's impression was that on take-off, Leslie looked as though he felt he needed to throw his weight forwards in an effort to encourage the horse to jump out and over the spread. But doing this actually throws too much weight onto the horse's front end and therefore compromises his ability to jump well; so Mark suggested to Leslie that if he felt the horse needed encouragement he should just touch him with his whip behind the leg on take-off to make him jump forwards rather than just up and down. George is pictured starting to throw a much more effective jump: on take-off Leslie has tapped him with his whip to send the jump forwards, and the low back rail has encouraged him to lower his head and neck and to reach forwards with his shoulders to clear the spread.

Mark then put three canter poles down on the approach to an upright fence; canter poles keep the stride elevated but also make the horse shorten up on the last three strides to the fence, again with the aim of teaching him to sit back on his hocks. The last canter pole encourages the horse to lift the hindleg more positively and to step forwards and under himself, which in turn produces a more powerful jump.

It is important to make sure that when the canter is soft and round, it still has enough energy in it; to this end, Leslie was to use half-halts around the arena to get the horse off his forehand, and then soften to him. When he rode up to the first canter pole he was to keep the leg on but soften the hand, leaving the canter poles to help lift

The canter poles on the approach help to shorten and elevate the stride. Over the last canter pole in particular you can see how George has had to lift and step under himself further with the hind leg

V-poles encourage the horse to snap up his forearms and fold his lower legs up tightly, thus giving himself the best chance of clearing the fence

and engage the canter. At his second attempt George cantered much more positively and confidently through the canter poles, which can be seen to make him really lift and step forwards with the hindleg.

Having worked on the technique required in the approach and take-off, it is important to make sure that, with this new-found power and energy, the horse is still careful to snap his front end up quickly. The use of V poles will achieve this, and here they have obviously helped George to produce an excellent jump over the planks: he is soft and round through his back and neck, he has lowered his head to produce the classic bascule, and has snapped up his forearms as well as his lower leg to make sure his front end is clear of the fence.

George is a laid-back character, and Mark explained that with such a horse the energy in the canter must be created for him; thus the rider has to work harder than on a fizzier type of horse which creates its own energy and can therefore be ridden more quietly. He suggested that Leslie did more work at home jumping George from trot because it is easier for the rider to keep the stride up together and light in front in trot.

Leslie also took Sidney's King to Mark, and Sid is much more of a live wire. His problem is that he tends to

To encourage Sid to land on the right lead Leslie was told to open his right hand and to slide his left leg back slightly

RIGHT: Each time Sid rushed to a fence Leslie had to pull him up and start again. He was only allowed to continue to a fence if he stayed soft, round, and in a rhythm

get very fast on the approach to his fences, and consequently jumps very hollow. Mark had various exercises to try and counter this difficulty. First, he was adamant that Leslie should be very strict about keeping Sid straight as he approached a fence, and in an even rhythm. Then he made him canter on a small circle over a little filler, but each time asking him to circle away on the other leg; this gave Sid something else to think about, rather than just rushing up to the fence.

Sid found it harder cantering away on the right lead, and Leslie found it difficult to keep him round – he was having to pull him to the right in mid-air, with the result that Sid hollowed badly as he jumped. Mark suggested that in the last couple of strides Leslie should slide his left leg back slightly and just open the right hand rather than pull with it. He wanted Leslie to stay soft and relaxed through his shoulders and elbows – but Leslie found this almost impossible to do when Sid insisted on throwing his head up and rushing at the fence. Mark advised that he should do more work with the canter before approaching the fence; often an effective exercise was to flex the horse left, then right, to shorten him up for a stride or two, then let him go on again – anything to keep his mind on the rider rather than rushing the fence.

Mark then moved to another exercise designed to keep Sid soft and round on the approach, and to teach him to wait and listen to his rider. Leslie had to canter in over a small one-stride double followed by three strides down to a small upright. Mark anticipated that Sid was quite likely to land over the double, throw his head up and rush for the next fence; if he did, Leslie was to pull him up in front of it, pat him, then turn away and come down the line again. He was only allowed to continue to the final fence when he stayed soft and in a rhythm, waiting for *Leslie's* instruction to continue.

Sid, however, seemed intent on rushing more times than he was prepared to behave, so Mark took the exercise back a stage, replacing the final fence with just a pole on the ground. Leslie was to land over the double, bring Sid back to walk and then let him walk on over the pole. Once he settled to this exercise he would be allowed to stay in canter down to, and over the pole; eventually he did so calmly. The pole was on a three-stride distance, and Mark moved it out a few yards and told Leslie to fit in four strides to it. Once Sid allowed himself to be shortened without fighting back, the pole was replaced with a small fence. But if at any point he rushed he was pulled up as before.

The session finished with Leslie cantering to a small upright, followed by seven strides to a gate. Mark instructed that as he landed over the upright he should just think slow, slow, slow, and hold with the hand only as much as was absolutely necessary to fit the seven strides in. The first time Leslie tried this Sid forgot the aim of the exercise and rushed at the first fence, so he was pulled up again. At his next attempt he was more co-operative, and stayed softer in his approach and jump over the first, and managed to contain and control his rhythm down to the gate. He did not produce such a round jump as George because he was still not round enough through his back; but in general his technique was far better.

Finally Leslie had to ride for a more forward jump over the planks, and then – still thinking 'slow, slow' – just allow the canter to flow forwards over the seven strides to the gate. This exercise was intended to show Sid that when he did stay soft and round, and listened to his rider without rushing at the fence, he would not be held up all the time. It was to show him that when he co-operated he had an easier time than if he rushed.

Mark suggested to Leslie that a horse with a problem such as Sid's should be ridden for a short time every day over two small fences on a related distance, with the rider being strict to pull him up every time he tried to rush.

It is always a pleasure and an education to watch Mark Todd ride in any phase of the three-day event. At Badminton in 1995 he provided an unforgettable exhibition of how he copes so calmly when things go wrong. The photographs on the opposite page show Mark and Bertie Blunt tackling the fence at the Badminton Lake. Mark talks us through the fence:

'On the approach to the Lake I really wanted to burst out laughing, the situation was just too ridiculous for words. Here I was galloping along, minus one stirrup and with very little control, heading for a very difficult cross-country fence. I concentrated on getting the horse to the right spot to take off, and could only hope for the best after that. Bertie was very, very good through this combination; he kept going forwards to the fence, picked up very cleanly in front over both elements, and turned smoothly in the water and out over the exit fence. I had just hoped that if I could meet the fence right then I would get the smoothest jump possible and would have most chance of staying in balance with the horse, particularly for making the turn once we were in the water. At a fence like the bounce into the Badminton Lake you are usually worse off if you under-ride it than if you over-attack. This distance measures only about twelve feet [3¹/₂m] which is quite short for a cross-country bounce, but because of the vast expanse of water facing the horse, and the big drop into the lake, it rides longer than you would think – so you need to attack it more than you might imagine was necessary'

Bruce Davidson

IN TRAINING

■ Bruce Davidson's selection for the Open European Championships marked his tenth team appearance for the United States, and his preparations were highlighted by a long sought-after win at Badminton in 1995. Twenty-one years after first competing there on Irish Cap when he finished third, Bruce claimed victory on the ten-year-old Eagle Lion.

Eagle Lion's jumping was the envy of all those who appreciate a horse that knows and loves its job. Bruce has been heard to say many times that 'There are four things Eagle Lion loves: breakfast, lunch, tea and jumping.' William Fox-Pitt, the overnight leader at 'Bruce's Badminton' until his horse Chaka failed the final horse inspection, commented that Eagle Lion is so good at his job that all Bruce has to remember to do is say 'Jump' – but then he mustn't forget to say 'Down' otherwise the horse might just keep going higher and higher! He is certainly less heart-stopping to watch in the final phase of a three-day event than many other horses; he always looks as if he is going to jump, and to jump clear.

So how do you prepare a horse such as Eagle Lion for a major championship? Bruce obviously adores the horse, and is prepared to accept his bad points as well as his good ones. 'The horse is very Irish and loves to jump,' explains Bruce 'but concentrating on anything else is very difficult for him. He is a very strong character and wants to do his own thing. He has his own balance which he is comfortable working in, and he doesn't really see why he should do things any differently. So for Eagle Lion, preparation is a case of working on his flatwork and just giving him enough jumping to keep him happy, but not so much that his flatwork falls to pieces.'

FLATWORK

Eagle Lion is a short, compact little horse but he has his own ideas about how he likes to work. He is naturally onward bound and does not want to have to sit down on his hocks more, as is needed in the collected work. Bruce does a lot of work on transitions within the pace, going from working to collected to medium trot to encourage the horse to bring his hindquarters further underneath him

Watching a jumping machine like this in action is fascinating. As he trots to his warm-up fence of a placing pole to a single 3ft 6in (1.3m) rail, Bruce leaves him very much alone. Eagle Lion's eye is fixed on the top rail, never leaving it until he takes off; and as the rail goes up he remains totally focussed on it, never faulting once. In his jump work Bruce leaves him to work in his own balance, and it is interesting to see that as he comes to the fence his nose is far above the vertical; then as he comes to take off, he lowers and stretches his head and neck forwards from this position before springing up effortlessly to clear the fence. This is quite a different style to the far more collected, round approach which many horses need in order to help them create a clean jump. Perhaps it is the difference between the natural jumpers, and those whose performance is 'man-made'.

After warming up over what seemed quite a sizable rail, the fences were quickly hoisted up higher and Eagle Lion was in his element. Cantering down to some planks set at an angle a few strides from a large parallel, Bruce had to interfere with the horse only

FLATWORK
ABOVE: On a circle the horse has to work harder because the inside hind leg has to come further under him. In the first picture Eagle Lion comes back against Bruce and doesn't stay round and soft through his top line. The second picture shows him working through from behind, and therefore staying soft and round

RIGHT: To encourage Eagle Lion to carry himself more in the canter, Bruce rides him on a circle but bends him to the outside. This forces the horse to carry more of his weight on the inside hindleg. Once he gets used to working in this type of balance he will find it easier to step under himself further with the inside hind, and will begin to work in greater self-carriage

JUMPING
When the stakes are raised the professional is in his element: Eagle Lion devours the bigger fences. Notice how, on the approach to the spread, Bruce places a hand on the horse's crest to encourage him to lower and stretch forwards with his head and neck

The final team training concentrates on exercises that simulate what will be met in the competition itself. Here Bruce and Eagle Lion practise a bounce combination. The whole way through the sequence the horse's eye is fixed on the top rail of each fence he has to jump

Bruce with Dr Peaches at The Vegetable Farm, Seoul 1988

once; when he first turned back to the spread the horse's enthusiasm got the better of him so that he made up too much ground on the approach to the fence and arrived at it rather too close for a comfortable jump. After that he held his rhythm and took everything in his stride.

Team trainer Mark Phillips had the confidence of a man who knows he has a secret weapon in his army; 'There is little you need do or say when you have a horse with a jump like that, other than just to let him do enough to keep him happy but sharp. It's his flatwork that needs the attention!' Bruce's answer as to how he produces a horse with such a jump is deceptively simple: 'At home, all my horses are introduced to jumping by jumping through grids; I think this is the best way to teach a horse to jump in a correct and athletic manner. After that the rider is responsibile for bringing the horse to the fence with the appropriate balance and pace, and to see the right take-off spot.' Barely had the question left my lips when Bruce

informed me that, 'Yes, I've always been able to see the right spot.'

Bruce has always enjoyed breeding and bringing on young horses. After his win at Badminton he recalled sitting in the start box and thinking back to when Eagle Lion was a youngster and the first day that he rode him: 'He bucked me off real quick!' Bruce bought the horse as a three-year-old. He is by the HIS stallion Gipfel, out of a Grade A showjumper, Stream Lion, and was bred by Patricia Nicholson in Co Meath, Ireland. Bruce has had three other horses out of the same dam, Pirate Lion, Regent Lion and Dandy Lion.

'Young horses have always been a part of my life. In any horse you want to see a good structure: a balance, athleticism, good hock placement and a good eye. There are certain things you can forgive in a horse, but with experience you get to know the balance that you like. Because once you have bought or bred a horse you still have to make it – even if it is bred for the job it can't do it unless you train it properly. But you have to start with the right animal, a really nice horse. After years of work you might make it into a really great horse; but it's no good starting with anything less, because if you do, having spent just as much time and probably even more work on producing it, you still wouldn't have a great horse.

'It is important that young horses are put to work and asked questions and taught certain things. But I don't spend countless hours teaching a young horse to do dressage. If he has the movement, by the thime he gets to a three-star CCI I start to do more with his dressage. The young horse needs more making in the other two phases than he does in the dressage. If he does the jumping well, then you can spend the rest of his life improving his dressage, but if he can't jump I don't really care if he was leading after the dressage!'

Bruce's youngsters are introduced to eventing as five-year-olds, when they take part in so-called 'preliminary competitions' (these are the equivalent of Britain's Novice horse trials.) They are first introduced to jumping through gridwork, and then compete in pure showjumping and hunter classes. Gridwork, or gymnastic jumping, teaches them how to use themselves properly and to respect the fences. The idea is to instil in the horse the knowledge that he can use himself correctly and athletically, so that good technique becomes habit. They also go hunting (Bruce is Field Master to his mother-in-law's pack, Mr Stewart's Cheshire Foxhounds) where they meet hedges, rails and ditches.

Depending on family commitments and the level at which his current bunch of horses are competing, Bruce usually flies a few of them over to England each season. His Advanced horses will come over for Badminton and Burghley, and he will often bring some of his less experienced horses over to gain more competition experience, perhaps aiming them at a three-star event such as Blenheim. It is only a six-hour flight and seems to take very little out of them; Eagle Lion flew to the UK only ten days before Badminton.

Bruce has continued to compete long after most of his contemporaries have turned to quieter lives, and each year he seems to prove himself to be as fit and able as ever. He has won two Olympic team golds and a silver, and has the title of individual world champion twice. He has won Lexington CCI six times, and if he is selected for Atlanta it will be his fifth Olympic Games and his eleventh team appearance.

Asked which have been his most memorable wins, he makes a philosophical reply: 'As you get older you enjoy every win; when you are younger you take so much for granted. You think that if you do everything right then you will win, but that isn't the way it happens because so many things out of your control can go wrong. And different wins mean a lot to you for different reasons. It may have been a minor event, but if it was that horse's best-ever performance then it would mean a great deal. You have to enjoy every little victory because as you get older so much can get in the way to stop you succeeding. I can name 1974 as being pretty special: I won my first World Championship title (and the team gold) on Irish Cap. I loved that horse more than I could love any other, and that weekend he did all three phases better than you could have expected any horse to. It was also the year I married my wife Carol [Hannum] and we rode at Badminton as part of our honeymoon. I finished third, Carol was eliminated at the Park Rails – and yes, our marriage did survive!'

7
Behind the Scenes

The organisation and infrastructure which allows each Olympics to proceed smoothly is enormous, as is the effort required just to allow the three-day event to go ahead; and in this chapter we are still only dealing with a small part of the 'behind the scenes' structure. For Hugh Thomas, the technical delegate, the pressure is at its greatest during the build-up to the games. For John Killingbeck, the team veterinary surgeon, the same applies. One might imagine that his task would be harder during the Games themselves but as he explains, once the horse starts the competition there is very little a vet can do within the rules to keep him in the competition. The hardest job is getting the team horses safely through their preparatory events and team training.

Hugh Thomas

TECHNICAL DELEGATE TO THE ATLANTA OLYMPICS

■ When Hugh Thomas, director of Badminton Horse Trials, stands up at the annual press conference and jokes about designing fences he would be too frightened to jump, it is easy to forget that not only did he compete at Badminton, he also took part in an Olympics: he rode Playamar in Montreal at the 1976 Games. Luck was not favouring the British on that occasion. 'It was very, very good until I found that, having gone well across country, my horse had sprained a tendon,' is Hugh's brief summation of events. Lucinda Green's horse, Be Fair, also went clear but slipped a hock tendon at the very last fence and could not complete the competition, so as a team Britain was eliminated. Of his other team-mates, HRH Princess Anne had completed despite a crashing fall, and Richard Meade had gone clear on Jacob Jones eventually to finish fourth.

Although as far as the three-day event was concerned it was all a great disappointment, those Olympics sparked a fascination in the Games which remains with Hugh Thomas today. 'In Montreal, as in some other Olympics, the equestrian site was completely separate to the rest of the Games so although you were well aware that you were competing at a major international event, it was easy to feel slightly divorced from the other athletes. At that time there had never been such a thing as a World Equestrian Games and so it certainly felt more of an occasion than the World Three-Day Event Championships. And I, for one, became completely hooked on the Olympic Games and what it meant as an ideal and as a competition. For a while I harboured ambitions of riding at another Olympics, although I soon decided against that – but I very much wanted to be a part of it somehow.'

Since then his involvement has included going to the Los Angeles Olympics as a team selector and official, being course designer at the 1988 Seoul Olympics, and cross-country controller at the 1992 Barcelona Olympics, and his experience has undoubtedly stood him in good stead for his role as technical delegate to the Atlanta Olympics. In Atlanta horses will have to compete in potentially the hottest and most humid conditions experienced so far, making this a job which many would have chosen to avoid.

The technical delegate must oversee the organisation of, and approve, the stabling, accommodation, practice areas, dressage and showjumping arenas, the roads and tracks, steeplechase and cross-country courses. He must ensure that adequate numbers of

sufficiently experienced officials are employed for the event itself, he must oversee the competitors' briefing, and in turn must brief the ground jury before handing over responsibility to them for the duration of the competition itself.

'At every international three-day event someone is appointed as technical delegate,' explains Hugh, 'and how much time and effort is required to carry out the task varies enormously from one event to another. When a technical delegate comes from overseas to Badminton, for example, if he is good he will ask a few questions to convince himself that all is as it should be, but he does not have to worry too much about whether or not we know how to run an event. For an Olympics, however, you are normally dealing with an organising committee or team which has never run a three-day event, or at least not as a team, and you are looking at a site where there has never been a three-day event before. This is one of the reasons why we insist that, a year or two before the Games, an event of some kind is held on the site; then any shortcomings or problems will be highlighted and can be corrected before the Olympic competition itself.

'Another major factor that influences the organisation of the event is the fact that the equestrian disciplines are just one sport amongst many others. All the

---

The technical delegate has to oversee the organisation of suitable facilities for the equestrian disciplines. The stabling complex at Seoul 1988

general arrangements such as transport and accommodation have to fit in with all the other athletes and officials. There will be around 15,000 personnel representing twenty-five other sports and they all need feeding, transporting and housing, so the arrangements you want to make for your own particular sport have to fit within the limitations of the system.

'It is not the technical delegate's job actually to organise all these different things – it is more a case of asking the right questions and knowing whether to be satisfied with the answers. At the moment for example I am not happy about the arrangements for getting the public into the event, and my job is just to keep pushing for what I want and making sure it happens. I try to make sure that people are motivated and organised in the right direction.

'The technical delegate for an Olympic Games is appointed by the FEI immediately after the previous Games. This is not a moment too soon, and ideally the person should be appointed as soon as the next host city has been chosen. I had a slight head-start as far as Atlanta was concerned. In 1991 someone had to go and approve the choice of equestrian site in Georgia. My appointment had not been confirmed at that stage, although it had been discussed, and when I was asked to go to Georgia I told the committee that the person who inspected the site should be whoever was going to be selected as TD. I was still asked to go, so knew I had got the job!

'The Atlanta Committee had pre-selected a number of sites which I was shown. Unusually, for this particular Olympics the first concern was whether or not there was any climatic difference between the sites. Given that there was none, my next hope was that the site nearest to the rest of the Games would be the most suitable. In this respect it was important to look at the basic type of ground, its soil structure and therefore the sort of going it would provide. You needed to be sure that the site was big enough, and then you looked for things such as attractive natural features which would help to create an interesting and flowing cross-country course.

'The site we decided on has the best basic soil structure and is the nearest to the rest of the Olympics. It will be quite tight fitting everything in; the site was originally about 1,500 acres [607ha] but at the time I was not told there would be a golf course built on it, the result being that there is now no room for on-site parking – hence the discussion as to how best to get the spectators in.

'One final consideration that the Atlanta Committee had to bear in mind was the attitude of the local community and of the people who owned the site itself, how receptive they would be. In this case the site is owned by a consortium which includes the equivalent of a city council, and their idea was to establish a permanent equestrian facility which would serve the surrounding states. For the duration of the Olympics the Atlanta Committee effectively takes over the site, but in many ways it is a joint venture between the Atlanta Committee and the local community. Already this has resulted in certain mutual benefits for both parties: for example the local city council needed somewhere to dispose of its treated sewage, and this will provide excellent irrigation for the cross-country course!

'I am sure that the finished centre will be one of the finest equestrian facilities in the world, and the largest; for the Olympic Games we need stabling for about three hundred horses, but there are plans for the permanent site to have stabling for seven hundred.

'What could appear to be a mammoth task is made easier by the fact that I deal effectively with just two people, Kate Jackson who is director of the equestrian events, and Roger Haller the course designer. It is a channel of communication that I am used to because at a three-day event you tend to deal direct with the event director or organiser and the course designer, and it is a system that works well.

'The biggest problems nearly always come with aspects that are not very well specified or thought out beforehand, such as accommodation for grooms and officials. The other area of difficulty is that every major event always attracts a lot of people who want to influence what goes on, in other words, people outside the Atlanta Committee. Problems have been caused in the past when, for example, the FEI had made arrangements directly with the committee and nobody has informed the technical delegate. I don't expect to make every single decision, but I do need to know when somebody else has made one!

'At the Atlanta Olympics the climate is obviously an added factor – we are likely to experience the most difficult conditions since the Kentucky World Championships in 1978 – and I have been very involved in deciding how to adapt the competition to allow for this. When I first inspected the site I reported back to the FEI that they must accept, there and then, that the competition would have to be modified, otherwise we would have to pull out of the Games. The decision was taken to try to go ahead and find a way of still producing a fair result.

'Research showed that Phase C would have more influence over the horse's well-being than many of us had realised. Before this research was undertaken the generally accepted modification was to shorten the

Hugh Thomas and Playamar, Montreal 1976.
Playamar strained a tendon and was unable to showjump on the final day

steeplechase if conditions were bad. The steeplechase has been shortened slightly for Atlanta, but we have also altered Phase C quite radically. In a cool climate Phase C does exactly what it is meant to – it enables the horse to recover from the steeplechase. But in hot conditions the horse will start to heat up again during Phase C, which then adds significantly to the endurance factor and it is no longer a recovery phase at all. Some experienced horsemen had felt all along that this was the case all along; but outside England, people are more prepared to listen to a scientist than a horseman, and so it is a great advantage that the facts are now proven scientifically. The cross-country course

has also been shortened, and towards the end of the course the fences and distances will be thoughtfully designed – there won't be any tight turns or short distances in combinations.

'Summaries of all the research findings have been published in FEI bulletins and are available to all national federations. As soon as we know exactly which countries are sending competitors we will take more assertive action to make sure that all team officials and riders are aware of what they need to be doing. There is much less ignorance around the world today than there was five years ago, and the qualifications needed to compete at this level get tighter all the time. But it would be wrong to assume that everybody will know exactly how to cope. For this reason there will be teams of trained grooms at the rest stop on Phase C and in the ten-minute box, who know exactly how to wash down and cool a horse in these conditions. It is very difficult to interfere too much with individuals, as each one has his or her own ideas on caring for the horse; but we would take a lot of convincing to let a horse through the rest stop without it having been washed and cooled by the grooms provided. I acted as technical delegate in May at a two-star event in New Jersey and was amazed at how few competitors knew how to cool down their horses correctly in such conditions; I suggested that twenty-minute seminars on the subject were held at all three-day events after the dressage phase. An event was held on the Olympic site in August 1994, and another in September 1995 and these provided excellent research opportunities. We also held an open forum for competitors and any other interested parties to discuss how best to deal with the climatic conditions.

'Everything is out in the open – what I know, you are welcome to know; there are no "confidential" reports, and that is the way it should be.

'Inevitably not everybody will agree with the decisions that have been taken or with the ones yet to be made, but at least everyone will be able to see the reasons why we have made those decisions. By the time we actually get to the Olympic three-day event I want to be able to say to riders and officials "this is the basic competition which includes the modifications we have discussed…and if the heat and humidity reaches X or Y then we will make such and such a modification".

'It is essential that everybody knows exactly what is planned. In the past there has been criticism of occasions when experienced riders have voiced concern about the conditions but have been told "not to worry, we have a plan up our sleeves". However, they were not told what the plan was, even though the organisers knew exactly what they intended to do – they just didn't see why they should tell competitors before they were ready to. That is wrong, because it simply breeds suspicion and affects people's confidence in the system; I hope those days are gone.

'By the time of the competition we will have put in place everything that we possibly can to safeguard the welfare of the horses. However, that does not absolve the rider from his responsibility and duty to pull up his horse if necessary.

'There are two "types" of exhausted horse: one is the horse that is going fine and then, a few strides later, drops the bit and gives up. If the horse has been ridden sensibly up until then, you cannot really blame the

rider for this happening because he would not have felt it coming. For example the Russian horse in Barcelona which fell, exhausted, at one fence had had its progress monitored by officials and fence judges: the report received just before its collapse was that it was still on the bit and looked to be going strongly – but a hundred yards later, at the next fence, it had had enough and fell.

'The other type of horse is the one which is gradually finding it harder and harder to keep going, and the rider of that horse would be expected to pull it up because he would certainly be able to feel its condition deteriorating underneath him. The question of whether or not an official should step in and order a rider to pull up is a difficult one, especially when it concerns a tired horse which is being carefully ridden and has so far gone clear.

'But since Barcelona there has been a growing feeling that "if in doubt the horse should be stopped", and that is a good thing. One or two riders may feel they have been unfairly stopped, but in the long term it is better for the sport and better for the horse.'

Many people imagine that the technical delegate is paid for his troubles, but in fact he is an unpaid volunteer; only hotel and travel expenses are reimbursed. Even someone of Hugh Thomas' experience has been surprised at the amount of work involved, especailly paperwork such as approving the documentation of guidelines and rules. In spite of this he is against the idea of a technical delegate being paid for his role, believing that the present system leaves the individual in a position where he can remain true to his beliefs and principles: if he can't get people to do things in the way he wants, or if he disagrees strongly with a decision that is made, he can walk away from the situation. He is not losing an income, only some pride and a good deal of prestige.

This is good news for all those who have felt some cynicism over the great lengths that have been taken to ensure that event horses do compete in Atlanta. Whilst appreciating the arguments of all those who maintain that the sport would suffer if it left the Olympic movement, it is also true that the sport will suffer a great deal more if the public does not enjoy the spectacle placed before it. And so it is a relief to realise that those who are very much involved in pushing ahead with the idea of competing in Atlanta do not stand to gain financially from the decision. So whilst Mr Thomas, and those who have stood before him, probably do deserve recompense for their efforts and expertise, it is better, as the man himself says, that they remain unrewarded.

John Killingbeck

THE ROLE OF THE TEAM VET

■ The British team vet's main role is to advise the selectors in their task of choosing horses suitable for the team which will contest the major championship being held that year. Specific involvement with the team horses does not begin until Badminton Horse Trials in May; here the selectors look at the horses that have performed well, draw up a longlist of potential team members, and a veterinary inspection by the team vet is carried out on the Monday after Badminton. There are then various short training courses for the selected riders before the final trial, where the shortlist is drawn up. The shortlist consists of the four likely team members, two reserves and per-

haps one other horse. These horses and riders go into team training at Badminton for a few days before flying out to the international championship.

Alongside the training of the actual team members, there is also a programme of short training courses for riders whom the selection committee wishes to encourage and help in the hope that they will progress to become future team members. The team vet is involved in these courses as well; he watches the horses perform, talks to the riders, and arranges or gives presentations on matters of interest with the aim of continually feeding the riders with up-to-date horse-care facts and ideas on nutrition, fitness, soundness and so on.

A horse taking part in the controlled environment trials at the Animal Health Trust in Newmarket in preparation for Atlanta

John Killingbeck MRCVS was appointed team vet to the British three-day-event team in 1992, a role which sees him working with the present selection committee through to the 1996 Olympics in Atlanta. Another aspect of his job is to liaise between the various veterinary and regulatory bodies to ensure that the selectors and riders are kept up-to-date with such matters as travel regulations and health requirements in the various countries the team might travel to. He explains that because Atlanta is such an unusual and difficult venue there has probably been more to do than usual. A tremendous amount of research has been carried out by the Animal Health Trust in Great Britain, and in other veterinary centres throughout the world in an effort to make sure that everyone is as educated as possible regarding the effects of both heat stress and dehydration on the horses, what can be done to help prepare them for the conditions, and how the event can be modified to ensure that they can perform safely in the prevailing climate.

The team vet's role and aim is clear: he has to do his best to make sure that fit, sound horses are selected and prepared for the championship; he must try to educate the riders as much as possible on matters relating to the care, welfare and performance of those horses; and at the competition itself he is responsible for their physical welfare. What makes the job difficult, as John explains, is that the team vet is dealing with experienced riders who have reached the top on their own merits, who have their own grooms, their own stable management ideas and their own vets and farriers. 'You come to them very much as a stranger,' says John. 'I would like to be able to have a bigger input but that only comes slowly as you gain their confidence. There is certainly a quest for knowledge now. But it has to be remembered that in most top eventing yards there are still only three or four three-day-event horses, so there is a limit to the experience that a rider gains and therefore as to how much he knows. A vet does sometimes expect more from the riders than is perhaps fair because of this.

'Riders are naturally anxious about their horses. It is very difficult to produce a world-class event horse. He has to be an all-round athlete; he is very brave and usually has a very good temperament, but he needs an awful lot of training. On top of that, eventing is an extremely tough discipline in terms of the physical stress that the horse has to stand. They have to be fit enough to run round the equivalent of Aintree or Cheltenham and yet still be disciplined and obedient enough to perform a dressage test.

'Once a horse is aimed at a major three-day event it means everything to the rider to get it there, because the gap until the next chance that he might get is greater than, say, in the racing world, where you might only have to wait a week or two for another race of the same standard. Because of all these pressures, the slightest lump or bump often causes a disproportionate amount of worry! On the plus side, because it takes so long to produce a good event horse, a rider will not risk him by competing if something is not quite right. So riders tend to be quite open in discussing their concerns about a particular horse, and are usually very good at sticking to veterinary advice on the treatment of the problem.

'Knowing that there is so much that can go wrong on the road to the Olympics does make the job of team vet a very stressful one. There is enormous emotional strain, as you just sit and wait for the phone to ring and the news that something has gone wrong. And this is made harder by not being involved with the horses on a day-to-day basis.

'I was team vet to the Japanese prior to the Seoul Olympics. They based themselves in Britain at one training centre, I vetted each horse that they bought, and then saw them on a daily basis – that way you knew exactly what was happening with each horse. It would be difficult to work this system for the British team because the riders are based in their own yards all over the country, but it would certainly make the task easier and more effective. As the system stands, my job is best carried out by helping to keep riders as informed as possible about new and up-to-date ideas, and hope that this is of help to them in training and managing their horses at home.'

INVOLVEMENT WITH THE TEAM HORSES

'One of my most important tasks is to advise the selectors so they don't pick unsound horses. So hopefully, by the time you get to a competition most of the groundwork has been done, and it is then a matter of dealing with competition-induced problems.

'When injuries occur at an event we are very limited as to what we can do to keep a horse in the competition as we are not allowed to use drugs. Riders sometimes hope you can work miracles, but it is not always possible. The other problem at a major championship is that there are always rumours flying around about some wonderful substances that somebody else's vet is using. Riders need to remember that everything, but *everything*, is detectable, and that when a horse fails a drug test at that level it is usually because someone has tried to be clever and administered a human drug in the hope that it won't be detected.

'We have a team physiotherapist Amanda Sutton, and she can play an important role in easing certain problems. In this respect physiotherapy can sometimes be of more direct use at an event because it can put some things right without the need for drugs, and hopefully the horse is then able to complete the competition.

'One of the added problems of an Olympic Games is the time involved – the horses are usually at the venue for about three weeks, and that is a long time to be in a strange environment. Atlanta, the site of the 1996 Olympics, obviously poses additional problems because of the high heat and humidity factors which are to be expected. The horses will have to be very, very fit, and I would hope to be more involved in the preparation of those horses, in the run-up to the Games, than would usually be the norm.

'Everybody has to be aware of the critical difference that the climate is going to have on the way the horses perform. In temperate climates a horse can still compete successfully while carrying minor health problems, but in a difficult climate these problems will surface and will affect him. As vets, we will have to go looking for those problems: racehorses have routine bloodtests, scoping and tracheal washes so when they race the trainer knows they have no hidden clinical problems, and this approach should be adopted for the Atlanta team horses. We will also need to monitor diet, water intake and electrolyte levels so that we know what is normal and healthy for each horse. This procedure started at the 1995 European Championships in Italy.

'In 1994 some horses were flown out to Atlanta for a trial one-day event. Those horses lost up to 45lb [20kg] of bodyweight, most of which was water, and that equates to about four gallons [20l] of water intake; it takes a horse several days to redress this imbalance so sufficient recovery time must be allowed after the journey out. The present plan is that, having flown out to Atlanta, the horses then have to spend a few days in quarantine before starting an acclimatisation period. Monitoring the horses for those first few days in Atlanta is going to be critical, because it is vital that they are not asked to work before they have adjusted to the local climate. Because if the horse has not acclimatised, one of the first systems to suffer is the respiratory system.

'The riders must be as aware as we can make them of the effects of heat and humidity. In recent years we have occasionally seen horses ridden to the point of distress and it is often lack of rider judgement and sensitivity that has been of more significance than the prevailing climatic conditions. Thankfully this has not involved any British riders. At the same competitions other riders have been seen on very tired horses but they have ridden them sympathetically and the horses have completed the competition with no adverse effects. Where there have been problems it has been because the rider was not aware soon enough that something was wrong. If you look back to the 1978 World Championships in Lexington where the climate caused a lot of problems and many horses failed to complete Phase D, Jane Starkey rode Topper Too, a horse which was not an ideal type for such conditions – she took him round the course at a very steady pace and completed safely, but if she had ridden him fast it would have been a very different picture. But as a rider Jane was aware of her horse's limitations and of how he felt. At the Atlanta Olympics the riders will need to be responsible enough to show that same sensitivity.

'The FEI has been tremendously helpful in taking on board the advice and suggestions of the veterinary profession, and in particular the findings of David Marlin at the Animal Health Trust, and the course and the competition have been adapted accordingly, without reducing its difficulty. Basically, when the horse's body temperature goes above a certain level, his body tissues cease to function and he rapidly goes into metabolic shock. Secondary to this you have dehydration caused by sweating, and this also causes the body tissues to stop functioning. The sweat from a horse is hypertonic, meaning it has more concentrated levels of electrolytes in it than, say, the sweat from a human which is hypotonic. The difficulty is that the horse does not register that he is becoming dehydrated because dehydration in a horse does not stimulate thirst: he starts to seize up, and rapidly goes into shock.

'The other problem secondary to dehydration is that the mucous membranes lining the lungs and the respiratory tract dry out and become much more viscous. The lungs then function less efficiently and become more susceptible to infection. So monitoring the horse's water intake is of paramount importance.

'The difficulty with heat and humidity stress is that it happens very quickly in a competition situation, as could be seen with King William at the World Championships in the Hague. He seemed to be powering his way around the course, but about two-thirds of the way round, having confidently jumped the bounce into the water, he was unable to find his usual fifth gear with which to finish and looked increasingly wobbly; Mary had to nurse him home. And that's how quickly it can happen – the horse can jump a fence and then be pulling himself up in the next two or three strides. For this reason the last part of the course will

Riders sometimes expect miracles but there is very little a vet can do during the event to keep the horse in the competition. Matt Ryan and Kibah Tic Toc, eventual gold medallists Barcelona 1992

be carefully designed to prevent the situation where a tired horse may jump into a combination fence quite happily but be unable to jump out.

'The Atlanta Research Project headed by Dr David Marlin of the Animal Health Trust has also proved what the true influence of Phase C would be in Atlanta. It is meant to be a recovery phase after the steeplechase but in hot, humid conditions, although the horse's body temperature would start to drop at the start of Phase C, after a few minutes it would start to rise again, with the result that Phase C would add quite significantly to the endurance element instead of relieving it. So in Atlanta there will be a stopping point part-way along Phase C. The horses will have the chance to start their natural cooling process, and will then be washed down at this point before their body temperature starts to rise again. The remainder of Phase C should then still serve its purpose as a further recovery phase. This modification will be a very real safeguard to the welfare of the horses. The rest period between Phases C and D has also been increased from ten to fifteen minutes.

'The Atlanta project has also prompted much discussion within the horse world about the best way to cool horses once they are in the ten-minute box. Again, Dr Marlin's work has proved that aggressive cooling – using bucket after bucket of iced water and then scraping it off quickly, and repeatedly – is the fastest way to bring down the horse's temperature, and that iced water does *not* cause muscle cramps as many people have suggested.

'A great deal of the information that is coming out today is not new. Our grandfathers, who relied on horses for their living, knew how to keep them fit and well. We are simply relearning a great many things that were common knowledge to horsemen in the past. And much of the research work is proving what many people thought was correct, which is reassuring.

'Personally I have never been desperately alarmed at the prospect of our horses competing in Atlanta. The main worry is for the less experienced equestrian nations taking part, who may not have had access to, or the necessary finance to enact the information that is available to us. But as long as everything is done to make sure that riders and team officials are fully aware of all the possible problems then I think we will have a safe and successful Games which will enhance rather than damage the reputation of the sport.'

8
Team Selection

In the sport of three-day eventing there is an international championship competition held every year: the Europeans run every two years, and the Olympic Games and World Championships every four years. The Senior Selection Committee is elected for a four-year period, the elections taking place at the end of each Olympic year; the culmination of each successive committee's efforts and policies is therefore to get a team to the Olympics which fall within their term of office. One of the problems for any selection committee is that, because they take over the job soon after an Olympic Games, if the team at that Olympics was successful then those horses and riders are very much in the public eye, and in the minds of the new team of selectors. But by the time the next Olympic Games comes round, those horses are four years older and maybe starting to feel the wear and tear of their long competitive career. But it takes a brave committee to overlook the 'obvious' team candidates at some stage and to put in a couple of younger horses or riders to see how they cope at that level; it is very tempting just to keep going with the combinations which are known well and which have proved themselves in the past at international level.

There is also the British principle of team medals being more important than ndividual glory. When a team is chosen for a championship, the aim is to win team gold, and for its members that may sometimes mean sacrificing their chance of personal glory. Therefore when the selectors are considering certain riders for teams, they have to be confident that each rider will be a good 'team' player; the very best individuals do not always find the transition to team player very easy and some find it impossible – so the task of choosing the best possible team is not always as straightforward as it looks. Add to that the uncertainty associated with all horse sports, such as whether or not your selected horses will remain fit and healthy in the build-up to the championship and not suffer any unexpected upsets in their training and preparation, then the selectors' responsibility begins to look increasingly fraught with problems!

Jane Holderness-Roddam

COMPETITOR AND SELECTOR

■Jane Holderness-Roddam (née Bullen) was elected as chairman of the selectors from 1989 to 1992, having had a remarkable and consistent career herself in top-level three-day eventing. At the 1968 Mexico Olympics, at the age of twenty, she became the first female rider to represent Britain in the sport of Olympic three-day eventing. Riding a little horse of barely 15hh, Our Nobby, Jane was part of the gold medal-winning team. Talking about the build-up to those Olympics she recalls 'The biggest surprise for everybody was that I won Badminton that year with Our Nobby. We had been fifth the previous year at our first Badminton, and took third place at Burghley, but to actually win in the Olympic year was quite unexpected. I was working as a nurse in London at the time and after our Badminton victory it was straight back to work on Monday morning as usual. Even though things had obviously been going well I hadn't had time even to think about whether we might get picked for the Olympic team. But the British media picked up on the idea and the build-up began then.'

Jane's potential Olympic partner, Our Nobby, was exceptional in that he was so small. 'It was very difficult to get him to measure 15hh, which is the minimum size for affiliated event horses,' confesses Jane. 'He was a terrible weaver, which meant you could never effectively build up any muscle to make him look bigger than he really was. People gave us all kinds of advice about how to help him reach the magical 15hh mark when the vet came to measure him, such as shutting him in his stable and making lots of loud noises to make him stand very upright! But even then it took several attempts before we found a vet who agreed to him being 15hh! He was a full Thoroughbred by Bewildered out of a Happy Landing mare, so he was classically bred with Derby winners on both sides of his family. He was fourth in a race at Bath but hadn't really made the grade for racing.

'He arrived on our doorstep led by a farmer who thought mother might like to buy him for one of us children. My mother actually thought he might suit Frank Weldon's son George who was looking for a pony, but he proved to be too difficult and nappy for us ever to sell on. We had seen him jump, but other

than that he was completely uneducated when he came, and once he had some food inside him he became very naughty and nappy; my older brother and sister, Mike and Jennie [now Jennie Loriston-Clarke] did their best to sort him out so that he could be passed reasonably safely to me! But he did just love his jumping; his dressage used to let him down, but in those days you earned bonus marks at the major three-day events if you took the hardest routes and made good time across country, and so we used to wipe out our dressage deficit quite effectively.

'After winning Badminton we were longlisted and asked to ride in the final trial at Burghley. We had a period of team training with Bertie Hill, and my sister Jennie had also been trying to improve Nobby's dressage. He had begun to show some progress, but by the time he got to Burghley he had had enough, and did the most awful dressage test – we lay 33rd out of thirty-six after the dressage! I was told to go slowly across country, which was very difficult as Nobby only had one speed which was flat out, and that's the speed we went at! We finally hauled our way up to finish third.

'There were quite a few problems among the other main team contenders; some horses had gone lame, and Bertie Hill was trying to swap several horses and riders – which he achieved with great success when he partnered Richard Meade with Mary Gordon-Watson's Cornishman, and Ben Jones with Martin Whitely's The Poacher (see Chapter 5). Amongst all this carry-on, we were named for the team. We had three weeks of team training before leaving for Mexico on 3 September. It is amazing now to think that our horses were expected to complete Burghley and then, only a few weeks later, travel out to Mexico for another championship three-day event.

'We knew that the altitude would be a problem, and that it would be very hot. As the first girl to be chosen for a British Olympic three-day event team I was determined not to let the side down, and had made sure I was very, very fit; for the last two months I was running five miles a day. Even so, the altitude did affect us when we got there. It made your chest feel very tight, but as a team we seemed to cope with it pretty well because it completely wiped out some horses and riders. We were given pills which helped us to cope, and Peter Scott-Dunn, the team vet, had looked into ways of safeguarding the horses' well-being and had instigated certain precautions. For example they wore very wide aluminium shoes which minimised effort because of their light weight and protected their feet from the very stony ground because of the extra width, and we took out water filters to make sure their drinking water was as pure as possible. A good many other horses developed problems because they would not drink the water.

'As was often the case then, the cross-country fences were made of very thin timber, which made the jumps look worse than they really were. Looking back, however, there were plenty of fences which would not be allowed today, such as the 3ft 11in rails onto a concrete bridge! Everything was made worse by the torrential rain which turned the ground to a bog – by the time Ben Jones and Richard Meade had to ride, the course was completely flooded in places and you couldn't see the take-off points at all! British supporters were running onto the course and placing sticks in the ground in front of one fence to mark the lip of the ditch! Ben Jones' horse had to paddle through floods on the approach to the completely submerged waterjump, and they only knew they'd found it when they fell off the edge and into it.

'I had two falls with Our Nobby, both caused because he crumpled up on landing when he couldn't pull his feet out of the mud and water quick enough. But we completed the course and still finished with the second fastest time of the day! At the end of speed and endurance day, Britain was leading as a team, and a Russian was leading individual. Sadly for him he took the wrong showjumping course, thus eliminating himself and losing his team any chance of a medal. Our Nobby had two fences down – in all his three-day events at home he had showjumped clear, but in Mexico I think he was very stiff and sore from

OLYMPIC SCRAPBOOK 1

TOP: *Jane with her sister Jennie at Heathrow, just before flying out to Mexico*

CENTRE: *Jennie gives Loppy (Our Nobby) a last-minute polish while Peter Scott-Dunn, the British team vet, makes a few last-minute checks – not least whether Jane could remember the dressage test*

RIGHT: *A very intense British team during the walk round, looking slightly horrified on discovering Phase A consisted of climbing uphill for almost 1,000 feet*

his falls; Richard Meade had two fences down as well, but Ben Jones and Derek Allhusen jumped clear.

'The scores were not officially announced until about ten o'clock that night – we had won the team gold, and Derek Allhusen took the individual silver. However, Our Nobby was retired after the Mexico Olympics, and I am very glad I made that decision for him because he remained very suspicious of water, even out hunting which he loved. Derek Allhusen's horse was eliminated at Badminton the following year, and I'm sure that was as a result of his experience in Mexico – it all took a lot more out of the horses than we realised.'

Jane remains a popular and successful horse trials competitor, and in 1995 also started a performance horse stud at the family home in Wiltshire. 'On today's cross-country courses so much more precision is needed,' comments Jane. 'Before, you could get away with quite a lot but much more in the way of accuracy is needed now; the horses must be schooled to a higher standard, and be more athletic to cope with today's more technical combinations. I don't think the standard of dressage at the very top has changed much, though – Ben Jones, for example, always rode a beautiful test; it is just that today there would be more riders of that same standard.'

Looking to her own future, Jane concludes: 'I am quite sure that one day I will lose my nerve for cross-country jumping, but today's courses are so well built – the bigger timber makes them look much more inviting and so for the time being I still love jumping them.'

OLYMPIC SCRAPBOOK 2

TOP: Fence 34 The flood water rose to above the take-off lip and the twigs pushed into the edge – by enthusiastic British supporters – gave the only indication of the take-off point

CENTRE: Ben Jones riding The Poacher wade through the floods at the last fence

LEFT: The stables at Avandaro were simple in design but well-built. On Peter Scott-Dunn's advice the British team brought their own water filter – the only team to do so. The horses wore specially designed aluminium shoes and were all eating specially prepared nuts which they had been eating for some weeks. (Only concentrated foods were allowed into Mexico.) We were stabled next to the Mexican team and opposite the Australians. The 'river' running down the centre is the result of the floods on cross-country day

ON THE SELECTION COMMITTEE

■ 'When I came onto the selection committee there was a set system which hadn't really changed for many years, whereby the top horses and riders more or less selected themselves and it was difficult for younger riders to get any help or recognition on their way up the ladder. With funding from the Horse Trials Support Group and the Worshipful Company of Saddlers, we introduced extra training courses with the aim of identifying and encouraging the up-and-coming talent; this initiative has been successfully continued by Bridget Parker, who succeeded me as chairman of the selectors in 1993.'

Prior to Jane's election Britain had won team silver, with Ian Stark winning individual silver and Ginny Leng bronze at the 1988 Seoul Olympics; Jane's first challenge was putting together a team for the European Championships at Burghley in 1989; this culminated in a confidence-boosting result when Britain won the team gold and all three individual medals – Ginny Leng gold, Jane Thelwall silver and Lorna Clarke bronze.

The World Championships in Stockholm 1990 threw up a new problem for the selectors. As Jane recalls, 'The heat in Stockholm surprised everybody, and very nearly bottomed Ian Stark's powerful grey Murphy Himself. Although we ended up with team and individual silver, it proved to us that in hot, humid conditions you really need very clean-bred horses, ideally full Thoroughbred, to cope with the climate.'

The World Championship team was a good mix of experience and new faces at international level. Ian Stark and Murphy Himself gave their usual display of excessive jumping to go clear. But on reflection it must have been a difficult competition for poor Ginny Elliot [then Leng] to stomach. It was she who had found and trained the young Murphy Himself, working hard to contain and challenge the powerful young horse's seemingly endless energy. But she had become increasingly beleaguered with the problem that he was becoming just too strong for her to hold; until finally at Badminton he had thrown a spectacular leap off the ski jump, a daunting enough fence when just popped quietly, and Ginny had been thrown off. After much deliberation she agreed to let Ian take over the horse, while she took Ian's horse Griffin in exchange. In an unusually frank moment Ginny has since described Griffin as the least generous horse she has ever ridden. At Stockholm, despite some very positive riding, he had a runout coming out of the water, and later put his feet down in the middle of the birch parallel which he presumably mistook for a bounce. Ginny was thrown off, but remounted to finish the course.

Karen Dixon, still relatively young as team members go but a veteran of the Seoul Olympics, had one stop at the water but was otherwise clear, and Rodney Powell had a runout on The Irishman, the horse on which he was to win Badminton the following year. So in spite of the fact that Ian was the only team member to go clear, Britain's overall performance was good enough for team silver, behind New Zealand. And Ian was a popular winner of the individual silver behind New Zealand's Blyth Tait, the new world champion.

Britain enjoyed a good build-up to the 1991 European Championships in Punchestown. At Badminton that year, the usual 'hunting ground' for the British selectors, British riders took the first four places, with Rodney Powell the winner, Ian Stark and his silver medal winner Murphy second, Helen Bell and Troubleshooter third, and Lorna Clark with King's Jester fourth. You might have thought that there you had your four team members, but even if that is what the selectors would have liked, it was not to be. Rodney Powell, faced with the dilemma of all full-time event riders of how to earn his living in this sport, decided to sell The Irishman to America for Bruce Davidson to ride. Sadly for all concerned very little was seen of The Irishman in international competition after that, and he certainly did not make it to the Barcelona Olympics which is what his new rider had hoped for.

Murphy Himself had been longlisted for the team but went lame during final training; Ian, however, was selected on Glenburnie who had finished sixth at Badminton. King's Jester suffered foot problems; he was eventually left out of the team but was selected to compete as an individual, although fate was harsh again on the seemingly luckless Lorna who had to withdraw the horse because of his lameness after the dressage phase. Ginny Elliot (then Leng) was another possible choice with Master Craftsman, but they had had to miss Badminton because the horse was recovering from a leg injury, and then Ginny herself broke her ankle riding at a one-day event; so although Crafty was fit to go, his rider was not. And so the selectors' dilemmas multiplied.

The eventual team proved ultimately successful: Ian Stark rode Glenburnie to take individual gold, Richard Walker – who still [1996] holds the record of being the youngest rider to win Badminton when only eighteen, in 1969 – took individual silver, and Karen Straker on Get Smart took bronze, in spite of a stop at the first water. The immensely popular Mary Thomson had been named as fourth team member on the relatively inexperienced eight-year-old King William. At his first Badminton earlier in the year he had been particularly impressive across country, although he had incurred sixty penalties for a fall on the flat at a point which unfortunately was still within the penalty zone area; they had also won the British Open Championships at Gatcombe. They made a great start at Punchestown by taking the lead after the dressage. The pair looked as if they were going to keep that lead with an impressive cross-country round when, all set to finish inside the time, disaster struck at the penultimate fence: young and exuberant, William stood off and threw much too big a jump off the big drop into the final water; his legs buckled on landing and Mary was tipped off. They finished the course, but Mary had injured her knee and was unable to showjump William the next day.

Of the two individuals there was Lorna Clark whom we know had withdrawn after the dressage; and Katie Meacham, riding Montana Blue, who had an eventful ride: she had a runout at the arena fence, and was thrown out of the saddle when her horse hit another fence very hard, although somehow she scrambled back on again. She showjumped clear on the final day to finish fifteenth.

In spite of this tremendous success, particularly welcome in the year prior to the Olympics, Jane and her selection committee had begun to realise that the current training system was still failing to bring through sufficient young talent to give the selectors a wider range of both horses and riders to choose from. 'We knew that we had got some outstanding horses,' explained Jane, 'but the obvious choices for these Olympics, based on past performance, were either getting old, such as Murphy Himself and Get Smart, or were not the type of horses thought suitable for the hot, hard conditions that would prevail in Barcelona, the site of the 1992 Olympics. But we did also have some outstanding riders who were all very good team members.'

With Master Craftsman again going lame during final training, the eventual Olympic team proved to be the same as the one that went to Punchestown. It had been hoped that Ian Stark would ride Glenburnie rather than Murphy Himself; Glenburnie, being full Thoroughbred, would have been better suited to the climatic conditions, but he had suffered a virus in the weeks before Barcelona and although he travelled out with the team, he was not considered as fit as Murphy.

The team's fate is discussed in detail in Chapters 3 and 5; let it just be said here that the lack of a medal, either team or individual, brought vociferous criticism of both the team and its selectors.

As Jane explains, with quietly suppressed anger reserved not for the treatment of herself but for that of the team: 'If Murphy had passed the vetting on the final day we would have been in a medal-winning position and nobody would have criticised anything. As it was, the media had been delighted with the British performance on the night of the cross-country. We were praised for our quick thinking, for the sympathetic way in which the horses had been ridden, and for our tactic of making Karen take some longer routes to try to ensure a safe clear, particularly after Richard's unexpected fall. But by the final day, when Murphy's score had had to be dropped and Richard's included, the press was very quick to savage the team and its officials.'

It has to be said that, in the circumstances, the only people to emerge showing any degree of dignity and sportsmanship were the team and its officials. Competing at any level, and at the Olympics in particular, is all about 'if only' stories, and the only riders without such tales are those with the gold medals. And even the sagest critics would do well to remember that hindsight is a wonderful thing; selectors may be blessed with many qualities, but foreseeing the future is not one of them!

As Jane explains, 'During my time as chairman of the selectors we were lucky to have a lot of outstanding horses competing at the time. Some were young horses which we hoped would be stars of the future, such as Montana Blue whom we took to Punchestown as an individual. But predicting whether a young horse will succeed consistently at four-star level is just as difficult as knowing whether or not your experienced horses will pass the final vetting. Sadly Murphy failed the vet in Barcelona because he struck a previously injured fetlock on the exit fence from the water. If a younger horse had hit the same fence with the same force he may also have failed the vet. And with Murphy's record of clean extravagant jumping it was equally hard to predict that he would injure himself in this way.

'It all comes down to timing – from my own experience I know that I was only selected for the Mexico Olympics because I won Badminton that year. If it had been a year earlier, or a year later I am confident that someone else would have taken my place. The timing and venue of the World and European Championships also limit or extend your selection possibilities. For example the 1989 European Championships were held at Burghley, so as the host nation we were allowed to send twelve horses and riders instead of the usual six. If, however, we had had that opportunity in 1991 we would have had the chance to test a far wider range of horses and riders, and would hopefully have broadened our choice. Horses are extraordinarily unpredictable – who would have thought that King William, winner of the British Open Championship in 1991 and winner of Badminton 1992, would choose Barcelona as the place to tell Mary he needed a stronger bit. [King William's hard-pulling and headstrong attitude obliged Mary to ride many of the longer routes because she found she could neither contain nor balance him sufficiently for the big combination fences.] You can plan everything out on paper, but once horse

and rider leave the start box, only the rider truly knows what feel his horse is giving him and he has to plan his round accordingly.'

Looking to the future and to the question of whether or not it is right to compete in Atlanta, Jane feels it would be a desperate shame to lose the opportunity to ride in an event as unique as the Olympics. 'The Olympic ideal is wonderful, and it is still the competition to win – everybody understands the value of an Olympic gold medal. But it does worry me that politics play far too much part in deciding where the Games are held; and this brings up the other problem, of whether it is right to compete in such unacceptable conditions, conditions which will affect not only the horses but the athletes as well.'

Bridget Parker

COMPETITOR AND SELECTOR

■ After the disappointment of Barcelona, it was obvious to any new chairman of selectors just how fine a line there can be between success and failure, and between congratulations and a savaging by the media. Bridget Parker nevertheless accepted the role happily and was chairman of selectors from 1993 to 1996, bringing to it a background and depth of experience similar to that of her predecessor Jane Holderness-Roddam.

Bridget rode in the gold medal-winning team at the 1972 Munich Olympics. As she recalls: 'I was long-listed with my horse Cornish Gold after Badminton of that year, where we finished third. We then had to ride at the final trial at Eridge horse trials before going into team training at Ascot. We lived in Eton school because Martin Whitely, then chairman of selectors, was a housemaster there, and the horses were ridden in Windsor Great Park all the time; Bertie Hill and Dick Stilwell were training us during this period. When we flew out to Munich I was down as reserve rider, the team being Richard Meade, Captain Mark Phillips, Mary Gordon-Watson and Debbie West. I walked the course and the roads and tracks with them, but as I never actually believed I would be riding I didn't study it in great detail. In those days you were allowed to take

a team of four, two reserve combinations, plus a spare horse, and the whole lot went through the first veterinary inspection.

'I had spent the afternoon just playing around with my horse, popping a few jumps and generally amusing myself in the practice area, but by that night we knew there were concerns as to the soundness of Debbie's horse Baccarat. Colonel Lithgow called me to his office and told me that if the horse wasn't right by the morning then I would be taking that team place. Baccarat was trotted up very early next morning and was still lame, and I received a call at 6am to tell me I was now in the team. My dressage wasn't until 4pm, so I did have time to re-walk the course and was again driven round the roads and tracks. I was probably luckier than my team-mates in that I just didn't have time to worry about any of it. Cornish Gold was never brilliant at dressage and so in that respect he performed a reasonable test; and in spite of a stop on the cross-country he still achieved one of the fastest rounds of the day. We won team gold, and Richard Meade took the individual gold; Mary Gordon-Watson finished fourth and I was ninth – although poor Mark Phillips and Great Ovation had a terrible time on the cross-country, suffering two falls and two refusals before completing.'

Bridget Parker and Cornish Gold at the water jump in the 1988 Munich Olympics

Bridget continued to compete – winning a team silver medal at the 1974 World Championships – until 1991; when she was bucked off a four-year-old at home and broke her back. For some hours she was paralysed but conscious, and when she proved lucky enough to recover fully she made the decision not to ride again. Her involvement with horse trials continued through her work as BHS steward, technical delegate and dressage judge, and to an even greater degree through her daughter Katie, who completed her first Badminton in 1995.

THE PREREQUISITES
OF SELECTING A TEAM

■ 'When selecting potential team members it is most important to take into account the temperament of the riders. They must train, travel and compete as a team, and a disruptive individual could have a disastrous effect on the others.

'The horses we are looking to select are those which are competing regularly at four-star level and which can prove their soundness and well-being after a three-day event. That is why we have a veterinary inspection for longlisted riders on the Monday following Badminton. On the Sunday, showjumping day, a lot of horses are still running on adrenalin – they pass the veterinary inspection and showjump all right, but by Monday morning they can be looking very different because any stiffness or tiredness will have caught up with them by then. At an international championship event the conditions now tend to be hot and hard, so any horses that look doubtful on the Monday after Badminton may well show that tiredness earlier in a hotter climate, and could well fail the final veterinary inspection at such an event in such conditions, and not be able to showjump. So we need to be as confident as we can that the horses selected will be able to complete the whole competition looking and feeling sound and well.

'After each Badminton we take two or three less experienced riders onto the championship team longlist, provided they have had a good Badminton. For the 1996 Atlanta Olympics our selection will be based on performances at Badminton 1995, Burghley 1995 and Badminton 1996, the last of which will also be the final trial. So we are looking for the proven combinations – somebody coming out and doing well at Badminton in 1996 but with no previous experience at that level, would not be selected for Atlanta. The other limiting factor with regard to selection for the Olympics is the type of horse that will cope best with the heat and humidity, and research so far shows this to be the smaller, wiry Thoroughbred. We saw in the Hague at the World Championships that Caroline Sizer's big horse, Ghost Town, was unable to cope with the conditions – he just didn't cool down enough after the roads, tracks and steeplechase. Similarly Mary Thomson's King

Bridget Parker

William was struggling by the end of the cross-country course – although he did come out fighting fit the next morning. But horses with a large body mass seem least able to cope.

'Whether it is the Europeans, the Worlds or the Olympics, whatever international championship it is in any particular year, I am a firm believer in going out with the team you think will win. The Worlds and Europeans are not a dress rehearsal for the Olympics: each team is picked with the aim of winning that competition. Winning the team gold in the Hague gave the whole equestrian world a tremendous boost, so that has to be your aim – to go out and win.

'The main difficulty with the job of senior selector is the comparatively short time you have to get to grips with things. Four years go by very quickly. The first year you are getting a feel of what's involved; you will have been given your predecessor's notes, but you are still finding your way – it is definitely a learning process. I certainly feel far more capable of handling the job now [1995] than I did in the first year I was in office. But then just as you feel comfortable with what you are doing, the job is over and it's someone else's turn.'

MIXED FORTUNES
Bridget was put up for selection by Christopher Schofield, chairman of the Young Rider Committee. Once the chairman is elected he chooses his own team of selectors, chef d'équipe, team vet and trainers; although this has to be done in consultation with the chairman of the Horse Trials Committee. Bridget's team consisted of Mike Tucker, Janet Norton and David Merret, all of whom had competed in horse trials; the chef d'équipe was Charlie Lane who had formerly commanded the King's Troop; and the team vet was John Killingbeck, who had already been involved with various international teams competing at home and abroad.

They did not, however, have the golden start that Jane Holderness-Roddam enjoyed because at the 1993 European Championships in Achselschwang the team did not complete the competition. It had several new faces, all of whom had had a successful Badminton that year. Charlotte Bathe and The Cool Customer, who had won Burghley the year before, went steadily but clear. But Nick Burton and William Fox-Pitt, both making their senior team début, failed to complete the course. Nick and the young Bertie Blunt fell, and Nick thought it best not to continue; he suffered severe criticism for this decision once back in England. However, Bertie Blunt was later sold and with Mark Todd on board, he has proved to be a very classy horse. William Fox-Pitt retired the exhausted Chaka who was later found to be suffering a virus. Many people considered Chaka was not genuine, but William remained loyal to the horse and they had a good win at Burghley a year later. And at Badminton 1995 they were in the lead after cross-country day, only to fail the final veterinary inspection. Chaka rewarded William's continuing faith in him with a succession of wins at Advanced one-day events, culminating in victory in the British Open Championship at Gatcombe in 1995. Chaka has since been retired.

Tina Gifford, riding as an individual, exonerated the selectors' faith in the 'young' by riding with a maturity and sensitivity belying her twenty-two years to take the individual silver medal. Ginny Elliot (then Leng), riding Welton Houdini, was the senior member of the team but suffered a totally unexpected runout on the steeplechase phase. Ginny was convinced that Houdini had been spooked by the mass of photographers with flash cameras on the approach to the fence but her critics were unsympathetic, some going as far as to say the horse had put in a 'dirty stop'. It is one of the less attractive aspects of the horse world that when Heather Holgate called for the banning of flash photography at events she was dismissed as trying to find excuses for her horse's behaviour. But only a few months later when yet another horse was clearly upset by flash photography when competing, those same sections of the media started clamouring for action to stop the use of flashguns. It is sad that the press was not prepared to support Heather Holgate and Ginny when they gave the same explanation for Houdini's runout. Surely the horse had proved its honesty by winning Badminton earlier that year?

Coming so soon after Barcelona, the disastrous result for Britain's team gave the 'armchair brigade', as they had become known through the flurry of critical letters received on the subjects of Barcelona and team selection, a second chance to pour scorn on what they saw as the decline of British eventing. It must therefore have been with some trepidation that Mrs Parker and her committee began to plan for the World Championships in the Hague the following year, 1994. New Zealand were hot favourites for the team title and anything else

that was going – but on this occasion they suffered the bad luck that had so far been the lot of Great Britain: Blyth Tait, reigning World Champion, retired his little mare Delta after a crashing fall, and Mark Todd and Andrew Nicholson were both thrown from their horses at the same fence, the step up out of the water. There was some consolation in the performance of Vaughn Jeffries and Bounce, who sailed through to take the individual title of World Champion.

The inclusion of Mary Thomson and King William in the British team had invited yet more criticism thanks to William's capacity for knocking showjumps, but in order to qualify for the Olympics, Britain had to compete as a team and William has always come through every three-day event looking fighting fit. Charlotte Bathe and The Cool Customer reproduced their reliable form from the Europeans, this time with more speed and attack to go fast and clear. Tina Gifford's style and determination which had been rewarded with the individual silver in the Europeans, continued in similar vein when she gave the relatively inexperienced nine-year-old, General Jock, a wonderful ride to produce another clear; and Karen Dixon with her team veteran Get Smart at last left her water jump jinx behind to go clear, to take the individual bronze. The team won gold to tumultuous applause and congratulations from a now very appreciative audience.

For Bridget Parker the 'mid-term' report is good, but the greatest challenge is still to come. In spite of their reliability, there must be some doubts about the wisdom of sending older horses such as The Cool Customer and Get Smart (both will be sixteen) to compete in the heat of Atlanta. And the powerful King William, although still relatively young, is not the ideal build for withstanding the climate, although Mary does have another impressive four-star horse in Star Appeal. Helen Bell and Troubleshooter, who went well as individuals to finish 22nd, are also in the category of 'the older horse'. Of that particular World Championship squad, therefore, the realistic choice is already down to one – General Jock, unless the selectors risk taking the older horses, a decision which did not pay off for their predecessors when Murphy Himself was sent to the Olympics.

And so the selectors' dilemma continues. The 1995 Europeans saw another team gold for Britain, and individual bronze for Mary King and King William. Her team-mates were Tina Gifford, William Fox-Pitt and Charlotte Bathe. There will be yet one more opportunity at Badminton 1996 to assess and select, but it is no easy task. Everyone, the critics especially, would do well to remember the words of Jane Holderness-Roddam: '...it all comes down to timing.'

9

Team Training

Different countries prepare in different ways for major championships. Although each may have an official team trainer, some leave their riders to prepare in their own way, while others organise a concentrated team training session just prior to the event. For example, in the build-up to the 1992 Barcelona Olympics the twenty-six participating nations (eighteen of which fielded teams) prepared in a number of different ways. Britain, Australia, Germany, America and Korea organised several weeks of training, with the team members settled all together in a 'base camp'. This gives them the chance to get to know each other as a team, it removes them from every day 'domestic' worries and allows them to concentrate fully on the task ahead.

The disadvantage is that some riders cannot afford to leave the rest of their horses for that length of time, and in particular the concentration period may not suit the way in which they like to prepare for a major event. For some, being at home amongst people they are close to, and having other things to occupy their mind in those last few weeks, reduces the build-up of tension that is inevitable, particularly amongst the less experienced team members. The New Zealanders followed a more individual approach, their riders preparing at home in their usual way, with visits from the team trainer and vet during the final build-up. The Irish kept to the individual approach, apart from organising a couple of training weekends which included dressage, showjumping and fastwork. The Swiss and the Swedish left their riders to their own devices, although a few official team training days were arranged for those based in Switzerland. The host nation, Spain, had riders based with Mark Todd and Lars Sederholm, as well as some who prepared from their homeland. But the whole team spent a few days in training at Gatcombe under the eye of their then team trainer Captain Mark Phillips.

Whilst attitudes to team selection have altered dramatically since, say, the days of Bertie Hill when riders and horses were swapped to produce the ultimate partnership, the approach taken during team training has remained much the same: it is a time or fine tuning and confidence building. Here, riders and trainers give an insight into what is involved.

Bertie Hill

COMPETITOR AND TRAINER

Bertie and his pony Robin in 1940

■ Born in 1927, Bertie Hill became one of Britain's greatest horsemen, his riding and training skills helping to shape what was a golden era for British horse trials. He first rode at the Olympics in 1952, won team gold at the 1953 European Championships, team and individual gold at the 1954 World Championships, and team gold at the 1956 Olympics. He also rode at the 1960 Rome Olympics, and finally was asked to train a British team for the 1968 Olympics in Mexico, where Britain took team gold and individual silver.

Bertie was not an early convert to eventing: his first love as a child was showjumping, and later he became a very successful point-to-point and National Hunt jockey; he was fortunate to ride many good horses, one of the most outstanding being the 14.3hh Brownie on which he won thirty-three point-to-points. Thus he had very soon gained an excellent reputation for his race riding and showjumping. His conversion to three-day eventing, however, came about in an unusual and most flattering way. Early in 1951 he received a letter from Captain Tony Collings who was in charge of putting together a team for the 1952 Olympic Games in Helsinki. The letter invited him to be trained at the Porlock Vale Riding School with the aim of competing at Badminton that year; Collings' long-term aim was to use this exercise to prepare a team for the Olympics. As Bertie says, 'I looked on it as a great challenge, besides which Tony Collings had painted a very rosy picture of what it would be like!'

Bertie had an immense natural talent for showjumping and riding across country, but he was desperately frustrated by the lack of progress he was making with his dressage. After three months of training at Porlock he told Tony Collings that he was giving up. Tony was appalled, and Bertie remembers him rising from his chair, looking him in the eye and saying 'Bertie, you have two great assets – you can showjump and you can ride across country. Please,

just for me, learn the dressage.' The next day Bertie was assigned two different horses to ride, horses which were easier on the flat than those he was used to, and he had dressage lessons twice a day from Richard Watjen the German trainer. 'Racing had made my hands hard,' explained Bertie 'and I just hadn't been able to feel what the trainer kept telling me I should be feeling. But as soon as I learnt to feel through my hands I became intrigued with the discipline of dressage.'

Bertie had ridden in only one event before he was entered for the Badminton three-day event, along with fellow Olympic hopefuls Lawrence Rook, John Miller (later Sir John Miller), Reg Hindley, John Oram and Michael Naylor-Leyland. They competed *hors concours* because they were all riding to the strict instructions of Tony Collings. Bertie and his mount, Banbridge Boy, produced a workmanlike test but they showed their true flair with clear rounds across country and showjumping. Asked whether he ever experienced any nerves about riding a cross-country course in those days, Bertie's reply was a tribute to the calibre of horse he rode; 'I was lucky in that I trusted the horses I rode at that level, and so I rarely worried about the fences.' He then quickly adds, 'Mind you, I'm talking about the horses I evented – I certainly didn't trust every horse I rode!'

One of Tony Collings' greatest assets as a trainer was that he had the courage to ensure that the best horses had the best jockeys. It didn't matter which horse you personally arrived with, if someone else rode it better then they got the ride on it. Bertie was chosen for the Helsinki Olympics, and given the ride on John Miller's mare Stella. The mare had been unable to perform one of the canter movements without going unlevel when ridden by her owner, but with Bertie on her back she performed perfectly. Bertie and fellow team-mate Reg Hindley became the first civilians to represent their country in the Olympic three-day event; until Helsinki

Countryman III who was sold to HM the Queen; but Bertie was able to retain the ride

RIGHT: At the Stockholm Olympics 1956, Bertie and Countryman III

In 1953 Bertie was selected for the European Championship team. He rode a different horse, Bambi V, and the team took the gold medal, and Lawrence Rook made up for his persoanl disaster in Helsinki by winning the individual title. The European Championships of 1954 were again a walkover for Britain; Bertie rode Ted Marsh's Crispin to take the individual gold, and the team won gold.

So far Bertie had enjoyed team successes on other people's horses, but a couple of years before the 1956 Olympics he bought one for himself: Countryman, a horse which turned out to be world class. Bertie takes up the story: 'I had gone to a yard near Exeter to look at a showjumper for my sister. I looked across the yard and saw a lovely head surveying me – but when I asked about the horse I was told he would be useless for me. The owner had seen him jump every type of

it had always been the domain of the military.

The team came very close to winning Olympic gold: Bertie had gone well to finish the day in seventh place, Reg Hindley wasn't far behind and as Lawrence Rook galloped to the last fence, that gold medal was in the British sights – but Starlight put his foot in a ditch and fell, badly concussing his rider. Lawrence Rook somehow remounted and successfully jumped the last fence, only to pass a flag on the wrong side before the finish; this eliminated him and, consequently, the team – in those days the team consisted of three riders, and all three scores had to count. It was only in 1960 that the rules changed and allowed four to a team, with the best three scores to count.

fence in Ireland bareback, but having brought him home and tried to put a saddle on him, he proved to be impossible to mount. The owner had ridden him just once, and was stood in front of me on crutches as testimony to the result.

'Nevertheless I was very taken with him, and on being told his price was £250, I offered £90; but to no avail. Then the very first thing the next morning I had a phone call telling me to bring my £90 and to take the horse away! I had a job to ride him with a saddle – he really hated having the girth done up, but I persevered and succeeded. After a season's hunting he won his first race over banks, and having already showjumped him with some success, I knew I had a three-day event

Chicago, who in one season took three different riders round three different three-day events

horse on my hands; and within a year he had indeed become a very successful event horse.'

At the European Championships of 1955 Countryman had earned himself a team place, and the British were highly successful: the team took gold, Frank Weldon won the individual title and Bertie took bronze. And Countryman earned himself a new owner: HM the Queen had expressed an interest in owning an event horse, and a syndicate led by the Queen bought him; Bertie, however, kept the ride. Nor did they disappoint either Queen or country when, in spite of an unexpected fall on the cross-country, the team won Britain's first Olympic gold for three-day eventing. The only disappointing factor was that Tony Collings, who had done so much to push British three-day eventing in the right direction, and who was personally responsible for Bertie's involvement in the sport, did not live to see his efforts rewarded at this, the ultimate level. Tony was killed in the Comet air disaster in 1954.

By the time the 1960 Rome Olympics came round, Bertie considered himself quite old enough not to expect to ride there; however the selection committee asked him to ride Wild Venture. This was the first Olympics when countries could field a team of four; for Britain this was Bertie, Frank Weldon, Mike Bullen and Norman Arthur. These Olympics were won by the Australians, but they were not a happy occasion as far as horses were concerned: the heat was oppressive, the ground extremely hard, and most of the fences were trappy and not very substantially built. One team horse, Norman Arthur's Blue Jeans, split a pastern bone on the cross-country, Frank Weldon fell four times and Bertie twice. As Bertie recalls: 'I was riding an old horse which had already completed an Olympic Games. One of our falls was at a fence with a big drop – he cleared the fence all right, but didn't put down his landing gear. This can happen to an old horse when he is tired, and in the hot, hard conditions this was a very tired horse. Interestingly, the winning Australian team were mounted on relatively young horses.' Rome was the last time Bertie took part in an Olympics as a rider, although he was involved in training riders and teams for subsequent Games. He established the Rapscott School of Equitation at his farm in Devonshire, and kept his own competition career to the national scene.

His last three-day event was Badminton in 1970, where ten of his pupils were also competing. Bertie was riding Chicago, a horse with which he had won the Chatsworth senior event the previous year. 'Chicago was a terrific horse,' says Bertie enthusiastically. 'He was by a Dartmoor pony colt out of a little eventing mare but I liked him the minute I saw him. I have always believed that if you see a horse that you think has got what it takes to reach the top you should buy it, even if you don't need it at the time. When I saw Chicago I needed another horse like a hole in the head, but I bought him – because when they are that special you never see them again. He was a terrific

horse to ride across country; once he knew his job he would cock his ear back towards me about fifty yards from the fence as if to say, "Don't worry, I've seen it, you just sit quiet and let me get on with it!".

'In that particular year, 1970, Chicago competed in three three-day-events: my son Tony rode him in the Junior Championships, Mark Phillips rode him in the gold medal-winning team at the World Championships in Punchestown, and I rode him at Badminton!' Having gone beautifully across country to finish in second place just one fence behind Richard Meade, almost unbelievably Bertie Hill then made a rare mistake: 'I had been helping my pupils to warm up and prepare for their showjumping rounds, and my mind wasn't really on my own job. I jumped the stile in the wrong direction and was therefore eliminated. I knew in mid-air what I'd done, but it was too late!' It is good to see that Bertie can still smile at his own fallibility. He rode in one more event after that...'One of those veteran classes,' chuckled Bertie, 'and I made sure I won it!'

BERTIE AS TRAINER

■ After his death in 1954, Tony Collings' system of team training and selection – ensuring that the best horses had the best jockeys – seemed to be abandoned. A wider range of riders was considered for selection but the influence of a strong leader was missing, a leader with the courage to mix and match horses and riders, and to keep an eye on the overall fitness and performance of potential team members. Britain did not perform well at the Tokyo Olympics of 1964, and Bertie was approached by the chairman of the selectors, Colonel Babe Moseley, to help prepare a team for the next Olympic Games. Bertie had three years in which to find and train a team fit to win team gold.

'I watched a large number of riders compete at Badminton and reported to the selectors the ones I wanted to take into training. Those horses and riders would come into team training three weeks before a major championship. One thing I did know was that to overcome the heat and humidity of Mexico, the site of the next Olympics, both horses and riders would have to be very fit. Although my riders were riding their own horses, skipping, running and playing tennis, I am a firm believer that there is nothing like riding to make you riding fit. So a lorryload of horses was brought in from Rapscott for the riders to use. But my greatest asset was knowing that Colonel Babe Moseley

accepted and supported the concept of pairing the best horses with the best riders. This was something I really wanted to do in two cases. However, having the committee's support doesn't make it any easier when you have to approach a rider to tell him or her that you don't want him but please can we have your horse!'

Bertie considered Mary Gordon-Watson to be an excellent rider, but felt that she was still too young at that point in her life to possess the physical and mental toughness that would be needed to compete successfully at the high altitude which prevailed in Mexico. Mary sportingly handed Cornishman over to Richard Meade, a decision which fate made easier when Mary broke her leg at about the same time.

The other swap was not so willingly accepted. Bertie did not think that Martin Whitely was fit enough for the challenge of the Games, and wanted Ben Jones to ride his horse The Poacher. As Bertie recalls, 'Martin was not at all happy about being taken off his own horse, but I think in his heart he knew it was right. And so it proved when we came away with the team gold.' Team member Derek Allhusen won the individual silver, Richard Meade finished fourth and Ben Jones was fifth. The fourth team member, Jane Bullen (now Holderness-Roddam) had two falls on the cross-country (see Chapter 8) but survived to complete the competition. It had been a very tough championship – much of the course had flooded, obscurring take-offs and landings, but all the riders rose to the challenge. Bertie is convinced that they succeeded because the best were partnered by the best.

Despite this success, when Martin Whitely took over as chairman of the selectors later that year there was again a move away from central control over team training and selection. As it was, Bertie trained half of the next Olympic team in that Bridget Parker and Captain Mark Phillips were pupils of his, whilst Richard Meade and Mary Gordon-Watson, now back on her own Cornishman, were trained by Dick Stilwell. The team took the gold medal in Munich and Richard Meade the individual title.

The system fell apart again at the Montreal Games of 1976. Bertie was not involved officially in any way, but watched quietly from the side-lines. Whilst he was in agreement with the riders chosen – HRH Princess Anne, Lucinda Prior-Palmer, Richard Meade and Hugh Thomas – he personally had doubts about the fitness of two of the horses chosen. Lucinda's horse Be Fair slipped the tendon off his hock, and Hugh Thomas's horse Playamar strained a tendon; both had jumped clear across country but could not complete the competition so Britain as a team was eliminated.

Bertie is the first to admit that the sport has changed tremendously since his heyday as rider and trainer. Sponsorship and the fact that so many riders are now trying to make a career out of their sport has led to a far more 'individual approach'. Financial pressures, and the sheer number of horses that many of the top riders have in their yards, make it difficult for them to find time for training of any kind, let alone weeks of intensive team training. When Bertie was being 'prepared' for his first Olympics in 1952 the team was in training at Porlock Vale for six months. This was only possible because his family were prepared to release him from his duties on the farm to give him this wonderful chance. Also the training of that particular team was supported financially by a private family, something that is probably impossible to repeat in today's fraught economic climate.

Nevertheless from his own experiences, and from what he has witnessed over the years, Bertie remains faithful to the principle that to win gold medals, the best must be on the best. 'A great horse deserves a great chance,' says Bertie, 'and a true horseman will accept that, even though his pride may be hurt. It happens in racing all the time – when it comes to the big race, it is usually a top jockey given the ride, and this is an accepted part of the system. Richard Meade rode

many horses owned by other people because he was recognised as a great horseman. Most of the horses I rode at international level belonged to other people and, in spite of having also suffered the down side myself, of being "jocked off" in the racing world, I still stand by that principle. It could still work today – all it needs is a respected person to appoach the owner of the horse and explain that the horse is good enough but only if it is ridden by another jockey.'

Simple as this suggestion sounds, it would be very difficult to implement, largely because the aims and ambitions of today's professional riders, and their need to stay in the front line in order to make a living, to attract rides and sponsorship, would probably overshadow any idealistic views they might have regarding duty to Queen and country! Today it is money that makes the world go round, and even the most idealistic rider knows only too well that he will gain not a jot financially by agreeing to hand his horse over to someone else, indeed his reputation might even be diminished.

Bertie competed in the days of true amateurism, but as he says, the training was taken extremely seriously. Many of the riders had careers to follow at the same time: Richard Meade was working in London prior to the 1972 Games; his horse was kept in Reading with his trainer Dick Stilwell, and he rode each morning before continuing into London to work. 'Three weeks of team training is sufficient prior to an international championship, as long as you are working with sound, fit horses. That means,' says Bertie, 'that the horses should have completed their last three-day event sound, and have remained sound since then. There is no point in training lame horses or, when the conditions are going to be hot and hard, old horses.'

Regarding his role as team trainer, Bertie considered it was not for him to try to change a rider's style, but to give him or her tips based on personal experience as to how to jump different fences. When walking a championship course, riders will usually turn to the trainer and ask if the way they plan to tackle it is the best way. And the experience of having watched those horses and riders for some time helps the trainer to anticipate how each horse is going to cope with the different fences. As Bertie explains, 'Different horses see fences in different ways and react accordingly, and their reaction is often more obvious to an observer on the ground than it is to the rider on board. And whilst it is probably wrong to insist that a rider tackles a fence in a certain way, you would hope that if he trusts your judgement he would see what you meant and would decide himself to tackle it the way you would like him to. In my experience if there was a

Bertie Hill as Master of the Dulverton West Foxhounds

particular fence that I didn't like for a certain horse, I was nearly always there to pick the rider up off the floor!'

Today, Bertie's own energies are devoted to enjoying life with his wife Mary in their Devonshire home, and to proudly watching the activities of his children and grandchildren. The Rapscott School of Equitation is in the capable hands of his son Tony, who is particularly popular with American clients who are seeking to improve their technique and boost their confidence. Daughter Sarah is married to the Minehead trainer Philip Hobbs, and race rides successfully herself; they have three children. But Bertie still keeps a keen eye on the world of eventing, and he is particularly encouraged by the success of British riders at the 1994 World Championships and the 1995 Europeans. 'Riders are starting to attack their courses again' he said, 'and this has been partly encouraged by the sort of courses that

Hugh Thomas has begun to provide at the Badminton three-day event. They are for the bold galloping horse, and this is the Olympic horse.'

Bertie will be going out to the Atlanta Olympics to spectate, and hopes dearly that Britain chooses a good enough team to win. He feels that as long as the horses and riders are as fit as they possibly can be, then along with the modifications that are being made to the speed and endurance phases, the competition should be successful. One further change he would like to see on the home front would be to see the appointment of Captain Mark Phillips as team trainer. At the present time the Americans are benefiting markedly from his teaching, and having had both Bridget Parker – the present chairman of the selectors – and Mark Phillips as pupils, Bertie would like to think that this combination would go a long way to keeping Britain at the top of the sport.

Stephen Hadley

SHOWJUMPING TRAINER

Stephen Hadley, the former showjumper to whom many event riders have turned for help in this phase

■ Stephen Hadley enjoyed a long career as a successful national and international showjumper, and his depth of knowledge and tactful, quiet style of teaching have made him an equally popular and effective trainer of both showjump and event riders. He has been involved in training Britain's three-day event team riders since 1989, the beginning of the build-up to the 1992 Barcelona Olympics. Steve gave up competing internationally in the late 1980s and concentrated on teaching, based at his farm in Warwickshire.

'I was lucky in that, although to begin with I trained mainly showjumpers rather than event riders, three of the people I did help in the early days went on to win two Badmintons and Burghley between them. They were Nicola Coe, Mary King and Charlotte Bathe, and they won these events within a couple of years of each other,' explains Steve. 'So my involvement with training eventers grew from there, really. Event riders are enjoyable to teach because they tend to be more trainer-orientated than showjumpers, and come to a showjump trainer to improve their jumping; they may not have any particular problems but they want to improve generally. A showjumper only tends to come to a trainer if he has a specific problem that he needs help with.

'Some riders come to me individually for help throughout the year, others I get involved with through the winter training courses. These are organised for riders who will almost certainly be in the team, as well as for competitors that the selectors think may make future team members. Some very talented riders seem to lie dormant for a few years and then suddenly find their form, and their way onto a team. The winter courses provide a different kind of training to that given at the team concentration just prior to an international championship. The winter training is more general – you are aiming to teach the rider something that is applicable to any horse he rides. The team concentration is very specialist – you are trying to help the rider get the most out of his team horse.

'By the time a rider is good enough to be considered for a team place, he or she has already developed his or her own style and it obviously works successfully for that person. My aim is not to change a rider's style radically, but to alter it to suit the particular horse he is riding. Every horse varies in terms of what suits it best when it comes to jumping, and the trainer's objective is to help horse and rider to become more efficient as a partnership, with the ultimate aim of leaving more showjumps up. My task as trainer is to get the horse and rider right on the day. The final preparation on the last day of a three-day event is vital, but the last twenty minutes before the showjumping phase of a major championship is not the place to be giving the rider a jumping lesson. You just work on the horse, helping the rider to get the horse up in the air.

'Because the cross-country is the dominant phase in eventing, most event riders tend to have their horses a little too onward bound when it comes to showjumping – they tend to go for longer strides and find it hard to adjust to riding at a slower pace, with the horse rounder and deeper in the final phase. If you can make this adjustment then the horse makes a different shape over the fence; it achieves a different elevation which tends to leave more fences up. The trajectory of the average event rider is a little flatter and longer than is in the horse's best interest for a good showjumping round.'

THE BARCELONA OLYMPICS

■ 'At this stage in a horse and rider's career you rarely need to be doing specific exercises such as gridwork. It is more relevant to help the rider in his task of cantering to a fence in the way that it suits that horse to be ridden. If you watch the top showjump riders, although they all have their own distinctive style, they still ride each horse slightly differently, depending on what suits that horse best. Some horses need to come in with more power and pace, others are better if the rider sits quietly and gives them time to come up in front of the fence. If the last sort is ridden up to a fence with too much pace, he won't have room to pick up enough in front to clear it. Others use their power and pace to store up energy so they can spring up and over the fence.

'British rider Charlotte Bathe's horse The Cool Customer has to be ridden in a certain way to a showjump; he tends to be over-bold and takes his fences on too much. If you let him do this he makes up too much ground on the way to a fence and can then have it down in front. You have to sit quietly and encourage him to wait in front of the fence, then he has the room to get his forehand up and clear of the front rail. The bottom line is that to succeed, you have to ride each horse in the way that suits it best. They can't all be ridden in the same way.'

The Barcelona Olympics was Steve's first experience of an Olympic Games, and it sadly holds few happy memories for him. 'My abiding memory of Barcelona is Scotty [Ian Stark] walking away from the final vetting with Murphy having been failed. If Murphy had been able to jump on the final day he could have had two fences down and the team would still have won the gold medal – and he was a very clean showjumper, so team gold was a realistic prospect. For the team to have come home from a gruelling event like that and be faced with such an onslaught of criticism was unforgivable.'

The 'armchair brigade' as they came to be known, attacked the British team with furious verbal malice, describing them as anything from big girls' blouses to spineless wimps. Up until the final vetting the team were being praised for the sensitive and thoughtful way in which they rode their horses in what were very hot, hard conditions. Thus Richard Walker's fall was accepted as unlucky, Mary was praised for her sensible handling of a hot-headed King William, Scotty for his acrobatic display with Murphy Himself and for having nursed him home so skilfully once the effects of his earlier exertions caught up with him, and Karen for riding a safe clear just when it was needed. But the moment Murphy failed the vet the tables were turned: the team had not gone fast enough, they had been too cautious, and they should have gone for gold like those 'wonderful New Zealanders and Australians'.

It has already been said several times that you need luck to win. Matt Ryan, the eventual gold medallist, was lucky to survive a couple of sticky moments at two water complexes – although he would argue that it was his riding ability which enabled him to survive the mistakes. Blyth Tait, the eventual bronze medallist, was lucky that his horse recovered from lameness just moments before its dressage test and that it remained sound throughout the competition. Whereas David Green, one of those 'wonderful Australians who was going for it', had to retire when his horse slipped on the flat, knocked into itself and went lame; but before it had even got back to the ten-minute box it was sound again – that was bad luck. And so it goes on. Had the British riders 'gone for it' in the reckless manner the public seemed to want, they would have been crucified if they had made a mistake as a result. Hindsight is a powerful weapon, and the 'armchair brigade' used it unrelentingly.

Even three years after the event Steve feels the same anger and sense of injustice, not for himself but for the team. He has sat through dinner parties when he has been the only person who had actually been to Barcelona, and yet his fellow guests simply refused to accept that the riders did their best. They ignore the fact that if Murphy had passed the vet we would almost certainly have won team gold.

'I know personally that every member of that squad gave it their best shot – they all did their job professionally and well. As someone who has been generally involved with horses all my life, and in particular involved in the extreme pressures of preparing for and riding at a big event, I *know* that the job was done right. We were just extremely unlucky. In thirty-five years of international competition I have never experienced a disappointment like it. I stayed out there after the three-day event to commentate on the showjumping which started a few days later, and when I walked back into the showjumping stadium for the first time my stomach just turned over – the disappointment still felt that strong.'

In the furore that followed Barcelona, it was the team and selectors who bore the brunt of the criticism. But one crucial aspect of the team's failure completely escaped criticism, and that was why Murphy Himself

ABOVE: Mary King (then Mary Thomson) and King William for Great Britain during their disastrous showjumping round at the Barcelona Olympics 1992
LEFT: Captain Mark Phillips (see page 180) and Cartier on the steeplechase phase at the Seoul Olympics, 1988

failed the vet. Here was a horse at the end of its career, which needed to be fit enough to jump just one course of showjumps (on sand) so he could then retire in reflected glory rather than in undeserved shame – but he failed the vet. Other horses which had taken far worse knocks on their way round the course came out sound the next day. Moreover there were plenty of unsound horses leaving the showjumping arena at the end of the day, which indicates that they, too, were unsound at some point after the cross-country phase.

Drugs cannot be used to help a horse if he is to stay in the competition but there is physiotherapy, laser treatment and cold therapy. All these things constitute a vet's ammunition, and other teams obviously used them in such a way as to get their horses through the final horse inspection. Steve feels very strongly that more could have been done to keep Murphy sound.

Several others since then have quietly voiced the same opinion – although most share the very British trait of just allowing things to pass by uncontested. John Killingbeck, the new British team vet for the Atlanta Olympics, comments in Chapter 7 that riders sometimes expect vets to perform miracles; but one gets the feeling that Murphy Himself didn't need a miracle, just a little more thought and attention.

Barcelona will long remain a bone of contention between those who felt that the team tried their very best and were unlucky to fail, and those who are convinced that they never tried at all. Having watched the team in training and having travelled out to the event itself, I would certainly share the view of Stephen Hadley, a far more informed observer than many of the critics, that in his own words, 'Barcelona was a case of four hard-fought-for gold medals that got away'.

Mark Phillips

COMPETITOR AND TEAM TRAINER

■ As a horseman, Mark Phillips has always been admired and judged kindly by the horse world, and his commitment to the sport of eventing has long been in evidence. He enjoyed considerable success as a competitor, and more recently has become deeply involved in event organisation and course design, in team and individual rider training, and in various other voluntary commitments such as his chairmanship of the British Equestrian Olympic Fund.

Mark's most successful individual performances as a competitor have always been at Badminton, which he has won four times on three different horses. His first win at this great event was in 1971 on Great Ovation. The following year it looked as if he would have to settle for second place: after the cross-country phase he was lying a mere 0.6 penalties behind Richard Meade, and although he showjumped clear, he fully expected Richard to do the same. Sure enough Richard did jump clear, but he fractionally misjudged the time and had to add 1.25 penalties to his final score. Mark and Great Ovation had won for the second time!

In 1974 he achieved the same result with Columbus, who was owned by HM the Queen; and in 1981, while sponsored by Range Rover as a member of the Range Rover team, he won again on Lincoln.

He won Burghley, where he is now course designer, in 1973; team gold at the Punchestown World Championships in 1970, riding Bertie Hill's Chicago; team silver at the 1974 World Championships on Columbus; and team gold on Great Ovation at the 1971 Burghley European Championships, when HRH Princess Anne and Doublet took the individual title.

Both his Olympic experiences have been desperately disappointing. His first ride was in Munich in 1972, of which he has clear recollections: 'During the build-up to the Games I was never satisfied with Great Ovation's dressage; I couldn't accept that it was good enough and kept working away, looking for more and more improvement. In the end Jennie Loriston-Clarke videoed the horse and made me watch it, and only then did I start to believe that perhaps it wasn't so bad. In fact the horse produced one of his best tests in Munich to lie third after the dressage – and then everything fell apart on the cross-country; the horse was going so well and felt so well that I think I became over-confident.

Great Ovation didn't have enormous scope and really hated being asked to stand off his fences, and at the third fence, a very wide parallel, I asked for a long one; but we didn't quite make it, he came down on the back rail and I was thrown off. Then I got back on in such a hurry that I didn't realise the rein was wrapped round his nose. So I continued on a very shaken horse with pretty ineffective steering and brakes, and we had another fall and several refusals. We did complete the competition but naturally enough were the discard score – the team, however, won the gold medal.

'My second chance came in 1988 when I went to the Seoul Olympics on Cartier, and on this occasion we fared no better: Cartier was lame behind at the end of the steeplechase, a lameness which I thought would wear off; but it didn't and it transpired he had pulled a muscle, so obviously was unable to continue. I suspect this was partly to do with his feeding. The horses were fed on hydroponic grass once they were in Seoul and he probably had too much protein in his diet, something which we take far more notice of today; because of this the muscle tightened up, and then it got pulled during the 'chase. Happily for us all as a team, Great Britain won the team silver, and two of the individual medals – silver to Ian Stark, and bronze to Ginny Elliot (then Leng).'

Cartier was the last horse on which Mark Phillips competed internationally. Soon after that he gave up competing at the highest level to concentrate on cross-country course designing and training of event riders: 'When I was first involved in training for a team in 1968, Bertie Hill was the "team trainer", a role that shortly afterwards he shared with Dick Stilwell; but as time went on we were moving further and further away from the team trainer scenario. There were, and still are, team training concentrations before the major championships, but these training periods have got shorter over the years.

'Riding at an Olympic Games is a very different experience to any other type of competition, mainly because you are there amongst the world's top athletes; it is a tremendously emotive experience, and it has to be the pinnacle of a sportsperson's career. I personally would far rather have gone to one Olympics than to any number of World Championships.'

CHEF D'EQUIPE AND TECHNICAL ADVISER

■ Captain Mark Phillips' official title is chef d'équipe and technical adviser to the American three-day event team, which capacity he has enjoyed since after the Barcelona Olympics. As he explains, 'The Americans have been through the same evolution as the British, in that they went from a situation where one man had total control – the Jack Le Goff era – to having no trainer at all when everybody did their own thing, only to find that that didn't work. They are now in a halfway-house situation: I am their technical adviser and chef d'équipe and have overall responsibility for the training and preparation of the team, but within that structure riders are free to train with people of their own choice.

'This has the advantage of ensuring that nobody feels obliged to work with anybody, yet their training is monitored to the extent that if I see something I am not happy about I am able to discuss it with the rider and his or her coach. In practice several of the riders do come to me, although there are always some that feel strongly about their particular system. And it can sometimes be frustrating because I don't get to work with the riders enough – maybe I can see things going wrong and can talk it through with the rider, but I don't always have the power to get to grips with the problem the way I would like. I think every trainer would like to be able to spend more time with the horses and riders they are preparing for a championship; there have been cases where I know we could have done better if there had been more time to work together.

'I think every rider needs help in the form of somebody standing on the ground watching him especially just before a major competition – and it is rarely too late to suggest to a rider that he adjusts something he is doing. For example, having watched the American riders at Gatcombe, which was only seven weeks away from the European Championships, I was quite happy to discuss with any of them anything that concerned me, even if the end result meant changing a rider's approach to something, because seven weeks is a long time. Closer to the competition you have to be more diplomatic.

'I watch riders competing across country as much as possible, because the more you can discuss with them in order to keep them honest about what happened and why, the better. Riders are very good at finding an excuse when something goes wrong, and

you need to have watched them to know whether or not it was bad luck, which it sometimes is, or whether, as is most likely, there was something they could have done to have avoided the problem.

'However once you are down to those last days before a championship then I think instilling confidence is more important than trying to get that last little bit of improvement out of somebody's performance. If you have had a chance to get to know the riders prior to the team concentration it is a great help, as you will know how much you can get out of them in terms of improvement, and when to be satisfied and settle for making them feel confident about the job they are doing. I am a great believer in the part that confidence plays in a rider's performance; nobody can afford to be over-confident, but you must be able to go into a big competition believing you can do it.

'The difficult part about being a team trainer is that you are a trainer, not a teacher, and so you have to accept that people are going to do things in different ways. As a nation the Americans have more of a trainer mentality than the British, particularly at grass-roots level; for example, young American riders expect to go to an event with their trainer. At the top level, at international events, personalities often play a greater part than perhaps they should. Thus how you handle people during the build-up to a championship affects whether or not you have a successful team. You have to feel your way a little bit, for instance not pushing too hard in one particular area if it is going to upset the balance, because you need to end up with a cohesive unit, not four disgruntled individuals.'

Given the opportunity, Captain Mark Phillips would have been delighted to have continued being involved with the training of British riders, but no such opportunity arose after Barcelona. His immediate loyalties may lie with his American team, but his roots are British and he cares immensely for the success not only of the British team, but for the future of the sport of horse trials in Britain, his country. One observation he does make, though feeling his way carefully: 'If anything is lacking in the British system at the moment it is somebody capable of keeping the riders honest with themselves on a regular basis. Riders need pulling up on their mistakes; it is too easy to say "the horse did this or that" – you need someone watching you who can say "Yes, the horse

Captain Mark Phillips,
former top class event rider, now course designer and
trainer to the American team

ATLANTA: THE CHALLENGE AHEAD

'We have to believe, to a point, what we are being told about the conditions and the prospects of competing successfully out there. A huge amount of money has been spent on research, too, with the result so far that the steeplechase and cross-country distances have been shortened, Phase C has been altered and includes two compulsory stops where the horses can be aggressively cooled, and the "ten-minute" halt has been increased to fifteen minutes. The organisers have the ability to shorten the distances even more, and to put in extra stopping points on Phase C if necessary. In fact, at the first field trial held on the Olympic site in 1994, the result was that the horses were starting the cross-country phase in better condition than many of the horses competing at Badminton in a temperate climate. Provided that is the case at the Olympic three-day event, then the horses should cope with the conditions during the cross-country phase.

'As far as the competition itself is concerned, I have to confess that I was far more excited about the Open European Championships where we could enjoy a genuine three-day event, than I am to Atlanta where it remains to be seen what sort of competition we will have. We may be lucky and get it absolutely right so that the best horses and riders come out on top; but it is possible that if we have a mild day then it could be won on the dressage, and if the climate is as hot as is expected it may be won by the horse best suited to competing in those particular conditions.

'Personally I will be delighted if I can take four horses and riders out there, and bring back four happy horses and riders.'

FINANCIAL SUPPORT

'American riders have some support from their national federation in that shortlisted riders are given the money to fly their horse to the venue of the particular champ-ionship and a little bit extra to help with their expenses. This is based on the understanding that they will turn up for the final trial; for example, for the 1995 European Championships in Rome, this was held at Thirlestane Castle in Scotland. Most riders use the money to fly to England early so that they can get in some valuable competition experience and training, but the cost of this extended stay has to be borne by the rider. There is a five-strong selection committee of which I am not a member. With the Atlanta Olympics in mind, the selection committee will probably expect the shortlisted riders to compete in Kentucky in June, after which they will go into team concentration for the build-up to the Olympic Games. Once they are in team training their costs are covered by the federation.'

did do this or that, but you could have done something about it!"

'All the time, from a trainer's point of view, the important thing is finding the balance that is acceptable to the riders, the balance between having total control and an acceptable degree of control in terms of the type of training and the time the riders can spend training. We will probably never return to the days of a "general-in-charge" with total control; besides, such a system has its handicaps in that one person cannot always get the best out of every individual. But with the present system, some people do not get as much help as perhaps they should. As ever, we live in a world of compromise.'

RIGHT: David O'Connor at Badminton on Wilton Fair

American Team Training

KAREN & DAVID O'CONNOR

Karen and David O'Connor

■Prior to the 1995 Open European Championships the Americans were based in Berkshire at Soley Farm Stud, the home of fellow countrywoman and dressage rider Sandy Pfleuger, and team concentration began three weeks before they flew out to Rome for the champ-ionship. Until this point the riders had followed their own programme, which took in a number of one-day events at which their selectors wanted to see them, such as Thirlestane Castle in Scotland (which the British were using as their final trial) and Witton Castle in Co Durham. During all this period they have been under the watchful eye of Captain Mark Phillips.

Before the Rome championships, Karen and David O'Connor had been based in the United Kingdom for five years, although they intended to return to live in America after the Open Europeans. Fellow team member Bruce Davidson has always worked from his base in Pennsylvania, flying his horses over to Britain for major competitions such as Badminton and Burghley. After winning Badminton in 1995 with Eagle Lion, he returned to Britain two months later with several horses to prepare for Burghley, Blenheim and the Open European Championships, basing himself for the whole time at Soley Farm Stud.

The team concentration period is usually used as a time for fine tuning the technique of the rider and his team horse, and for the building and nurturing of confidence and team spirit. David O'Connor, who hopes to make the team for the Atlanta Olympics, explains: 'Working closely with trainers of the calibre of Mark Phillips, and previously Lars Sederholm, is a very enjoyable part of team training. You don't often get the chance to work very closely with people like that and it is something I think we all look forward to. But the key to a successful preparation is not to get so caught up in the team training approach that you take your horse out of the programme which you know suits him best. This is more likely to happen at your first encounter with "team concentration". At the first one you tend to wait for people to tell you what to do, rather than getting on with it in your own way and only looking to your trainer to fine tune your performance. Then as you get used to the set-up, the communication between everybody improves and you concentrate on what suits you and your horse.

'Captain Mark Phillips is very confident in what he does and he respects the people he is working with. Nothing is forced on you, but things are suggested for you to do, and it is up to you to take them on board if they help.'

The horse with which David was chosen to ride at the Open Europeans – and the one he hopes may take him to Atlanta – is relatively new to him. 'I bought Custom Made at the end of last season, having seen him at the 1994 Young Rider Championships at Blenheim. He had a run-out on the cross-country there, and then had three showjumps down, but there was a lot to like about him. He has proved to be an excellent horse; it has been a step-by-step process seeing what he would be ready for, but he won the Lexington CCI in Kentucky USA earlier this season [1995] and went well at all his events in Britain in the run-up to the Europeans. There has been a lot to work on all the way through; he is quite a 'run-away', and I *did* get run away with at most events during the spring, but that was really a lack of confidence. Now he has more confidence that has sorted itself out, and it has also led to an improvement in his showjumping. He is a good mover, and is a real trier. He is an easy horse in the dressage as the crowds don't seem to worry him, but they do affect him in the showjumping when the pressure seems to get to him, and then he starts to get strong again.

'He is a big strong horse, and being successful with him comes down to not letting him use his strength against you. I hope to take him to Atlanta – he has a tremendous engine and is very straightforward about what he does.'

David's wife, Karen, had her first Olympic ride at Seoul in 1988, and is also hopeful of a ride at Atlanta. Her build-up to the 1995 Open Europeans had gone well, with the highlight being a richly deserved third place at Badminton in 1995 on Biko, the big-striding 17.3hh Thoroughbred with the striking white face.

During the team concentration period the American riders competed at Witton Castle, Co Durham, where Karen was delighted with Biko's performance. 'I was very happy with the horse in all three phases. He has been making steady progress throughout the season, and he finally feels strong enough in himself to manage the collected work more easily.

Karen in the showjumping with the enormous, white-faced Biko

'The facilities at Sandy Pfleuger's are superb, and having the use of an outdoor manège has made a big difference to the horse's way of going, and the confidence with which I feel I can ride him through the movements. The result is that our performance is much sharper and more precise now.

'Biko is a fairly straightforward horse to jump and so in the few weeks before a major championship we just have a final review of all the exercises we have worked on. We concentrate on exercises which simulate what we will meet in competition such as arrowheads, corners and angled fences, and combinations. We rarely jump anything too big until just before an event, and then it is a good idea to put up something of a decent height to get the rider's eye in. Because Biko is so big the main thing I have worked on is his adjustability – I need to be able to send him forwards, but I must then be able to collect him back up again. If he can do this it makes him faster across country and cleaner in the showjumping.

'Quite apart from the training exercises and fast-work, there are many other final details to work out, such as clipping and shoeing, before the horses are sent out to Italy for the championships. So the grooms play a vital part in the horses' preparation, too; they

often get to know the horse better even than its rider, and their knowledge is invaluable. My own preparation has been good in that my events with Biko have gone well, and I also had a good run round Blenheim on another horse before leaving for the Europeans.'

In many cases, being husband and wife in the same team would undoubtedly stretch the relationship to breaking point, but for Karen and David there seem to be only advantages: 'We draw from each other's strengths,' says Karen 'whilst allowing the other to be his own person. Everyone prepares for a competition in different ways, mentally and physically, and we give each other that flexibility, and as much advice as we can. I believe our marriage has made our careers.'

10
The Future

The recurring message throughout this book is that for those who have taken part in an Olympic Games, the experience is special: 'It's unique'…'The atmosphere is incredible, the thrill indescribable'…'The honour will remain with me always…' For the rest of us, the vast majority who can only wonder enviously just what it must be like to be an Olympic competitor, the Games continue to find a place in our hearts and imagination.

To run an Olympic Games millions of pounds must be raised both nationally and internationally by the Olympic

Association of each country, and by other groups such as, in Britain, the British Equestrian Olympic Fund and the Horse Trials Support Group. It takes an infinitely tolerant public, and one which cherishes the concept of the Games, to continue to afford such support. In the run-up to the Atlanta Games the British Olympic Association launched an appeal to raise four million pounds, and the British Equestrian Olympic Fund aims to raise £250,000 for the purpose of 'supporting, training and sending British riders to the Olympic Games'.

LEFT: The 1992 Olympic Gold medallist, Matt Ryan
INSET: The author, Debby Sly, with the Ledbury Hunt's Granite

■Once the Games are underway, the competitors' expenses are largely paid for by their own Olympic Association; but there are many costs still to be met. For example, the horses going to the Atlanta Olympics will require a three-week acclimatisation period before the start of the Games and the costs of this stay, together with those of their attendant grooms, officials, vets and trainers, will have to be covered. During the Games themselves, only a limited number of 'officials' have their expenses paid by the Olympic Association; for example only one 'official' team trainer is catered for, yet two or three different trainers may travel out with the team – their expenses have to be met by the appropriate Equestrian Federation.

Fund-raising is therefore an on-going and 'Olympic' effort in itself, but it is obviously a price considered worth paying by all those involved and it all makes the future of the Olympic three-day event appear very rosy. Things did indeed look somewhat shaky for a while after Barcelona when it was rumoured that the three-day event would be dropped from the Olympic movement because of the expense of providing stabling and the cross-country course. But the announcement that, from 1996 onwards, there will be separate team and individual competitions within the three-day event would appear to make its future look secure. After all, this format allows countries to send more riders than they were able to in the past – a move that is unlikely to have been made if the sport were about to be discarded by the International Olympic Committee.

It would seem that the greatest threat to the future of the Olympic three-day event is not the officialdom that governs the Olympics, but the increasingly difficult climatic conditions in which the Olympics are held. Time and again, experienced Olympic three-day event riders have said they would far rather be riding in suitable conditions than having to battle once again with a hot, humid climate and hard ground conditions for the sake of staying in the Olympic movement. The rumours that followed Barcelona obviously dented the confidence of the powers-that-be in the equestrian world and successfully planted in the minds of riders and officials the fear that, if we had pulled out of Atlanta because of the conditions, then the three-day event would lose its place in the Olympic Games. Increasingly, however, riders seem to want to rise above that threat. Bruce Davidson makes this comment:

'I am not worried about the horses losing their Olympic status. It is more important that they should be allowed to perform and show their lifetime's efforts under the best conditions. The equestrian Olympics should be held where they belong, in a temperate climate. The public enjoys seeing things done well, which means seeing competitions held in an environment which is constructive towards the effort, not destructive.'

The tremendous amount of research that has been undertaken prior to Atlanta will no doubt benefit competition horses and ponies all over the world, and in many respects it was long overdue. But whilst research and veterinary expertise may make competing in Atlanta 'safe', it cannot possibly make it comfortable. Track athletes have commented that the climatic conditions in Atlanta are 'disgusting' to train and compete in, and so horses and riders are likely to find the whole experience fairly uncomfortable. Although research is reassuring, it doesn't always make the reality any more palatable; it is rather like saying that although scientific evidence has proved that a person can survive in desert conditions with no water for x number of days, it still doesn't make the experience any more attractive.

It is wrong to point the finger only at Atlanta. For far too long the equestrian world has been willing to sit back and allow three-day event championships to be held in climates which have proved to be uncomfortable. The World Championships in Kentucky and Stockholm are two examples. We have all learnt a great deal since then in terms of caring for the competition horse in hot, humid conditions, but why can't we learn a better lesson altogether and choose more appropriate venues?

Let us return to the contentious issue that if we stay away from the Atlanta Olympics it will jeopardise the place of three-day eventing in the Olympics, and that if we are no longer part of the Olympic movement then the sport will lose out financially. I have yet to see how well founded that argument is. Spectator interest in the sport will grow if the public sees it performed well, and as Bruce Davidson has pointed out, that means performing in suitable conditions. Moreover as far as the riders are concerned, whilst it is a personal honour to compete, few can say they have benefited financially from their involvement. Mark Todd, double Olympic gold medallist, has stated quite categorically that although he became better known as a result of his wins, it made not a jot of difference to him financially, and he has been no better able to maintain or secure sponsorship than any other rider. Matt Ryan, the 1992 gold medallist, comments that his performance at *Badminton* that year brought him far greater acclaim than his win at the Olympics.

This may be too simplistic a view, but if gold medallists fail to gain any more sponsorship than the rest of us, then potential sponsors are obviously not specifically attracted by the prospect of their protégé winning an Olympic gold medal. Furthermore a fundamentally healthy, appealing sport has far more chance of winning long-term public and commercial interest than one which sacrifices its long-standing attributes in an attempt to attract attention in the short term. The Olympic Games are staged only once every four years and are attended by the world's top event riders; but these represent a tiny minority of the riders that make up the sport as a whole. More significant is the fact that every time a three-day event championship is held in unpleasant conditions, it opens the door for adverse criticism and ammunition, and surely it is wrong to gamble the whole structure of a healthy, happy sport against competing at just a few, high-profile competitions. The Olympic three-day event is not bigger than the sport of eventing itself: to be sure, the Olympic ideal encompasses perfectly the sport of three-day eventing, but the sport deserves better than to have to 'modify' itself to suit a less-than-ideal venue. As Andrew Nicholson put it so succinctly: 'I am not a great fan of sitting in competitors' briefings and being told how hot/humid/hard it is going to be. The event should not be held in such conditions in the first place.'

A great deal more is at stake in Atlanta than the welfare of the horses that are selected to compete there. America hosts a strong animal rights movement, some factions of which consider eventing to be a cruel sport in itself; they have a following which is easily swayed, and are backed by vast funds, and they don't need the additional factor of hot, humid conditions to give them grounds to object to the sport. But without any doubt at all, if we allow horses to compete in Atlanta and the climate has a blatantly adverse effect, we will be giving them all the ammunition they could possibly envisage to cast against us. It has to be fervently hoped, therefore, that the Olympic three-day event in Atlanta is a great success, and even those who are strongly against horses being sent there will be praying that their fears are unjustified. It will be no pleasure for anybody to be able to say 'I told you so'.

Even if Atlanta proceeds without incident, the sport should not become complacent about what it is willing to accept. It is probably true that if you haven't competed at an Olympic Games you cannot appreciate its true value, but times, attitudes and conditions do change, and having had the priviledge of speaking to a large number of riders who *do* know the true value of

the Olympics, it is interesting to see how their attitudes differ. It is not too much of a generalisation to say that those who competed during the early Olympics, and probably right up until Montreal (1976) are wholeheartedly in favour of participation and consider that it is an honour and an experience which no one has the right to deny to future competitors. But the present generation of riders seems more concerned with the suitability of the venue, rather than the occasion itself. They would rather compete where the conditions are most suited to the sport so that they can perform to the best of their ability. This is more a reflection of the growing professionalism within the sport than a flowering sense of idealism! Most of today's top riders have made their sport their career, and in order to earn their living they need to go out and win. They have a much better chance of doing that if they are competing in good conditions, than if they are worrying about whether or not their particular horse is suited to the prevailing climatic conditions at the event.

Were we to follow this line, however, and only compete where we felt the conditions were appropriate, the sport would possibly become increasingly insular; for example, championships could then only be hosted in a limited number of countries – and even then some would argue that those climates can be unpredictable and might still make fools of us. But at least the odds would be limited, and any 'adverse' conditions would still be relatively more comfortable than those in climates which are known and expected to be harsh. Great Britain hosts more events than any other country and for that reason attracts large numbers of visiting foreign riders. Her climate can be a little unpredictable, but it is never unbearable; in 1995 Badminton experienced unusually hot conditions, but whilst competitors and officials excitedly reported how well the horses were coping with the hot, hard conditions, a voice of reason was heard in the form of Dot Willis, who tactfully pointed out that 'In Atlanta this would be considered a cool day'.

Whether or not Atlanta proves to be successful, the sport of three-day eventing will need a voice of reason to steer its path in the future. Hopefully in Atlanta the results of the recent research, combined with responsible riding and decision-making, will ensure a safe and successful competition. Assuming that is the case, let us hope that this is not used as an excuse for continually gambling with the welfare of our horses and thus with the future of our sport.

Index

ABOVE`: Sportsmanship, courage, skill and selflessness are the mark of a true Olympic sport. The British three-day event team after winning team silver, Seoul 1988
LEFT: Ian Stark with Sir Wattie, team and individual Olympic medallists at Seoul, 1988